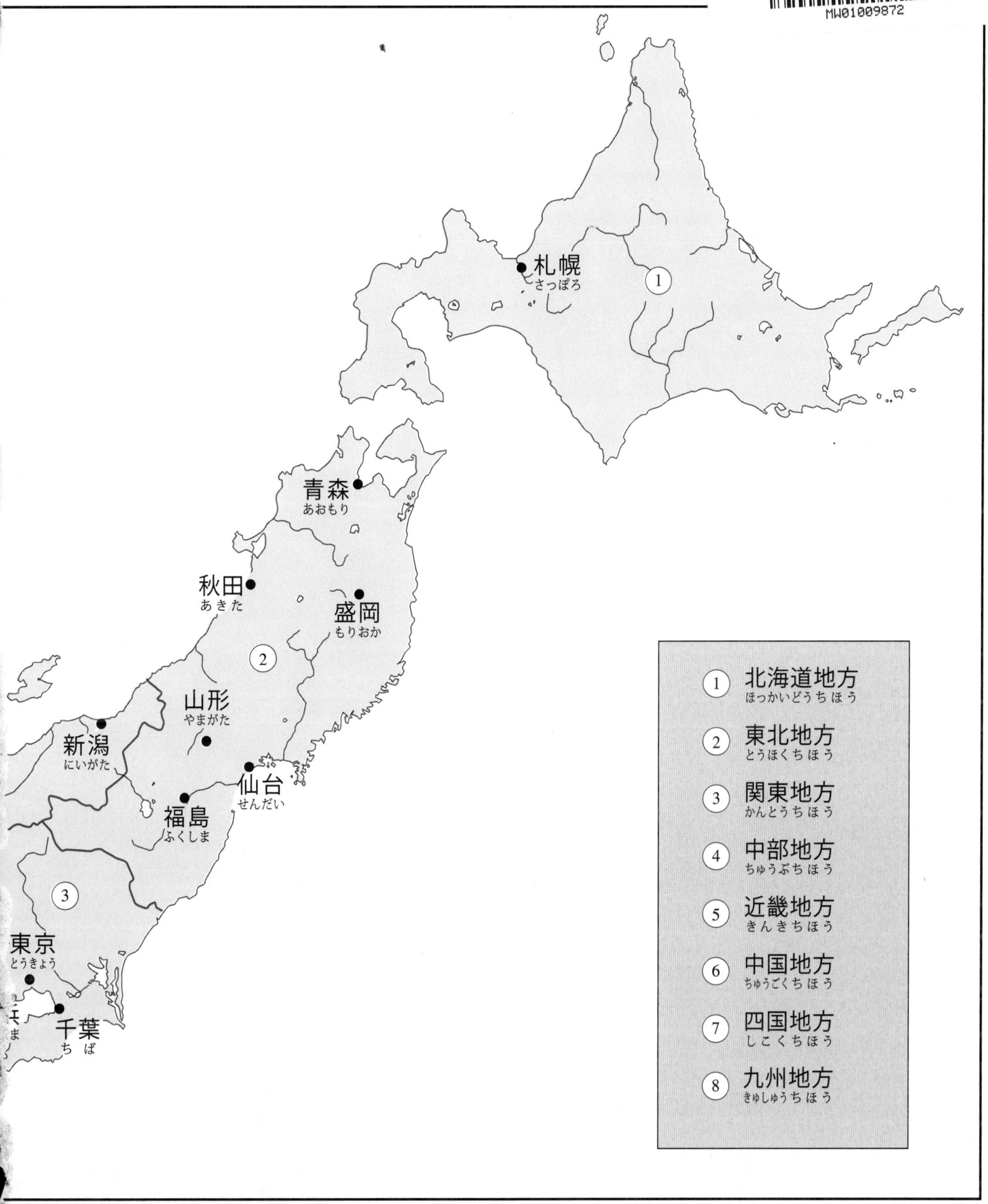

札幌
さっぽろ

1

青森
あおもり

秋田
あきた

盛岡
もりおか

2

山形
やまがた

新潟
にいがた

仙台
せんだい

福島
ふくしま

3

東京
とうきょう

千葉
ちば

1 北海道地方
ほっかいどうちほう

2 東北地方
とうほくちほう

3 関東地方
かんとうちほう

4 中部地方
ちゅうぶちほう

5 近畿地方
きんきちほう

6 中国地方
ちゅうごくちほう

7 四国地方
しこくちほう

8 九州地方
きゅうしゅうちほう

NAKAMA 1a

INTRODUCTORY JAPANESE: *COMMUNICATION, CULTURE, CONTEXT*

Second Edition

Yukiko Abe Hatasa
Hiroshima University

Kazumi Hatasa
Purdue University
The Japanese School, Middlebury College

Seiichi Makino
Princeton University

Houghton Mifflin Harcourt Publishing Company
Boston New York

Publisher: Rolando Hernández
Senior Sponsoring Editor: Glenn A. Wilson
Executive Marketing Director: Eileen Bernadette Moran
Discipline Product Manager: Giuseppina Daniel
Senior Development Editor: Judith Bach
Development Editor: Kim Beuttler
Senior Project Editor: Margaret Park Bridges
Senior Media Producer: Mona Singh
Senior Content Manager: Janet Edmonds
Cover Design Director: Tony Saizon
Senior Photo Editor: Jennifer Meyer Dare
Senior Composition Buyer: Chuck Dutton
Senior New Title Project Manager: Pat O'Neill
Marketing Assistant: Lorreen Ruth Pelletier

Cover image: Harold Burch, New York City

Page a-31: © Kayte M. Deimoa/PhotoEdit
Page a-45: © Christine Schneider/zefa/Corbis
Page a-83: © Gary Conner/PhotoEdit
Page a-134: © Kenneth Hamm/Photo Japan
Page a-176: © Teruyo Shimizu/Photo Japan
Page a-177: © Kenneth Hamm/Photo Japan
Page a-220: © Jeremy Hoare/Alamy
Page a-221: © Jeremy Hoare/Alamy

Printed in the U.S.A.

Library of Congress Control Number: 2007926500

Instructor's Annotated Edition
ISBN-10: 0-618-96630-7
ISBN-13: 978-0-618-96630-1

For orders, use student text ISBNs
ISBN-10: 0-618-96628-5
ISBN-13: 978-0-618-96628-8

3456789-DOW-12 11 10 09 08

ABOUT THE AUTHORS

Professor Yukiko Abe Hatasa received her Ph.D. in linguistics in 1992 from the University of Illinois at Urbana-Champaign. She is known nationwide as one of the premier Japanese methodologists in the United States and as an experienced coordinator of large teacher training programs. She has served as the coordinator of the Japanese language program at the University of Iowa and is currently a professor at Hiroshima University, where her primary responsibilities are teacher training and SLA research.

Professor Kazumi Hatasa received his Ph.D. in education in 1989 from the University of Illinois at Urbana-Champaign. He is currently a professor at Purdue University and Director of the Japanese School at Middlebury College. He is recognized internationally for his work in software development for the Japanese language and distributes most of his work as freeware over the Internet.

Professor Seiichi Makino received his Ph.D. in linguistics in 1968 from the University of Illinois at Urbana-Champaign. He is an internationally prominent Japanese linguist and scholar who is recognized throughout the world for his scholarship and for his many publications. Before beginning his tenure at Princeton University in 1991, he taught Japanese language, linguistics and culture at the University of Illinois while training lower division language coordinators. He is an experienced ACTFL oral proficiency trainer in Japanese and frequently trains Japanese instructors internationally in proficiency-oriented instruction and in the administration of the Oral Proficiency Interview. Professor Makino has been the Academic Director of the Japanese Pedagogy M.A. Summer Program at Columbia University since 1996. He also directs the Princeton-in-Ishikawa Summer Program.

CONTENTS

Chapter 4: Japanese Cities

Chapter 5: Japanese Homes

Chapter 6: Leisure Time

Reference Section

TO THE STUDENT

Nakama 1 is based on the principle that learning another language means acquiring new skills, not just facts and information—that we learn by doing. To achieve this goal, *Nakama 1* systematically involves you in many activities that incorporate the language skills of listening, speaking, reading, and writing. We believe that culture is an integral component of language, too. To help you become familiar with Japanese culture, your text includes high-interest culture notes and relevant communication strategies. New to this edition, an appealing story line video, featuring a Japanese-American exchange student in Tokyo, bring chapter dialogues to life.

ORGANIZATION OF THE TEXTBOOK

Nakama 1 consists of twelve chapters in two parts. *Nakama 1a* contains Chapters 1-6; *Nakama 1b* contains Chapters 7-12. In Chapter 1, you will learn the sounds of the Japanese language and a set of Japanese syllabary symbols called **hiragana.** You will also learn basic greetings and classroom instructions. A second Japanese syllabary called **katakana** is presented after Chapter 2. Chapters 2 through 12 each focus on a common communicative situation and contain the following features:

- Chapter Opener: Each chapter opens with a theme-setting photograph and chapter contents by section. Keeping in mind the objectives listed at the top of the opener will help you focus on achieving your learning goals.
- Vocabulary: The vocabulary is presented in thematic groups, each followed by a variety of communicative activities and activities in context. Supplemental vocabulary is also provided throughout the chapter, but you are not expected to retain it. All active vocabulary is listed by function at the beginning of each chapter, except for Chapter 1, where the list appears last, after you've learned to read **hiragana**.
- Dialogue: The lively dialogues center on Alice Ueda, a Japanese-American college student, who is spending two years studying in Japan. Through the dialogue and accompanying video, you will get to know a series of characters and follow them through typical events in their lives. The video, related activities, and interactive online practice will all reinforce your understanding of the content, discourse organization, and use of formal and casual Japanese speech styles.
- Japanese Culture: Up-to-date culture notes in English explore social, economic, and historical aspects of Japanese life that are essential to effective communication.
- Grammar: Clear, easy-to-understand grammar explanations are accompanied by sample sentences and notes that help you understand how to use the grammar appropriately. In-class pair and group activities let you practice immediately what you've learned. As there is a high correlation between successful communication and grammar accuracy, this section is especially important.
- Listening: Useful strategies and pre-listening activities for general comprehension precede the section's main listening practice. Post-listening activities concentrate on more detailed comprehension and apply what you have learned to other communicative purposes.

- Communication: This section will provide you with knowledge and practice of basic strategies to accelerate your ability to communicate in Japanese.
- **Kanji**: Chapters 4 through 12 introduce a total of 127 **kanji** (Chinese characters). The section begins with useful information such as the composition of individual characters, word formation, and how to use Japanese dictionaries. The presentation of each character includes stroke order to help you master correct stroke orders when writing in Japanese and to prepare you for the reading section.
- Reading: Each reading passage begins with a reading strategy, and includes pre- and post-reading activities designed to help you become a successful reader of Japanese. From Chapter 2, the text is written in all three scripts: **hiragana**, **katakana**, and **kanji**. **Hiragana** subscripts (**furigana**) are provided for **katakana** through Chapter 3, and for unfamiliar **kanji** throughout the textbook. The readings include a small number of unknown words to help you develop strategies for understanding authentic texts.
- Integration: Integrated practice wraps up every chapter using discussion, interviewing, and role-play activities that interweave all the skills you've learned in the current and previous chapters.

STUDENT COMPONENTS

- Student Text: Your Student Text contains all the information and activities you need for in-class use. It is divided into two parts encompassing twelve chapters plus a special chapter following Chapter 2 that introduces **katakana**. Each regular chapter contains vocabulary presentations and activities, a thematic dialogue and practice, grammar presentations and activities, cultural information, reading selections, writing practice, and ample communicative practice. Valuable reference sections at the back of the book include verb charts, a **kanji** list, and Japanese-English and English-Japanese glossaries.
- In-Text Audio CD: The In-Text Audio CD contains recordings of all the listening activities in the text as well as all active chapter vocabulary. The audio activity clips are also available as MP3 files and the vocabulary pronunciations can be found in the flashcards on the student website. These audio materials are designed to maximize your exposure to the sounds of natural spoken Japanese and to help you practice pronunciation.
- Student Activities Manual (SAM): The Student Activities Manual (SAM) includes out-of-class practice of the material presented in the Student Text. Each chapter of the SAM includes a workbook section, which focuses on written vocabulary, grammar, **kanji** and writing practice, and a lab section, which focuses on pronunciation and listening comprehension, including Dict-a-Conversation dictation activities.
- SAM Audio Program: The SAM Audio Program corresponds to the audio portion of the SAM and reinforces your pronunciation and listening skills. You may listen to this material in the lab or on CD. The audio is also available as MP3 files from the passkey-protected area of the student website.
- DVD: New for the second edition, the two-tiered Nakama video program includes a story line video, where the experiences of a Japanese-American exchange student, Alice Ueda, featured in the chapter dialogues are brought to life. A series of cultural segments that depict everyday situations are tied to

the theme of each chapter. You will be able to view the video in class, on DVD, on the student website as MP4 files, or while working on video comprehension activities found on the passkey-protected area of the site.

- HM JapaneseSPACE™: You will find a variety of resources on the student website at HM JapaneseSPACE™: A wealth of interactive exercises and games give you further practice with chapter topics. Vocabulary and grammar quizzes, audio flashcards for vocabulary, and **kanji** and pronunciation review help you monitor and assess your progress. Web search activities and Web links encourage further exploration of chapter themes. MP3 files for the text listening activities can also be downloaded from the site. The website is accessible at college.hmco.com/PIC/nakamaone2e.

ACKNOWLEDGMENTS

The authors and publisher thank the following people for their recommendations regarding the content of *Nakama 1*. Their comments and suggestions were invaluable during the development of this publication.

Noriko Akatsuka
Aloysius Chang
Len Grzanka
Hiroko Harada
Masako Hamada
Janet Ikeda
Mieko Ishibashi
Noriko Iwasaki
Kimberly Jones
Sarachie Karasawa
Hiroko Kataoka
Yukio Kataoka
Michiya Kawai
Chisato Kitagawa
Lisa Kobuke
Chiyo Konishi
Junko Kumamoto-Healey
Yukari Kunisue
Yasumi Kuriya
Akira Miura
Shigeru Miyagawa
John Mertz
Seigo Nakao
Hiroshi Nara
Machiko Netsu
Catherine Oshida
Yoko Pusavat
Yoshiko Saito-Abbott
Haruko Sakakibara
Kitty Shek
Ritsuko Shigeyama
Satoru Shinagawa
Zenryu Shirakawa
Shizuka Tatsuzawa
Miyo Uchida
Alexander Vovin
Paul Warnick
Yasuko Ito Watt
Kikuko Yamashita

The authors and publisher also thank the following people for field-testing *Nakama 1*. Their comments contributed greatly to the accuracy of this publication.

Nobuko Chikamatsu
Fusae Ekida
Junko Hino
Satoru Ishikawa
Yoshiko Jo
Sayuri Kubota
Yasumi Kuriya
Izumi Matsuda
Junko Mori
Fumiko Nazikian
Mayumi Oka
Amy Snyder Ohta
Mayumi Steinmetz
Keiko Yamaguchi

The authors are also grateful to the following people at Houghton Mifflin for their valuable assistance during the development of this project: Rolando Hernández, Glenn Wilson, Eileen Bernadette Moran, Lorreen Pelletier, Judith Bach, Kim Beuttler, Charline Lake, and Margaret Bridges.

They are especially grateful to Yoshiko Jo and Margaret Hines for copyediting, to Satoru Ishikawa, Bill Weaver, and Yoshiko Jo for proofreading, and to Michael Kelsey of Inari Information Services, Inc. Finally, profound thanks go to Noriko Hanabusa for her work on the Student Activities Manual and to Kazuko Yokoi for her work on the illustrations in this edition.

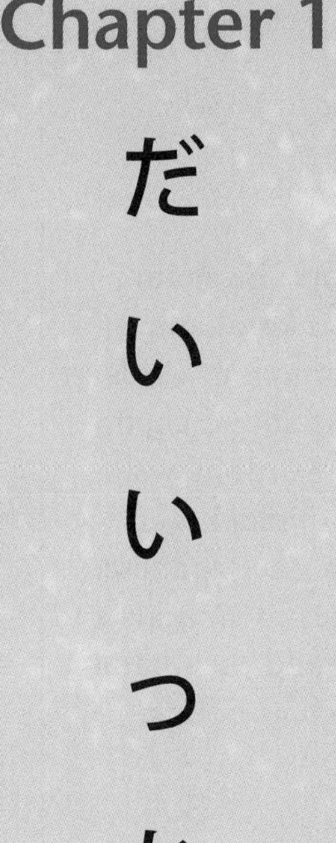

Chapter 1
だいいっか

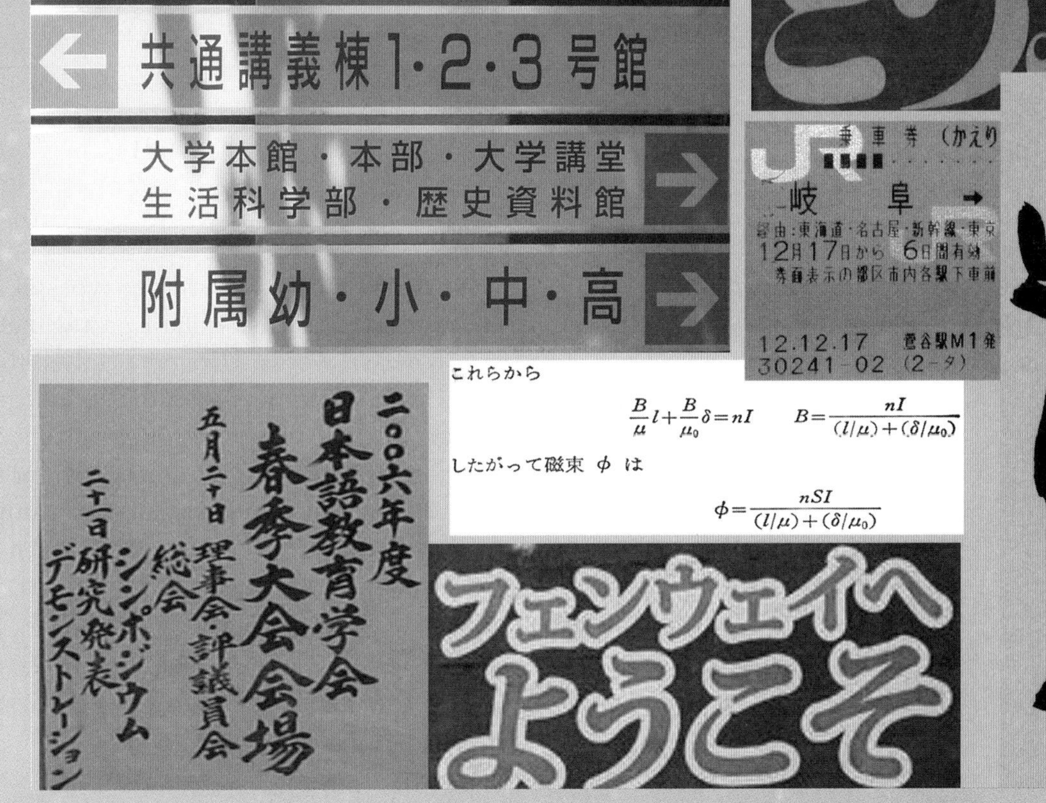

The Japanese Sound System and Hiragana

I. Introduction

Japanese is usually written with a combination of three types of script: **hiragana**, **katakana**, and **kanji** (Chinese characters). Individually, **hiragana** and **katakana** represent sounds, and **kanji** represent words. **Hiragana** is used for function words (words such as *in*, *at*, and *on*) and for inflectional endings (indicating sound changes used to express tense, negation, and the like), and for some content words as well. **Katakana** is used for words borrowed from other languages, for example, **keeki** (cake), for onomatopoeic words expressing sounds, such as **wanwan** (the Japanese word for *bow-wow*), and for some scientific terms, such as the names of animals and plants in biology textbooks. **Kanji** are characters of Chinese origin, and each **kanji** represents a morpheme or a word and is used for content words, such as nouns, verbs, and adjectives.

Hiragana

Like the individual letters in the English alphabet, **hiragana** represent sounds, but each **hiragana** character represents a vowel or a combination of a consonant and a vowel, such as **a, sa, ki, tsu, me,** and **yo. Hiragana** evolved through the simplification of Chinese characters during the Heian period (794–1185).

Having no writing system of their own, the Japanese began importing Chinese characters (**hanzi**) to write their own language in the late fourth or early fifth century. They employed two adaptation strategies to do so. One was based on meaning and the other was based on sound. The meaning-based strategy involved using an individual **kanji** to write a Japanese word that was synonymous with the Chinese word the **kanji** represented. For example, the Japanese word for "wave" was expressed using the Chinese character with the same meaning, 波. Its pronunciation in Chinese, *puâ*, was replaced with the pronunciation of the corresponding Japanese word, **nami.**

The sound-based strategy, by contrast, used Chinese characters to represent Japanese sounds rather than meanings. For instance, the character 波 in this context was used to represent the syllable *ha* because of its close resemblance to the sound *puâ* in Middle Chinese. (The character is currently pronounced [ha], but it was pronounced as [pa] in classical Japanese, similar to the middle Chinese [puâ].) In this usage, the meaning of the character 波 was completely ignored. This was a cumbersome system, however, because Japanese words usually contain several syllables and Chinese characters represent only one sound. In order to overcome this problem, Chinese characters were gradually simplified until they reached the forms used in present-day **hiragana**. These simplified characters appear in many women's literary works, including the famous *Tale of Genji*, and for this reason **hiragana** was once called **onna de** (*women's hand*).

Hiragana as written today consists of 46 characters (Figure 1). Two diacritical marks in the shapes of two dots ゛ or a small circle ゜ are used to show voiced consonants (Figure 2). The basic syllabary can also be used to represent *glides*, which are combinations of characters that represent more complex sounds (Figure 3).

Look at Figure 1 and pronounce each character by repeating it after your instructor and/or the accompanying audio. This chart should be read from top to bottom and right to left. Japanese may be written vertically in this manner or horizontally, from left to right, as in English.

Figure 1

n	w	r	y	m	h	n	t	s	k		
ん	わ	ら	や	ま	は	な	た	さ	か	あ	a
		り		み	ひ	に	ち	し	き	い	i
		る	ゆ	む	ふ	ぬ	つ	す	く	う	u
		れ		め	へ	ね	て	せ	け	え	e
	を	ろ	よ	も	ほ	の	と	そ	こ	お	o

Figure 2

p	b	d	z	g	
ぱ	ば	だ	ざ	が	a
ぴ	び	ぢ	じ	ぎ	i
ぷ	ぶ	づ	ず	ぐ	u
ぺ	べ	で	ぜ	げ	e
ぽ	ぼ	ど	ぞ	ご	o

Figure 3

p	b	d	z	g	r	m	h	n	t	s	k	
ぴゃ	びゃ	ぢゃ	じゃ	ぎゃ	りゃ	みゃ	ひゃ	にゃ	ちゃ	しゃ	きゃ	ya
ぴゅ	びゅ	ぢゅ	じゅ	ぎゅ	りゅ	みゅ	ひゅ	にゅ	ちゅ	しゅ	きゅ	yu
ぴょ	びょ	ぢょ	じょ	ぎょ	りょ	みょ	ひょ	にょ	ちょ	しょ	きょ	yo

II. Hiragana あ〜そ

In this section, you will learn fifteen **hiragana** and their pronunciation. The following charts show both printed and handwritten styles.

Note that some lines that are connected in the printed style are not connected in handwriting. For example, the vertical diagonal curved lines in the printed forms of き[ki] and さ[sa] are connected, but they are not connected in handwriting (き and さ). Also, the character そ[so] is written as a single stroke in the printed style, but as two strokes in handwriting (そ), where the diagonal line at the top is not connected with the rest of the character.

Printed style

s	k		
さ	か	あ	a
し	き	い	i
す	く	う	u
せ	け	え	e
そ	こ	お	o

Handwritten style

s	k		
さ	か	あ	a
し	き	い	i
す	く	う	u
せ	け	え	e
そ	こ	お	o

Learning hiragana

The mnemonic pictures and keys below have been provided to help you memorize the **hiragana** characters. Remember that the mnemonic pictures are not accurate representations of the shapes or the sounds of the characters.

a	あ	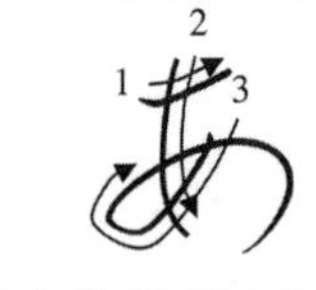 あ (strokes 1, 2, 3)	あ is similar to [ah] but is shorter.	 *Ah!* Ann is good at ice-skating.
i	い	 い (strokes 1, 2)	い is similar to the vowel sound in *ear* but is shorter.	 I have big *ears*.
u	う	 う (strokes 1, 2)	う is similar to the vowel sound in [ooh] but is shorter and the lips are not as rounded.	 *Ooh!* This is heavy.
e	え	 え (strokes 1, 2)	え is similar to the first vowel sound in *exercise* but the mouth is not opened as widely.	 I need *exercise*.

o	お	お	お is similar to the vowel sound [o] in *on* as the British pronounce it, but the lips are slightly more rounded.	The ball will land *on* the green.
ka	か	か	か is a combination of [k] and [a]. The Japanese [k] sound is less forceful than the English sound.	*Karate* kick.
ki	き	き	き is similar to *key* but the vowel sound is shorter.	This is *a key*.
ku	く	く	く is similar to the first syllable of *cuckoo* but the lips are not as rounded.	This is a *cuckoo*.
ke	け	け	け is similar to the sound [ca] in *cane*, but without the [y] sound.	A man with a *cane*.
ko	こ	こ	こ is similar to the sound [co] in *coin* without the [y] sound.	A ten yen *coin* is worth about a dime.
sa	さ	さ	さ is a combination of [s] and [a]. The Japanese [s] sound is not as strong as the English [s] sound because less air is forced out between the teeth.	Don't drink too much *sake*.
shi	し	し	し is similar to *she* but is shorter and the lips are spread wider. Japanese does not have the sound [si] as in *sea*.	This is how *she* wears her hair.
su	す	す	す is a combination of [s] and [u].	*Swimming* is fun in the summer.
se	せ	せ	せ is similar to the sound of *se* in *señor*.	Hello, *Señor* García.
so	そ	そ	そ is similar to *so* but is shorter.	This character zigzags *so* much.

Reading hiragana

Read the following words, paying attention to intonation and devoiced (whispered) sounds. Characters with a bar over them (for example, いけ) should be pronounced with a higher pitch than those without a bar. The [i] and [u] in き , く , し , す, ち , つ , ひ , and ふ may be devoiced between two voiceless consonants or at the end of a word. Characters with a small circle under them (き) contain a devoiced [i] or [u].

え	picture	いけ	pond
おかし	confectionery	いす	chair
き	tree	きく	chrysanthemum
かお	face	さけ	sake
あし	leg	えき	station
せかい	world	そこ	bottom
あさ	morning	しお	salt
あかい	red	あかい かさ	red umbrella
あおい	blue	あおい いす	blue chair

Useful Expressions

1. Forms of address

The Japanese always use a title to address people other than family members. Young people, however, sometimes refer to their close friends by name only, without using titles.

se n se i せんせい	se n se i ～せんせい	sa n ～さん
professor, teacher	Professor ～	Mr./Mrs./Miss/Ms. ～

Example: たなかせんせい　　やまださん

Professor Tanaka　　Mr./Mrs./Miss/Ms. Yamada

Notes

- The せい in せんせい (**sensee**) is pronounced by stretching the [e]. You will learn more about long vowels in a later section.
- It is customary to address an instructor simply as せんせい .

- The literal meaning of せんせい is "born ahead," which by extension means "honorable master." For this reason, it is used to refer to other people but never to oneself. Further, it can be used to address people in professions other than teaching, especially when the person in question has recognized expertise and performs a mentoring function. Patients refer to their medical doctors as せんせい. But せんせい should never be used in reference to oneself.
- The Japanese usually address each other using last names and titles, even when they have known each other for a long time. First names are used primarily among family members and close friends.
- ～さん is a generic term, but you cannot use it when referring to yourself or to someone who should be addressed with a title such as せんせい.

2. Introducing yourself

ha ji me ma shi te　　de su　do o zo　yo ro shi ku

はじめまして。　～です。どうぞ　よろしく。

How do you do? I am ～. Pleased to meet you.

(The English translation here is not a literal equivalent of the Japanese.)

Example:

A: hajimemashite yamada desu doozo yoroshiku

はじめまして。やまだ　です。どうぞ　よろしく。

B: hajimemashite sumisu desu doozo yoroshiku

はじめまして。すみす　です。どうぞ　よろしく。

Mr. Smith　　**Mr. Yamada**

NOTES

- The little circle at the end of each sentence represents a period in written Japanese.
- You cannot use a title or さん when speaking of yourself.

はなして みましょう Conversation Practice

1. Today is the first day of Japanese class. Introduce yourself to your classmates. Listen to your classmates as they introduce themselves and try to remember their names.
2. Did you greet your classmates with a bow? If you didn't, greet them again, and bow. If you don't know how to bow properly, ask your instructor to show you.

III. Hiragana た〜ほ

In this section, you will learn fifteen more **hiragana** and their pronunciation. Note that the right side of な [na] consists of a single connected line in the printed style, but consists of two strokes in the handwritten style な [na].

Printed style

h	n	t	
は	な	た	a
ひ	に	ち	i
ふ	ぬ	つ	u
へ	ね	て	e
ほ	の	と	o

Handwritten style

h	n	t	
は	な	た	a
ひ	に	ち	i
ふ	ぬ	つ	u
へ	ね	て	e
ほ	の	と	o

Learning hiragana

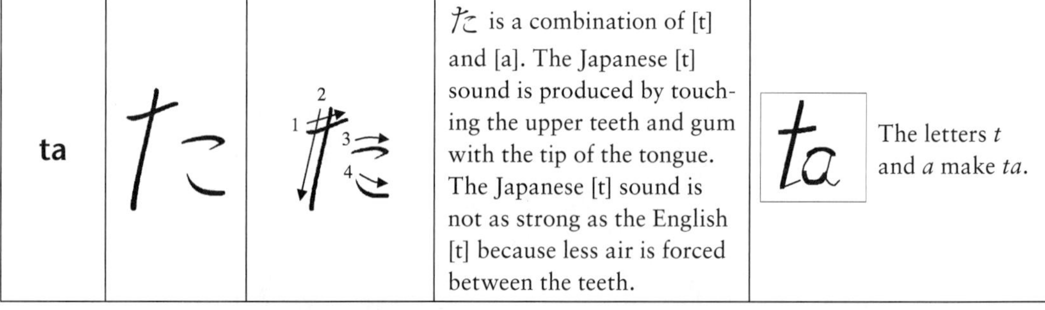

ta	た	た	た is a combination of [t] and [a]. The Japanese [t] sound is produced by touching the upper teeth and gum with the tip of the tongue. The Japanese [t] sound is not as strong as the English [t] because less air is forced between the teeth.	ta — The letters *t* and *a* make *ta*.

chi	ち	ち	 ち The sound is [chi] as in *cheer*. There is no [ti] sound in Japanese.	 Being a *cheerleader* isn't easy.
tsu	つ	 つ	つ is similar to the sound [t's] in *cat's*.	 A *cat's* tail.
te	て	て	 て is similar to the first syllable of *table*, but without the [y] sound.	 Fruit on a *table*.
to	と	と	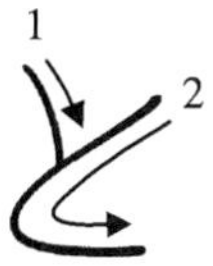 と is similar to the sound of *toe* but the [t] is softer.	 I've got a thorn in my *toe*.
na	な	な	 な is similar to the sound of [na] in *nap* in British pronunciation, but the vowel sound is more like [a] as in *ah*.	 This person is taking a *nap*.
ni	に	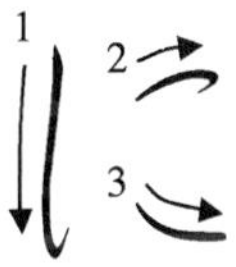 に	に is similar to the sound of *knee*, but the vowel sound is shorter.	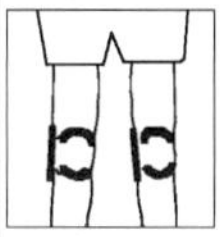 Look at my *knees*.
nu	ぬ	ぬ	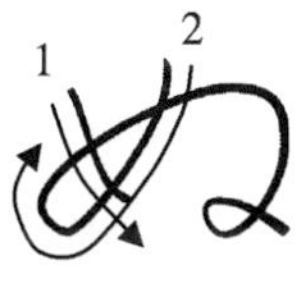 ぬ is similar to the first syllable of *noodle*, but the vowel sound is shorter.	 *Noodles* and chopsticks.
ne	ね	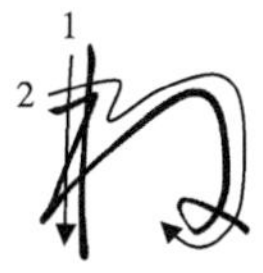 ね	ね is similar to the sound of *ne* in *net*.	 I caught a fish in my *net*.
no	の	の	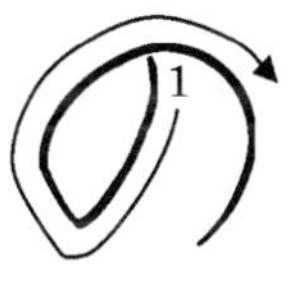 の is similar to the sound of the English *no*, but the vowel sound is shorter and the lips are not as rounded.	 See the *no* smoking sign.
ha	は	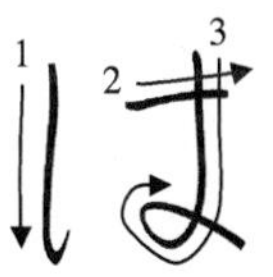 は	は is a combination of [h] and [a]. The Japanese [h] sound is much softer than the English equivalent.	 I bought a *house*.
hi	ひ	 ひ	ひ is similar to the sound of *he*, is but the vowel sound is shorter.	 This is Mr. Hill. *He* is strong.

fu	ふ	ふ (stroke order 1–4)	ふ is a combination of [f] and [u]. The initial consonant [f] is produced by bringing the lips together as if blowing out a candle.	Mt. *Fuji* is beautiful.
he	へ	へ (stroke order 1)	へ is similar to the sound of *head*, without the final [d] sound.	I have a *headache*.
ho	ほ	ほ (stroke order 1–4)	ほ is similar to the initial part of *home*, without the [u] sound.	A house isn't a *home* without TV.

Reading hiragana

Read the following words, paying attention to devoiced sounds and intonation.

て	hand	にく	meat
つき	moon	ひと	person
おなか	stomach	ねこ	cat
はな	nose	いぬ	dog
くち	mouth	ふえ	flute
たき	waterfall	ほし	star
たな	shelf	うち	house
たかい	high, expensive	たかい にく	expensive meat
ひくい	low, flat	ひくい こえ	low voice

Useful Expressions

Daily greetings

Greeting people properly is important in all cultures. In Japanese, the phrases used when greeting people vary according to the time of day.

In the morning:

o ha yoo go za i ma su

おはよう ございます。

Good morning. / Hello. (formal speech)

o ha yoo

おはよう。

Good morning. / Hello. (casual speech)

Examples: Student A: おはよう。(ohayoo)

Student B: おはよう。(ohayoo)

Student: おはよう ございます。(ohayoo gozaimasu)

Teacher: おはよう。(ohayoo)

Acquaintance A: おはよう ございます。(ohayoo gozaimasu)

Acquaintance B: おはよう ございます。(ohayoo gozaimasu)

In the afternoon:

ko n ni chi wa

こんにちは。

Good afternoon./ Hello.

Example: A: こんにちは。(konnichiwa)

B: こんにちは。(konnichiwa)

In the evening:

ko n ba n wa

こんばんは。

Good evening./Hello.

Example: A: こんばんは。(konbanwa)

B: こんばんは。(konbanwa)

Notes

- The よう in おはよう ございます [**ohayoo gozaimasu**] is pronounced by stretching the [o]. You will learn more about long vowels in a later section.
- In general, these phrases are used in both casual and formal situations. The expression おはよう ございます [**ohayoo gozaimasu**], however, has a less formal version, おはよう [**ohayoo**], which may be used with friends or family members. It is considered rude if used with superiors or in formal situations.
- If you see the same person more than once on the same day, using these phrases each time you meet would sound rather silly. In such cases, you should just bow slightly or talk about something else.

- The は in こんにちは [**konnichi wa**] and こんばんは [**konban wa**] is pronounced [wa] rather than [ha].
- こんにちは [**konnichi wa**] and こんばんは [**konban wa**] are not used among family members.

はなして みましょう Conversation Practice

1. It is morning. You meet an elderly neighbor on the street. Greet him/her.
2. Imagine that class is about to begin in the morning. Greet your instructor and classmates, nodding slightly rather than bowing.
3. Greet a friend in the morning. Greet your instructor in the afternoon. Greet a friend in the evening.
4. Walk around the classroom. As your instructor announces whether it is morning, afternoon, or evening, greet five classmates with the appropriate phrase. Don't forget to bow slightly.

IV. Hiragana ま〜ん

In this section, you will learn the remaining **hiragana**. Notice that the right side of む [mu] consists of a single connected line in the printed style but has two strokes in the handwritten style む [mu]. Similarly, while ゆ [yu] in the printed style is written in a single stroke with all lines connected, the handwritten style of ゆ [yu] is written in two strokes. In addition, り [ri] in the printed style is written in a single connected line, but り [ri] in handwritten style consists of two vertical lines.

Printed style

n	w	r	y	m	
ん	わ	ら	や	ま	a
		り		み	i
		る	ゆ	む	u
		れ		め	e
	を	ろ	よ	も	o

Handwritten style

n	w	r	y	m	
ん	わ	ら	や	ま	a
		り		み	i
		る	ゆ	む	u
		れ		め	e
	を	ろ	よ	も	o

Learning hiragana

ma	ま	ま (strokes 1, 2, 3)	ま is a combination of [m] and [a]. The Japanese [m] sound is like the [m] in *mom*, but is less forceful.	*Mom*! I can't sit any longer.
mi	み	み (strokes 1, 2)	み is similar to the sound of *me*, but the vowel sound is shorter.	Who is twenty-one? *Me!*
mu	む	む (strokes 1, 2, 3)	む is similar to the sound of *moo*, but the vowel sound is shorter.	Cows *moo*.
me	め	め (strokes 1, 2)	め is similar to the first syllable of *medal*.	An Olympic gold *medal*.
mo	も	も (strokes 1, 2, 3)	も is similar to the sound of [mo] in *more*.	Catch *more* fish with a hook.
ya	や	や (strokes 1, 2, 3)	や is a combination of the [y] and [a] sounds. The sounds [yi] and [ye] do not exist in Japanese.	A *yacht*.

yu	ゆ	 ゆ (stroke order 1, 2)	ゆ is similar to the first syllable of *ukulele*.		Can you play the *ukulele*?
yo	よ	 よ (stroke order 1, 2)	よ is similar to the first syllable of *yo-yo*, but the vowel sound is shorter.		*Yo-yos* were once very popular.
ra	ら	 ら (stroke order 1, 2)	ら The [r] sound in Japanese differs slightly from both the English [l] and [r]. To an English speaker's ears, its pronunciation lies somewhere between [r], [l], and [d]. It is produced by flicking the tip of the tongue against the gum behind the upper set of teeth. It is much lighter than the English [l].		A *rabbit*.
ri	り	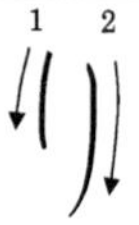 り (stroke order 1, 2)	り is similar to the first syllable of *ribbon*. The position of the tongue is the same as in ら.		A *ribbon*.
ru	る	 る (stroke order 1)	る is similar to the sound of *loop* without the [p] sound, but the vowel sound is shorter. The position of the tongue is the same as in ら.		A *loop* at the end.
re	れ	 れ (stroke order 1, 2)	れ is similar to the sound of *let's* without the [t's]. The position of the tongue is the same as in ら.		*Let's* dance.
ro	ろ	 ろ (stroke order 1)	ろ is similar to the sound *rope* without the [p] sound, but the vowel sound is shorter. The position of the tongue is the same as in ら.		A cowboy with his *rope*.
wa	わ	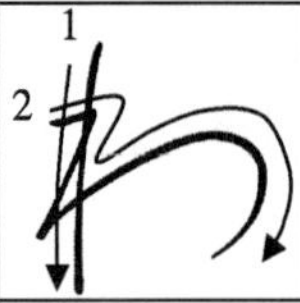 わ (stroke order 1, 2)	わ is similar to the English *wah*, but the lips are not as rounded or pointed.	 WAH	*Wah*!
wo	を	 を (stroke order 1, 2, 3)	を is pronounced like お.		*Oh!* I can ride a unicycle
n	ん	 ん (stroke order 1)	ん The pronunciation of ん changes according to the sound it precedes. It is [n] before [t], [s], [d], [z], [dz], [n], and [r], and [m] before [m], [n], [b]. It is a somewhat more nasal sound [ng], when it comes before [k] or [g], or at the end of a word.	 End	The *end*

Reading hiragana

Read the following words, paying attention to devoiced sounds and intonation.

あたま	head	はれ	clear (weather)
みみ	ear	とり	bird
め	eye	むすめ	daughter
ひる	afternoon	かわ	river
よる	night	やま	mountain
あめ	rain	からし	mustard
ゆき	snow	くすり	medicine
くも	cloud	うま	horse
しろい	white	しろい とり	white bird
くろい	black	くろい め	black eyes

Useful Expressions

Taking leave of friends and instructors

The phrase for good-bye differs according to the person you are addressing.

To instructors or social superiors:

shi tsu ree shi ma su

しつれい します。

Good-bye.

Example: Student: せんせい、しつれい します。 (sensee shitsuree shimasu)

Instructor: じゃ、さよなら。 (ja sayonara)

Notes

- The literal translation of しつれい します is *I am about to commit a rudeness* or *I am about to disturb you.*
- You should nod slightly when you say good-bye.
- しつれい します can also be used as a polite greeting (similar to "excuse me") when you enter the office of a professor or social superior.

To friends:

j a a ma ta
じゃあ、また。

See you later. (literally, *well then, again*)

Example: Student A: じゃあ、また。 (j a a m a t a)
Student B: じゃあ、また。 (j a a m a t a)

Note

- The 、 mark represents a comma in Japanese. Unlike English commas, Japanese commas always slant to the lower right.

To someone you do not expect to see for an extended period of time:

sa yo o na ra / sa yo na ra
さようなら。/ さよなら。

Good-bye.

Example: Friend A: さよなら。 (sa yo na ra)
Friend B: さようなら。 (s a y o o n a r a)

Note

- さようなら **[sayoonara]** or さよなら **[sayonara]** is usually used when you do not expect to see the person for an extended period of time, although these phrases, especially the more colloquial さよなら **[sayonara]** can be used more generally as well.

はなして みましょう Conversation Practice

1. Imagine that class is over. Say good-bye to your instructor and five classmates.
2. You are leaving your professor's office. Say good-bye to him/her.
3. Your friend is moving to a different city. Say good-bye to him/her.

V. Hiragana が〜ぽ： Voiced consonants

The consonants [k], [s], [t], [h] are voiceless, and they have voiced counterparts. The difference between voiceless and voiced consonants is the presence or absence of vibration. For instance, pronounce [k] and [g] one after another. The position of the tongue and the shape of the lips are identical for both sounds. In both cases you touch the back of your mouth with your tongue, then you quickly release the tongue to let the air flow. The only difference between the two is that your vocal chords vibrate when you pronounce [g], but not when you pronounce [k]. Feel the difference by putting your hand on your throat when you pronounce [k] and [g]. A voiced consonant is indicated by two dots (゛) and an unvoiced consonant by a small circle (゜) to the upper right corner of the character. For example, the voiced consonant [b] in ば has its voiceless counterpart [p] in ぱ。

					h		t	s	k	
ん	わ	ら	や	ま	は	な	た	さ	か	あ
		り		み	ひ	に	ち	し	き	い
		る	ゆ	む	ふ	ぬ	つ	す	く	う
		れ		め	へ	ね	て	せ	け	え
	を	ろ	よ	も	ほ	の	と	そ	こ	お

New hiragana

Printed style

p	b	d	z	g (ng)	
ぱ	ば	だ	ざ	が	a
ぴ	び	ぢ	じ	ぎ	i
ぷ	ぶ	づ	ず	ぐ	u
ぺ	べ	で	ぜ	げ	e
ぽ	ぼ	ど	ぞ	ご	o

Handwritten style

p	b	d	z	g (ng)	
ぱ	ば	だ	ざ	が	a
ぴ	び	ぢ	じ	ぎ	i
ぷ	ぶ	づ	ず	ぐ	u
ぺ	べ	で	ぜ	げ	e
ぽ	ぼ	ど	ぞ	ご	o

Note that [g] is sometimes represented as [ng] to reflect the softness of this sound.

Reading hiragana

Read the following words, paying attention to the voiced and voiceless consonants.

ひげ	beard	にほんご	Japanese language
ゆび	finger	かばん	bag
うで	arm	ちず	map
のど	throat	かぎ	key
ひざ	knee	かぜ	wind
からだ	body	えんぴつ	pencil
でんわ	telephone	てんぷら	tempura
ながい	long	ながい うで	long arm
みじかい	short	みじかい ゆび	short finger

Useful Expressions

Thanking, apologizing, and getting attention

Expressions of courtesy are important in every culture. Here are some of the basic ones in Japanese.

a ri ga to o go za i ma su
ありがとう ございます。
Thank you.

do o i ta shi ma shi te
どういたしまして。
You are welcome.

su mi ma se n
すみません。
I am sorry, excuse me.

a no o su mi ma se n
（あのう、）すみません。
(Um,) Excuse me.

NOTE

- ございます as in おはよう ございます [**ohayoo gozaimasu**] and ありがとう ございます [**arigatoo gozaimasu**] are polite expressions. The more informal おはよう [**ohayoo**] and ありがとう [**arigatoo**] are used in casual speech, among peers, but not with older people or with those of a higher social status.

はなして みましょう Conversation Practice

1. What would you say to your instructor if you forgot your homework?
2. Your instructor is talking to someone. You need to speak to him/her. How would you interrupt the conversation?
3. Your classmates are standing in front of the door. You want to leave the room. What would you say to them?
4. The student sitting next to you picks up the pencil you just dropped. What would you say to him?

VI. Hiragana **ああ〜わあ** : Long vowels

When the same vowel appears twice consecutively in a word, the two are pronounced as a continuous sound rather than as two separate vowels. This is called a long vowel.

In general, long vowels are written by adding あ to **hiragana** containing the vowel [a], い to **hiragana** containing the vowel [i] or [e], and う to **hiragana** containing the vowel [u] or [o]. Note that when い is added after the vowel [e] it is pronounced as [e]. (See the following chart.) Similarly, when う is added after the [o] sound, it is pronounced as [o]. There are some exceptions in which え and お are added instead of い and う, respectively, but you should not worry about them for now. You can learn them when you learn new vocabulary.

	w	r	y	m	h	n	t	s	k		
ん	わあ	らあ	やあ	まあ	はあ	なあ	たあ	さあ	かあ	ああ	aa
		りい		みい	ひい	にい	ちい	しい	きい	いい	ii
		るう	ゆう	むう	ふう	ぬう	つう	すう	くう	うう	uu
		れい		めい	へい	ねえ ねい	てい	せい	けい	ええ えい	ee
	を	ろう	よう	もう	ほう	のう	とお とう	そう	こお こう	おお おう	oo

Reading hiragana

Read the following words, paying attention to long vowels.

せんせい	teacher	がくせい	student
ふうせん	balloon	さとう	sugar
おうさま	king	こうこう	high school
ていねい	polite	とけい	clock, watch
おにいさん	elder brother	いもうと	younger sister
おとうと	younger brother	おとうさん	father
おかあさん	mother	おばあさん	grandmother
おじいさん	grandfather		
ちいさい	small	ちいさい とけい	small clock, watch

Here are some common exceptions that use え or お for long vowels.

ええ	yes	おねえさん	elder sister
とおり	street	こおり	ice
おおきい	big, large	おおきい とおり	big street

Useful Expressions

Understanding your instructor's requests

Here are a few common expressions your instructor will use in class. When you hear words you don't understand, try to guess what the teacher is saying from the context or situation or by observing gestures.

きいて ください。	Please listen.
みて ください。	Please look.
かいて ください。	Please write.
よんで ください。	Please read.
いって ください。	Please say it/repeat after me.
もう いちど いって ください。	Please say it again.
おおきい こえで いって ください。	Please speak loudly.

はなして みましょう Conversation Practice

1. Listen to your instructor's requests and try to determine what he/she wants you to do.
2. Working in pairs, take turns asking each other to perform certain actions, using phrases you know.

VII. Hiragana Small っ : Double Consonants

A small **tsu** っ indicates that the consonant that immediately follows it is preceded by a glottal stop and held for an additional syllable. This is called a double consonant. Double consonants often involve the glottis in speech, but may not necessarily require a full glottal stop. When written in a romanized form, they are indicated by a doubled consonant.

Horizontal writing

Printed style	Handwritten style
っか	っか
っき	っき
っく	っく
っけ	っけ
っこ	っこ

Vertical writing

Printed style			Handwritten style		
っく	っき	っか	っく	っき	っか

Reading hiragana

Read the following words, paying attention to double consonants.

にっき	diary	ざっし	magazine
がっき	musical instrument	せっけん	soap
がっこう	school	はっぱ	leaf
きっぷ	ticket	こっき	national flag
きって	stamp	さっか	writer
ねっとう	boiling water	しっぽ	tail
りっぱな	fine, magnificent	りっぱな がっこう	fine school

Useful Expressions

Confirming information and making requests

わかりましたか。 *Do you understand (it)?*

はい、わかりました。 *Yes, I understand (it).*

いいえ、わかりません。 *No, I don't understand (it).*

If you have trouble understanding your teacher because he/she speaks too softly or too fast for you, you can make requests using the following phrases.

To hear something repeated:

もう いちど おねがいします。

Please say it again. (literally, *Once more, please.*)

Example: Student : せんせい、すみません。もう いちど おねがいします。

Excuse me, Professor, could you say that again?

Teacher: あ、すみません。じゃ、もう いちど いいます。

Oh, sorry. Okay, I'll say it again.

To hear something spoken more loudly:

おおきい こえで おねがいします。

Please speak loudly. (literally, *Loud voice, please*) .

Example: Student: あのう、すみません。おおきい こえで おねがいします。

Excuse me, Professor, could you say that again a bit louder?

Teacher: はい、わかりました。

Okay.

To hear something spoken more slowly:

もう すこし ゆっくり おねがいします。

Please say it slowly. (literally, *A bit more slowly, please.*)

Example: Student: すみません、もう すこし ゆっくり おねがいします。

Excuse me, could you say that once more, a bit more slowly?

Teacher: はい、わかりました。

Okay.

Notes

- These phrases can be used with (あのう、) すみません、which makes your request sound more polite.
- おねがいします is more polite than ～てください (as in いってください) because the latter is a command form. It is more appropriate to use おねがいします with a social superior such as your instructor.

はなして みましょう Conversation Practice

1. Your instructor says something and checks your comprehension. Respond to him/her.
2. Your instructor says something you don't understand completely because it was spoken too fast, too softly, etc. Make the appropriate request so that you can understand what was said.

VIII. Hiragana きゃ〜ぴょ : Glides

Sounds containing a consonant and [y], such as [kya], [kyu], or [kyo], are called glides. Glides are written with a **hiragana** containing the sound [i] followed by a small ゃ、ゅ、 or ょ.

ぱ	ば	だ	ざ	が	ん	わ	ら	や	ま	は	な	た	さ	か	
ぴ	び	ぢ	じ	ぎ			り		み	ひ	に	ち	し	き	[i]
ぷ	ぶ	づ	ず	ぐ			る	ゆ	む	ふ	ぬ	つ	す	く	
ぺ	べ	で	ぜ	げ			れ		め	へ	ね	て	せ	け	
ぽ	ぼ	ど	ぞ	ご		を	ろ	よ	も	ほ	の	と	そ	こ	

pya	bya	dya	ja zya	gya			rya		mya	hya	nya	cha tya	sya sha	kya
ぴゃ	びゃ	ぢゃ	じゃ	ぎゃ			りゃ		みゃ	ひゃ	にゃ	ちゃ	しゃ	きゃ
pyu	byu	dyu	ju zyu	gyu			ryu		myu	hyu	nyu	chu tyu	syu shu	kyu
ぴゅ	びゅ	ぢゅ	じゅ	ぎゅ			りゅ		みゅ	ひゅ	にゅ	ちゅ	しゅ	きゅ
pyo	byo	dyo	jo zyo	gyo			ryo		myo	hyo	nyo	cho tyo	syo sho	kyo
ぴょ	びょ	ぢょ	じょ	ぎょ			りょ		みょ	ひょ	にょ	ちょ	しょ	きょ

There are some variations in romanization.

Horizontal writing

Printed style	Handwritten style
きゃ	きゃ
しゅ	しゅ
ちょ	ちょ

Vertical writing

Printed style			Handwritten style		
き	し	ち	き	し	ち
ゃ	ゅ	ょ	ゃ	ゅ	ょ

Reading hiragana

Read the following words, paying attention to glides.

こうちゃ	black tea	きんじょ	neighborhood
でんしゃ	train	ひゃく	one hundred
いしゃ	doctor	さんびゃく	three hundred
しゃしん	photo	りょこう	trip

A glide can be combined with a double consonant.

しゅっぱつ	departure	ちょっかく	right angle
しゃっくり	hiccup	しょっき	tableware

Add あ or う to form a long vowel within a glide.

きょう	today	びょうき	sickness
きゅうり	cucumber	みょうじ	last name
にんぎょう	doll	しょうがつ	New Year's Day
りょう	dormitory	ぎゅうにゅう	milk

Useful Expressions

Asking for Japanese words and English equivalents

1. Asking for a Japanese word
   Look at the objects in your classroom. Is there anything you do not know how to say in Japanese?

If the object is close to you:

これは にほんごで なんと いいますか。
What do you call this in Japanese?

Example: Smith: これは にほんごで なんと いいますか。
What do you call this in Japanese?

Yamada: 「ほん」と／って いいます。
You call it **hon.**

Smith

Yamada

NOTES

- To answer, say ～と／って いいます.
- The marks 「」 are the equivalent of quotation marks in English.

If the object is close to your interlocutor but at a distance from you:

それは にほんごで なんと いいますか。
What do you call that in Japanese?

Example: Smith: それは にほんごで なんと いいますか。
What do you call that in Japanese?

Yamada: 「いす」と／って いいます。
You call it **isu.**

Smith **Yamada**

If the object is at a distance from both you and your interlocutor:

あれは にほんごで なんと いいますか。
What do you call that (over there) in Japanese?

Example: Smith: あれは にほんごで なんと いいますか。
What do you call that (over there) in Japanese?

Yamada: 「でんわ」と／って いいます。
You call it **denwa.**

Smith **Yamada**

Note that これ, それ, and あれ refer only to objects, and never to people.

If you want to know the Japanese word for an object that is out of sight, for something intangible, or for any English word:

～は にほんごで なんと いいますか。
How do you say ～ in Japanese?

Example: Smith: せんせい、「love」は にほんごで なんと いいますか。
Professor, how do you say "love" in Japanese?

Teacher: 「あい」と／って いいます。
You say **ai.**

2. Asking for the meaning of a Japanese word or phrase

   Do you know what がくせい means? How about だいがく and せんこう? If you don't understand a Japanese word or expression, ask your instructor or a classmate:

〜って なんですか。

What does 〜 mean?

Example: Student: せんせい、「すいか」って なんですか。

Professor, what does **suika** *mean?*

Teacher: 「Watermelon」です。

It means watermelon.

To give the answer, say 〜です。

はなして みましょう Conversation Practice

1. Point at things that you are wearing and ask your instructor how to say them in Japanese.
2. Your instructor is in front of the class and you are sitting at a distance from him/her. What objects are near him/her? Ask your instructor what these objects are called in Japanese.
3. If the classroom has a window, ask your instructor the Japanese word for something you can see outside.
4. Ask your instructor the meanings of the following words: だいがく, せんこう, がくせい, つくえ, こくばん, まど, くるま.

たんご
Vocabulary

Nouns

せんせい　Teacher

Suffixes

〜せんせい　Professor 〜

〜さん　Mr./Mrs./Miss/Ms. 〜

Expressions

(あのう、)すみません。 (Um,) Excuse me.

ありがとう　ございます。 Thank you.

あれは　にほんごで　なんと　いいますか。 How do you say that (over there) in Japanese?

いいえ、わかりません。 No, I don't understand (it).

いって　ください。 Please say it. / Repeat after me.

おおきい　こえで　おねがいします。 Please speak loudly. (student request)

おおきい　こえで　いってください。 Please speak loudly. (instructor request)

おはよう。 Good morning. / Hello. (casual)

おはよう　ございます。 Good morning. / Hello. (polite)

かいて　ください。 Please write.

きいて　ください。 Please listen.

これは　にほんごで　なんと　いいますか。 How do you say this in Japanese?

こんにちは。 Good afternoon. / Hello.

こんばんは。 Good evening. / Hello.

さようなら。／さよなら。 Good-bye.

しつれいします。 Good-bye. / Excuse me.

じゃあ、また。 See you later. (literally, Well then, again.)

すみません。 I am sorry. / Excuse me.

それは　にほんごで　なんと　いいますか。 How do you say that in Japanese?

〜って　なんですか。 What does 〜 mean?

〜と　いいます。／〜って　いいます。 You say 〜, you call it 〜.

どういたしまして。 You are welcome.

はい、わかりました。 Yes, I understand it.

はじめまして。 ～です。 どうぞ よろしく。 How do you do? I am ～. Pleased to meet you.

～は にほんごで なんと いいますか。 How do you say ～ in Japanese?

みて ください。 Please look at it.

もう いちど いってください。 Please say it again. (instructor request)

もう いちど おねがいします。 Please say it again. (student request)

もう すこし ゆっくり おねがいします。 Please say it slowly.

よんで ください。 Please read.

わかりましたか。 Do you understand (it)?

Chapter 2

だいにか

あいさつと　じこしょうかい

Greetings and Introductions

Objectives	Meeting people for the first time, introducing people, identifying people, telling time
Vocabulary	Countries, nationalities, languages, year in school and academic status, majors, time expressions
Dialogue	はじめまして *How do you do?*
Japanese Culture	Meeting and greeting people
Grammar	I. Identifying someone or something, using ～は　～です
	II. Asking はい／いいえ questions, using ～は　～ですか
	III. Indicating relationships between nouns with の
	IV. Asking for personal information, using question words
	V. Using も to list and describe similarities
Listening	Listening for key words
Communication	Using あいづち: (attentive feedback) 1; classroom manners
Reading	Using format as a clue

たんご
Vocabulary

Nouns

アジアけんきゅう (あじあ)	アジア研究	Asian studies
アメリカ (あめりか)		America, the United States
イギリス (いぎりす)		England
いちねんせい	一年生	freshman, first-year student (The suffix せい may be dropped.)
いま	今	now
えいご	英語	English
オーストラリア (お すとらりあ)		Australia
がくせい	学生	student
カナダ (かなだ)		Canada
かんこく	韓国	South Korea
けいえいがく	経営学	management/business administration
こうがく	工学	engineering
こうこう	高校	high school
ごご	午後	p.m., afternoon
ごぜん	午前	a.m., morning
こちら		this person, this way
さんねんせい	三年生	junior, third-year student (The suffix せい may be dropped.)
しゅっしん	出身	one's native country, hometown, birthplace, alma mater
スペイン (すぺいん)		Spain
せんこう	専攻	major
だいがく	大学	college, university

だいがくいんせい	大学院生	graduate student
だいがくせい	大学生	college student
たいわん	台湾	Taiwan
ちゅうごく	中国	China
なまえ	名前	name
にねんせい	二年生	sophomore, second-year student (The suffix せい may be dropped.)
にほん	日本	Japan
ビジネス (びじねす)		business
フランス (ふらんす)		France
ぶんがく	文学	literature
メキシコ (めきしこ)		Mexico
よねんせい	四年生	senior, fourth-year student (The suffix せい may be dropped.)
らいねん	来年	next year
りゅうがくせい	留学生	foreign student
れきし	歴史	history

Pronouns

ぼく	僕	I (normally used by males)
わたし	私	I (used by both males and females)

Copula Verb

です		(to) be

Time Expressions

いちじ	一時	one o'clock
にじ	二時	two o'clock
さんじ	三時	three o'clock
よじ	四時	four o'clock
ごじ	五時	five o'clock
ろくじ	六時	six o'clock

しちじ	七時	seven o'clock
はちじ	八時	eight o'clock
くじ	九時	nine o'clock
じゅうじ	十時	ten o'clock
じゅういちじ	十一時	eleven o'clock
じゅうにじ	十二時	twelve o'clock
はん	半	half past いちじはん 1:30

Question words

どこ		where
どちら		where (more polite than どこ), which way
なに/なん	何	what

Particles

か		question marker
の		noun modifier marker (of), ('s)
は		topic marker
も		similarity marker (also, too)

Prefixes

お〜	御〜	polite prefix おなまえ polite form of なまえ (name)

Suffixes

〜ご	〜語	language
		にほんご Japanese language
〜じ	〜時	〜 o'clock
〜じん	〜人	-nationality アメリカ(あめりか) じん
〜せい	〜生	-student
		だいがくせい college student
		いちねんせい freshman
〜ねん	〜年	year いちねん first year

Interjections

あのう	uh, well . . .
いいえ	no, don't mention it, you're welcome
はい／ええ	yes

Expressions

いいえ、そうじゃありません／そうじゃないです	No, that's not so
はい／ええ、そうです	Yes, that's so
そうですか	Is that so? I see.
～から　きました	came from ～ [casual]
こちらこそ	It is I who should be saying that. Thank you.
～って　いいます	colloquial version of ～と　いいます

たんごの れんしゅう Vocabulary Practice

A. くに Countries

Starting with this chapter, loan words (foreign words used in Japanese) will be written in **katakana**. They will have subscripts in hiragana, except for the symbol ー, which indicates a long vowel. For example: コーヒー (こ ひ) (*coffee*) is pronounced with an elongated [ko] and an elongated [hi].

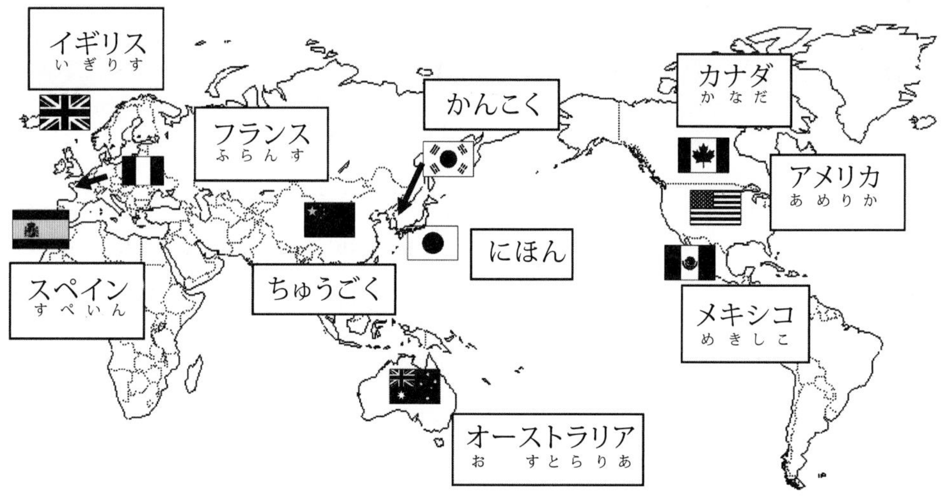

B. こくせきと こくご Nationalities and languages

Activity 1

In Japanese, identify the countries indicated on the map below, the nationality of the people from each country, and the principal language(s) spoken there.

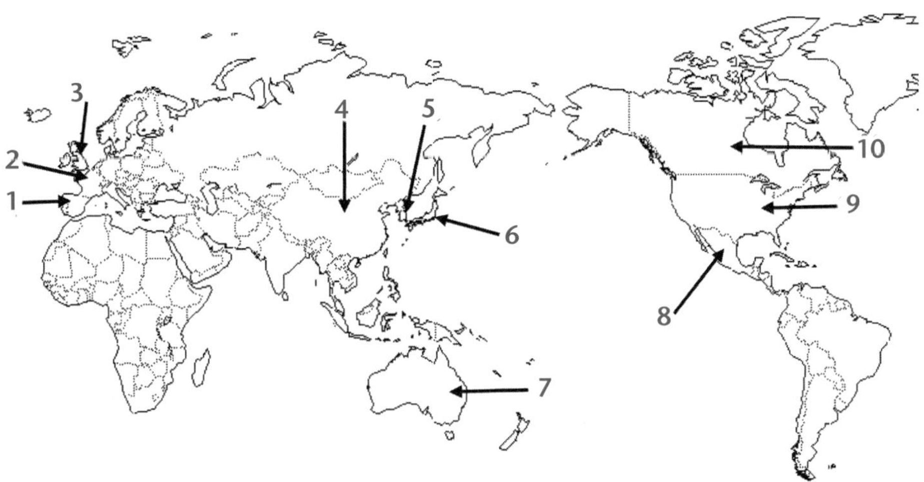

Activity 2

In Japanese, identify the countries represented by the flags below, the nationality of people from each country, and the principal language(s) spoken there.

Activity 3

Identify or guess the language of each of the following greeting phrases.

(a) Good morning.
(b) Bonjour.
(c) Buenos días.
(d) Ni hao?／Zao chen hao.
(e) An nyong haseyo.
(f) おはよう(ございます)。

C. ～ねんせい Year in school and academic status

1	2	3	4	G
いちねんせい	にねんせい	さんねんせい	よねんせい	だいがくいんせい
freshman	sophomore	junior	senior	graduate student

がくせい	student
りゅうがくせい	international student
だいがく	college
こうこう	high school

Activity 4

Write your answers to the following questions in **hiragana**.

1. いま、なんねんせいですか。 (*Which year are you in now?*)
2. らいねん　なんねんせいですか。(*Which year will you be in next year?*)
3. "high school student" は　にほんごで　なんと　いいますか。
4. "graduate student" は　にほんごで　なんと　いいますか。

D. せんこう Majors

アジアけんきゅう (あじあ)	Asian studies
けいえいがく	management
こうがく	engineering
ぶんがく	literature
ビジネス (びじねす)	business
れきし	history

Activity 5

Answer the following questions in Japanese.

1. Which of these disciplines are you interested in?
2. Which of these disciplines is the most difficult to learn, in your opinion?
3. Which of these disciplines is the easiest to learn, in your opinion?
4. Do you know how to say your major in Japanese? If not, ask your instructor and write it down.

Supplementary Vocabulary: Academic majors

いがく	医学	medicine (medical science)
おんがく	音楽	music
かがく	化学	chemistry
きょういくがく	教育学	education
けいざいがく	経済学	economics
けんちくがく	建築学	architecture
こくさいかんけい	国際関係	international relations
コンピュータこうがく (こんぴゅ た)	コンピュータ工学	computer engineering
しゃかいがく	社会学	sociology
じょうほうかがく	情報科学	information science
じょうほうこうがく	情報工学	information technology
しんりがく	心理学	psychology
じんるいがく	人類学	anthropology
すうがく	数学	mathematics
せいぶつがく	生物学	biology
せいじがく	政治学	political science
びじゅつ	美術	fine arts
ぶつりがく	物理学	physics

E. Time expressions

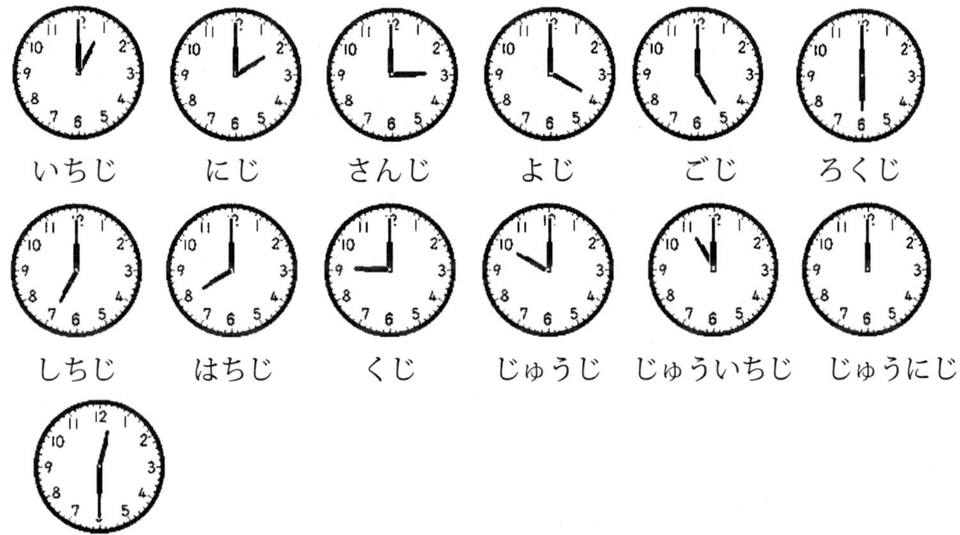

You can probably guess how to say the numbers “1” through “12” from the time expressions and academic years presented above. For a complete explanation of Japanese numbers, see Chapter 3, vocabulary practice D (pp. a-91–92).

Activity 6

State the time on the following clocks using time + です (*it's* 〜).

Example: Q: いま　なんじですか。

What time is it now?

A: いちじです。

ダイアローグ
Dialogue

はじめに Warm-up

Answer the following questions in English

1. When you meet a Japanese person for the first time, how do you introduce yourself? Do you shake hands?
2. Suppose you have just been introduced to your host family in Japan. What kinds of things would you talk about?

はじめまして *How do you do?*

Alice Ueda, a Japanese-American student, is attending an orientation session at the International Student Center at Joto University in Tokyo. A student sitting next to Ueda speaks to her.

リー： あのう、すみません。いま　なんじですか。

うえだ： いちじですよ。

リー： いちじですか。どうも　ありがとう ございます。

うえだ： いいえ。

リー： あのう。

うえだ： はい。

リー： おなまえは　なんですか。ぼく、リーって　いいます。

どうぞ　よろしく。

うえだ：　こちらこそ　どうぞ　よろしく。わたしの　なまえは
アリス(ありす)　うえだです。

リー(り)：　ああ、そうですか。ぼくは　たいわんから　きました。
うえださんは？

うえだ：　シカゴ(しかご)です。わたしは　ウエストサイド(うえすとさいど)だいがくの
さんねんせいです。

リー(り)：　そうですか。ぼくも　さんねんせいです。
せんこうは　なんですか。

うえだ：　ぶんがくです。リー(り)さんは？

リー(り)：　ぼくは　れきしです。

An International Student Center staff member and a Japanese man approach them.

りゅうがくせいセンター(せんた)の　ひと (International Student Center staff member)：
うえださんですか。

うえだ：　ええ、そうです。

りゅうがくせいセンター(せんた)の　ひと：　すずきさん、こちらは
うえださんです。うえださん、こちらは
ホストファミリー(ほすとふぁみり)の　すずきさんです。

うえだ：　はじめまして。　アリス(ありす)です。　どうぞ よろしく。

すずき：　すずきです。　こちらこそ、よろしく。

Dialogue Phrase Notes

- The particle よ (*I tell you*) in いちじですよ indicates the speaker's assertion and mild emphasis that he/she is providing information known to him/her but not to the listener.
- どうも can have many meanings. In the dialogue どうも means *very much*, so どうも　ありがとう　ございます (*thank you very much*) expresses a deeper appreciation than ありがとう ございます (*thank you*).
- いいえ means *no*, but in the above dialogue, it means *don't mention it* or *you are welcome*, as in いいえ、どういたしまして. This usage of いいえ is common in Japanese conversation.

- あのう is a hesitation marker. It expresses the speaker's reluctance to bother the person to whom he/she is speaking. This hesitation shows the speaker's respect and consideration for the person he/she is approaching. It can appear by itself as in the dialogue, or with other phrases such as あのう、すみません as in Chapter 1.
- ～と／って　いいます (*[something/someone] is called* ～) was introduced in Chapter 1. This phrase can be used in self-introductions, as in the dialogue.
- ああ、そうですか (*oh, I see*) and そうですか (*I see / is that so?*) is used by the speaker to acknowledge that he/she has understood what has been said. ああ may also be used as a shorter way to convey the same meaning.

ダイアローグ(だいあろぐ)の　あとで　Comprehension

Complete the chart with information about Alice and Li.

	くに／まち Country/city	～ ねんせい Year in college	せんこう Major
うえだ			
リー(り)ー			

にほんの　ぶんか
Japanese Culture

First name or last name?

How do you address your friends and classmates? How about your professors?

When you meet a Japanese adult for the first time, use your last name when introducing yourself. Also, it is not customary to use a Japanese adult's first name, especially when the person is older or higher in social status. However, it is not uncommon to find close friends calling each other by their first names. Since many Japanese are aware that Westerners usually use first names, a foreign student may be addressed by his/her first name, followed by さん, as in クリス(くりす)さん. In family settings, older family members address younger ones by their first names, though younger family members do not use the first names of older members. Instead, they use kinship terms such as mother, father, older brother, and older sister. When a foreign student stays with a Japanese host family, the parents will call the student either by his/her first name only, or will use the first name with さん. The host sisters or brothers will most likely use first name + さん. In general, senior members are referred to by kinship terms and junior members by their first name plus さん (unisex), くん (for a young boy) or ちゃん (for small children). When in doubt, ask the members of the host family how they want to be addressed.

Bowing? Shaking hands?

Why didn't Suzuki shake hands with Alice Ueda when he was introduced to her?

To be on the safe side, always bow when meeting a Japanese adult for the first time. Bow with your feet together, bending about fifteen degrees from your waist. Drop your eyes as you bow. You may bow more deeply and more than once if you wish to show greater respect. Shaking hands is not customary in Japan, but if someone extends his or her hand, then respond accordingly. Do not squeeze the person's hand too firmly.

名刺 (business cards)

Who uses めいし? When and how do people exchange めいし?

In Japan, exchanging business cards is an important part of the ritual of meeting people for the first time. Professionals always have business cards, as do many graduate students. Undergraduate students usually do not have them since they are not considered full-fledged members of adult society. When a person expected to have a card does not have one on hand, he/she usually apologizes for his/her oversight. A person given a name card takes it with both hands. It is important to read the card carefully in order to identify the person's title or position and the name of the organization to which he/she belongs. Such information is considered essential in socializing with the proper degree of formality or politeness.

ぶんぽう
Grammar

I. Identifying someone or something, using ～は　～です

The sentences X は Y です (*X is Y*) and X は Y じゃありません／じゃないです (*X isn't Y*) are used to identify or characterize a person or thing. Japanese uses particles in addition to nouns, verbs, adjectives, etc. Particles most often consist of one character (sometimes two), and they are placed immediately after a noun or at the end of a sentence. Those particles that appear after nouns assign a grammatical function to the noun they follow. Those that appear at the end of a sentence indicate the function of the preceding sentence or the speaker's attitudes or emotions. は, which is pronounced *wa*, indicates that the preceding noun X is the topic of the sentence.

Affirmative

Topic		Comment	
Noun	Particle (Topic)	Noun	Copula Verb
たなかさん	は	さんねんせい	です。

Mr. Tanaka is a junior.

Negative

Topic		Comment	
Noun	Particle (Topic)	Noun	Copula Verb
すずきさん	は	りゅうがくせい	じゃありません。 じゃないです。

Mr./Ms. Suzuki is not an international student.

In the above example sentences, the topic Xは represents information already known to both the speaker and the listener. Yです is a comment about the topic. That is, Y represents information concerning the topic X. For example, in the sentence たなかさんは　さんねんせいです。(*Mr./Ms. Tanaka is a junior.*), たなかさん is what the speaker wants to talk about, or the topic, and さんねんせい is what the speaker wants to say about the topic.

わたしは　いちねんせいです。でも、たなかさんは
　いちねんせいじゃありません。
I am a freshman, but Ms./Mr. Tanaka is not a freshman.

ロペスさんは　メキシコ じんです。がくせいです。

Mr./Ms. Lopez is Mexican. He/she is a student.

モネさんは　だいがくいんせいです。リーさんは
だいがくいんせいじゃありません。

Mr./Ms. Monet is a graduate student, but Mr./Ms. Li is not.

Notes

- The topic X は can be omitted if the speaker thinks the listener can identify what it is from the context. For example, わたしは is omitted in greetings such as はじめまして　～です。どうぞよろしく, because it is obvious that the speaker is talking about himself/herself.
- です and じゃありません／じゃないです do not change form according to either the number of persons or things being discussed or the voice (first person, second person, or third person) of the subject. Compare the following Japanese and English sentences.

  わたしは　だいがくせい<u>です</u>。
  I <u>am</u> a college student.

  うえださんは　だいがくせい<u>です</u>。
  Ms. Ueda <u>is</u> a college student.

  わたしたちは　だいがくせい<u>です</u>。
  We <u>are</u> college students.

- じゃないです is more colloquial than じゃありません.
- While the English verb *to be* sometimes indicates location, such as *Tokyo is in Japan*, です and じゃありません／じゃないです do not.

はなして　みましょう　Conversation Practice

Activity 1

Imagine that the following people live in your dormitory. Work with a partner and tell him/her about each person.

Example: たなかさんは　にほんじんです。
だいがくいんせいです。
せんこうは　かんこくごです。

Name	Nationality	Year in school	Major
たなか	にほんじん	だいがくいんせい	かんこくご
リー り	ちゅうごくじん	だいがくいんせい	アジアけんきゅう あじあ
ブラウン ぶらうん	オーストラリアじん おすとらりあ	よねんせい	ビジネス びじねす
スミス すみす	アメリカじん あめりか	さんねんせい	こうがく
キム きむ	かんこくじん	にねんせい	フランスご ふらんす
モネ もね	カナダじん かなだ	いちねんせい	ぶんがく

Activity 2

Complete the following chart by circling the appropriate words and by writing in your major (and nationality, if necessary) in Japanese.

Your name	
Status	だいがくせい　だいがくいんせい
Major	
Year	いちねんせい　にねんせい　さんねんせい よねんせい　だいがくいんせい
Nationality	アメリカじん　ちゅうごくじん　かんこくじん あめりか ＿＿＿＿＿＿じん

Activity 3

Introduce yourself to your partner and describe yourself using the words in Activity 2 and the X は Y です pattern.

Example: はじめまして。 (your name) です。どうぞ よろしく。

(わたしは) (college student/graduate student) です。
(year) せいです。

せんこうは ______ です。わたしは (nationality) じんです。

Now listen to your partner's self-introduction and complete the following chart.

Partner's name	
Status	
Major	
Year	
Nationality	

Activity 4

Introduce a partner and yourself to another classmate.

Example: わたしは________です。__________じんです。
__________せいです。

せんこうは____________です。

こちらは__________さんです。

______さんは__________じゃありません／じゃないです。

__________です。

II. Asking はい／いいえ questions, using ～は　～ですか

It is very easy to formulate questions in Japanese. All you have to do is add the particle か to the end of the sentence.

Asking the listener's identity

Question		
	Copula Verb	Particle
すずきさん	です	か。

Are you Mr./Ms. Suzuki?

Answer		
		Copula Verb
はい／ええ、	そう	です。

Yes, I am.

Asking about people and things

Question	
	Particle
キムさんは　かんこくじんです	か。

Is Mr./Ms. Kim Korean? /Are you Korean, Mr./Ms. Kim?

Affirmative Answer		
		Copula Verb
はい／ええ、	そう	です。

Yes, he/she is. / Yes, I am.

(literally, *Yes, it is so.*)

Affirmative Answer		
		Copula Verb
はい／ええ、	かんこくじん	です。

Yes, he/she is Korean. / Yes, I am Korean.

Negative Answer		
		Copula Verb
いいえ、	そう	じゃありません。 じゃないです。

No, he/she isn't. (literally, *No, it isn't so.)*

Negative Answer		
		Copula Verb
いいえ、	イギリスじん	です。

No, I am British.

おおき： うえださんですか。	*Are you Ms. Ueda?*
うえだ： はい、そうです。	*Yes, I am.*
おおき： うえださんは　にほんじんですか。	*Are you Japanese, Ms. Ueda?*
うえだ： いいえ、アメリカじんです。	*No, I'm American.*

Notes

- The Japanese pronoun あなた, although it is equivalent to *you*, is not used as commonly as its English counterpart. It is more common to use the name of the person being addressed. Thus, アリス(ありす)さんは　がくせいですか can mean either *Are you a student, Alice?* or *Is Alice a student?* depending on whether you are talking to Alice or someone else.
- はい／ええ、そうです is an affirmative answer to questions, and means *Yes, I am / you are / it is / he/she is / they are / we are.* いいえ、そうじゃありません／いいえ、そうじゃないです is a negative answer, and it means *No, I'm not / you aren't / it isn't / he/she isn't / they aren't / we aren't.*

はなして　みましょう　Conversation Practice

Activity 1

Answer the following questions, using ええ、そうです or いいえ、そうじゃありません／いいえ、そうじゃないです.

Example: がくせいですか。　　ええ、そうです。

1. がっこうは　ウエストサイド(うえすとさいど)だいがくですか。
2. いちねんせいですか。
3. せんこうは　にほんごですか。
4. アメリカ(あめりか)じんですか。
5. りゅうがくせいですか。
6. せんせいは　にほんじんですか。

Activity 2

Find out how many of your classmates are in the same year of school as you by asking ～さんは　～ですか. Also, find out how many have the same major as you.

Example: A: たなかさんは　いちねんせいですか。

B: ええ、そうです。／いいえ、そうじゃありません／いいえ、そうじゃないです。

A: そうですか。せんこうは　にほんごですか。

B: ええ、そうです。／いいえ、そうじゃありません／いいえ、そうじゃないです。

Activity 3

Work with a partner. Choose an identity from the chart below, but don't tell your partner. Your partner will try to guess who you are by asking questions using ～は　～ですか. Answer with ええ、そうです or いいえ、そうじゃありません／いいえ、そうじゃないです.

Examples: A: にほんじんですか。

B: いいえ、そうじゃありません。

A: アメリカ(あめりか)じんですか。

B: ええ、そうです。

A: せんこうは　えいごですか。

B: ええ、そうです。

A: スミス(すみす)さんですか。

B: ええ、そうです。

Name	Nationality	Year in school	Major
スミス(すみす)	アメリカ(あめりか) じん	さんねんせい	えいご
ブラウン(ぶらうん)	アメリカ(あめりか)じん	いちねんせい	アジア(あじあ)けんきゅう
ロペス(ろぺす)	アメリカ(あめりか)じん	にねんせい	ぶんがく
ジョンソン(じょんそん)	アメリカ(あめりか)じん	だいがくいんせい	ビジネス(びじねす)
ハート(はと)	アメリカ(あめりか)じん	よねんせい	スペインご(すぺいん)
たなか	にほんじん	いちねんせい	スペインご(すぺいん)
やまだ	にほんじん	だいがくいんせい	けいえいがく
さとう	にほんじん	にねんせい	こうがく
もり	にほんじん	よねんせい	ぶんがく
すずき	にほんじん	さんねんせい	アジア(あじあ)けんきゅう

III. Indicating relationships between nouns with の

The particle の allows the first noun in a phrase to modify the second noun. Because の can convey a variety of relationships between two nouns, such as possession, group membership, or location, the particle's meaning depends on the context.

とうきょうだいがくの	リー(り)さん	Mr./Ms. Li from Tokyo University
とうきょうだいがくの	がくせい	student at Tokyo University
わたしの	せんこう	my major
れきしの	せんこう	history major
わたしの	せんせい	my teacher
せんせいの	ほん	teacher's book; book written by the teacher
メキシコ(めきしこ)の	うち	house in Mexico
にほんの	ほん	book about Japan; book from Japan
にほんごの	ほん	book written in Japanese; book about Japanese
とうきょうの	おかださん	Mr./Ms.Okada who lives in Tokyo; Mr./Ms. Okada who is from Tokyo

すずき：はじめまして。すずきです。
How do you do? I'm Suzuki.

きむら：はじめまして。りゅうがくせいセンター(せんた)の　きむらです。
How do you do? I'm Kimura of the International Student Center.
うえださん、こちらは　うえださんの　ホストファミリー(ほすとふぁみり)の すずきさんです。
Ms. Ueda, this is Mr. Suzuki from your host family.

うえだ：はじめまして。アリス(ありす)　うえだです。どうぞ　よろしく。
How do you do? I'm Alice Ueda. Pleased to meet you.

すずき：こちらこそ。よろしく。
Same here.

たなか：ロペス(ろぺす)さんの　せんこうは　ビジネス(びじねす)ですか。
Is your major economics, Mr./Ms. Lopez?

ロペス(ろぺす)：いいえ。　わたしは　こうがくの　せんこうです。
No. I'm an engineering major.

Notes

- Possessive pronouns in English consist of one word, as in *my*, but the equivalent forms of Japanese consist of a pronoun followed by の, as in わたし/ぼく+ の. Also, the semantic relationship between the modifier and the word being modified is not always clear in this structure. The relationship depends on context and the meanings of the two nouns. For example, in the phrase たなかせんせいの ほん, Professor Tanaka may be the author or the owner of the book.
- The appositive relationship can also be expressed with の . The following example is translated into English as *Mr. Suzuki from my host family*. In contrast, すずきさんの ホストファミリー(ほすとふぁみり) is interpreted as *Mr. Suzuki's host family*.

ホストファミリー(ほすとふぁみり)の　すずきさん	*Mr. Suzuki, who is in (my) host family*
すずきさんの　ホストファミリー(ほすとふぁみり)	*Mr. Suzuki's host family*

はなして みましょう　Conversation Practice

Activity 1

Pretend that you are the moderator of a panel discussion on environmental protection. Introduce the following experts using Noun の Noun.

Example:　(やまだ)

こちらは　シカゴ(しかご)だいがくの　やまだせんせいです。

a-51 #1

1. いいえ, そうじゃありません.

2. ええ, そうです。

3. いいえ, そうじゃないです。

4. ええ, そうです。

5. いいえ, そうじゃないです。

6. ええ, そうです。

a-55 #3

1. リーさん

2. びじねす

3. こうがく

4 よんせいだいがく

Activity 2

You meet a student from another school. Introduce yourself in terms of your school by using Noun の Noun.

Example: はじめまして。(わたしは)__________だいがくの
__________です。

Activity 3

Complete the following dialogue, using the information from the chart below.

Example: A: たなかさんの　せんこうは　えいごですか。

B：いいえ、そうじゃありません。かんこくごです。

Name	School	Major
たなか	とうきょうだいがく	かんこくご
リー (り)	にほんだいがく	アジア (あじあ) けんきゅう
ケリー (けり)	UCLA	ビジネス (びじねす)
スミス (すみす)	ハワイ (はわい) だいがく	こうがく
キム (きむ)	ヨンセイ (よんせい) だいがく	ぶんがく

1. A: __________の　せんこうは　アジア(あじあ)けんきゅうですか。

   B: ええ、そうです。

2. A: ケリー(けり)さんは　アジア(あじあ)けんきゅうの__________ですか。

   B: いいえ、ビジネス(びじねす)の　がくせいです。

3. A: スミス(すみす)さんの__________は　ハワイ(はわい)だいがくですか。

   B: ええ、そうです。

4. A: キム(きむ) さんは__________の　せんこうですか。

   B: ええ、そうです。

Activity 4

Use Noun のNoun to tell a classmate your friend's name, school, and major.

Example: ________さんは　わたしの　ともだち (friend) です。
________さんの　だいがくは__________だいがくです。
せんこうは__________です。

IV. Asking for personal information, using question words

In Japanese, you don't have to change the word order of a sentence to form an information question. All you have to do is to use a question word, such as なん (*what*) or どこ (*where*), for things you want to ask about.

Asking about names and things, using なん

Question			Answer
	Question Word		
おなまえは	なん	ですか。	アリスです。 ありす
What is your name?			*I am Alice.*

Question			Answer
	Question Word + Suffix		
キムさんは きむ	なんねんせい	ですか。	さんねんせいです。
What year are you in, Mr./Ms. Kim?			*I am a junior.*

Question			Answer
	Question Word + Suffix		
いま	なんじ	ですか。	さんじです。
What time is it now?			*It's 3 o'clock.*

もり：すみません。いま なんじですか。
Excuse me. What time is it?

すずき：よじはんですよ。
It's 4:30.

もり：そうですか。どうも。
Oh, is it? Thanks.

すずき：いいえ。
You're welcome.

To specify a.m. and p.m., add ごぜん (a.m.) or ごご (p.m.) in front of the time expression.

とうきょうは　いま　ごぜん　じゅうじです。
In Tokyo it is 10 a.m. now.

ニューヨークは（にゅよく）　ごご　ろくじはんです。
It is 6:30 p.m. in New York.

Using どこ and どちら to ask about places

Question		
Question word (place)	Particle	
どこ	から	きましたか。

Where are you from?
(literally, *Where did you come from?*)

Answer		
Noun (place)	Particle	
にほん	から	きました。

I'm from Japan.
(literally, *I came from Japan.*)

やまだ： ソフィー(そふぃ)さんは　どこから　きましたか。
Sophie, where are you from?

ソフィー(そふぃー)： カナダ(かなだ)から　きました。
I'm from Canada.

やまだ： そうですか。なんねんせいですか。
I see. What year are you in?

ソフィー(そふぃ)： いちねんせいです。やまださんは？
First year. How about you, Mr./Ms. Yamada?

やまだ： わたしは　にねんせいです。
I am a sophomore.

Notes

- In Japanese, a question word cannot be used as a topic or come before the particle は. It is a part of the です half of the sentence, and replaces the word that is in question. For example:

  やまだ：　たなかさんは　なんねんせいですか。
  What year are you in, Mr./Ms. Tanaka?

  たなか：　わたしは　いちねんせいです。
  I'm a freshman.

- どこから　きましたか。 is a way of asking about someone's hometown, home state, or native country. から is a particle that means *from*. きました is the past tense form of the verb きます (*come*). In formal situations use the more polite どちらから いらっしゃいましたか (*where are you from*). When answering this more formal question, however, you should always use きました, and not いらっしゃいました.

- To find out the name of someone's school, use どこ. For example, やまださんの　だいがくは　どこですか。asks for the name of a school, and not the location of the school.

  A: やまださんの　だいがくは　どこですか。
  Where do you go to school, Mr./Ms. Yamada?

  B: とうきょうだいがくです。
  I go to the University of Tokyo.

  Do not use なんですか to ask for the name of a school:

  ~~やまださんの　だいがくは　なんですか。~~

はなして　みましょう　Conversation Practice

Activity 1

Begin a dialogue by asking a question that corresponds to each of the following answers.

Example: スミス(すみす)です。
　あのう、おなまえは　なんですか。

1. メキシコ(めきしこ)から　きました。
2. アジア(あじあ)けんきゅうです。
3. リー(り)です。
4. さんねんせいです。
5. フランス(ふらんす)ごです。
6. よじです。
7. だいがくいんせいです。
8. じょうとうだいがくです。

Activity 2

Ask your classmates about their majors and hometowns. Is there anyone who is majoring in the same subject as you?

Example: A: __________さんの　せんこうは　なんですか。
B: __________です。～さんは？
A: わたしの　せんこうは__________です。
B: ああ、そうですか。

Activity 3

Ask your classmates and your instructor about their majors and hometowns. Find out who comes from the most distant place.

Example: A: ________さんは　どこから　きましたか 。

B: ________ から　きました。~さんは？

A: ________ から　きました。

B: ああ、そうですか。

Activity 4

Work with a partner. Look at the map of world and ask each other what time it is in various cities.

Example: とうきょう (Tokyo)

A: とうきょうは　いま　なんじですか。

B: <u>ごぜん　じゅういちじですよ。</u>

A: そうですか。

1. ニューヨーク (New York) にゅ よ く
2. ホノルル (Honolulu) ほのるる
3. シドニー (Sydney) しどに
4. モスクワ (Moscow) もすくわ
5. バンクーバー (Vancouver) ばんく ば
6. ロンドン (London) ろんどん
7. バンコク (Bangkok) ばんこく
8. デリー (Delhi) でり
9. カイロ (Cairo) かいろ

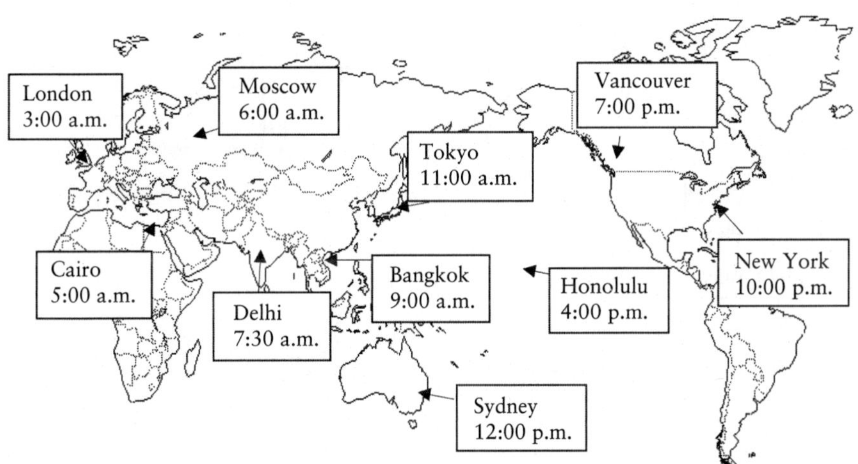

Activity 5

Work with a partner. You are traveling through a number of cities in the United States. Ask your partner what time it is in the city you are in now. The reference time indicates the current time in the last city you visited. Your partner will have to compute the time for the city you are asking about based on the reference time.

Example: Reference time: 7:30 a.m. EST
City you are in now: Chicago

A: あのう、すみません。いま　なんじですか。

B: ろくじはんですよ。

A: ああ、そうですか。どうも　ありがとうございます。

B: いいえ。

1. 7:30 p.m. EST, Denver
2. 9:00 a.m. CST, Seattle
3. 8:30 p.m. CST, New York
4. 2:30 p.m. MST, Anchorage
5. 1:00 p.m. MST., Atlanta
6. 11:30 p.m. PST, Salt Lake City
7. 1:30 a.m. PST, Honolulu
8. 11:00 p.m. PST, Boston

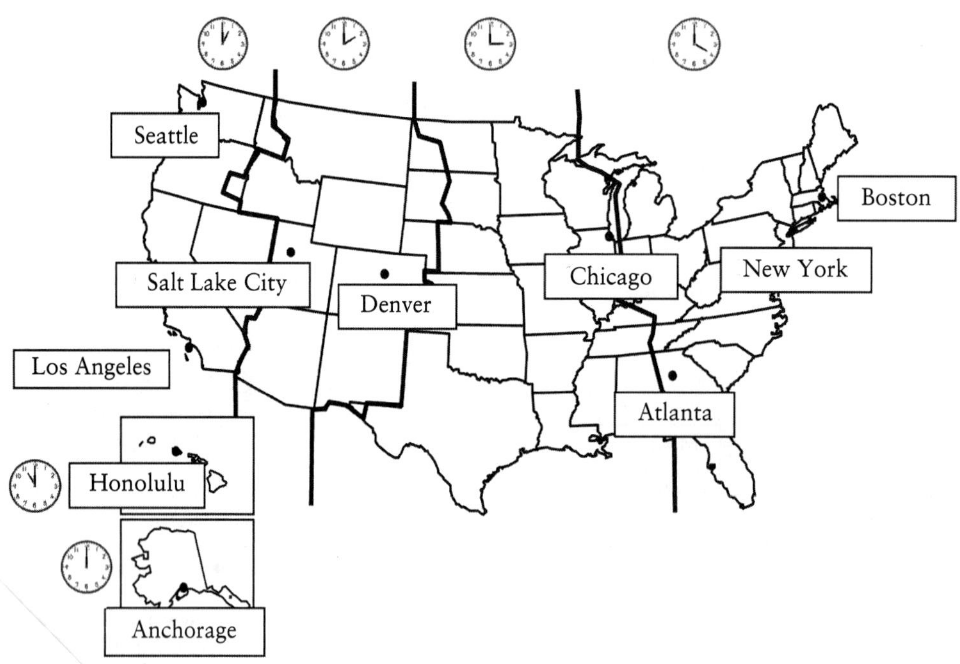

V. Using も to list and describe similarities

The particle も means *also* or *too*, and it is used to show the similarity between what has been just said and what you are saying.

Sentence 1		
	Particle	
わたしの　こうこう	は	ミルズ(みるず)　ハイスクール(はいすくーる)です。

My high school is Mills High School.

Sentence 2		
Noun Phrase	Particle	
トム(とむ)さんの　こうこう	も	ミルズ(みるず)　ハイスクール(はいすくーる)です。

Tom's high school is also Mills High School.

うえだ：キム(きむ)さんは　にほんごの　がくせいですか。
Are you a Japanese major, Mr./Ms. Kim? (literally, *are you a student of Japanese?*)

キム(きむ)：ええ、そうですよ。うえださんは？
Yes, I am. How about you, Ms. Ueda?

うえだ：わたしも　にほんごの　せんこうですよ。
I am a Japanese major, too.

キム(きむ)：ああ、そうですか。
Oh, is that so?

やまだ：すずきさんは　どこから　きましたか。
Ms. Suzuki, where are you from?

すずき：とうきょうから　きました。
I'm from Tokyo.

やまだ：そうですか。ぼくも　とうきょうから　きました。
Is that so? I'm from Tokyo, too.

すずき：ああ、そうですか。とうきょうの　どこですか。
Oh, really. Where in Tokyo?

やまだ：あさくさです。
Asakusa.

はなして　みましょう　Conversation Practice

Activity 1

Work with a partner. The following is a list of new students at the International Student Center. Introduce one of the students to your partner, and your partner will then introduce you to a student who shares the trait you have just described in the first introduction. Take turns making the introductions.

Example 1: A: こちらは　キム(きむ)さんです。キム(きむ)さんは　フランス(ふらんす)ごの　がくせいです。

B: こちらは　ロペス(ろぺす)さんです。ロペス(ろぺす) さんも　フランス(ふらんす)ごの　せんこうです。

Example 2: A: こちらは　ワット(わっと)さんです。ワット(わっと)さんは　イギリス(いぎりす)から きました。

B: こちらは　モリス(もりす)さんです。モリス(もりす)さんも　イギリス(いぎりす)じんですよ。

Name	Country /Nationality	Year in school	Major
キム(きむ)	かんこく	いちねんせい	フランス(ふらんす)ご
イー(い)	かんこく	だいがくいんせい	ぶんがく
リー(り)	ちゅうごく	よねんせい	こうがく
チョー(ちょ)	ちゅうごく	にねんせい	かんこくご
ブラウン(ぶらうん)	オーストラリア(おすとらりあ)	さんねんせい	れきし
スミス(すみす)	オーストラリア(おすとらりあ)	にねんせい	かんこくご
ロペス(ろぺす)	メキシコ(めきしこ)	よねんせい	フランス(ふらんす)ご
ガルシア(がるしあ)	メキシコ(めきしこ)	だいがくいんせい	こうがく
ワット(わっと)	イギリス(いぎりす)	いちねんせい	れきし
モリス(もりす)	イギリス(いぎりす)	さんねんせい	ぶんがく

Activity 2

Work with the class. Find a person who went to the same high school you attended.

Example: A: わたしの　こうこうは　セントラル(せんとらる)　ハイスクール(はいすくーる)です。
～さんの　こうこうは　どこですか。

B: わたしの　こうこうも　セントラル(せんとらる)　ハイスクール(はいすくーる)です。

or わたしの　こうこうは　ミルズ(みるず)　ハイスクール(はいすくーる)です。

Activity 3

Work with a partner. Ask your partner the time in the cities on the list.

Example 1: ペキン(ぺきん) (Beijing)　ホンコン(ほんこん) (Hong Kong)

A: ペキン(ぺきん)は　いま　なんじですか。

B: じゅういちじですよ。

A: そうですか。じゃあ、ホンコン(ほんこん)は　いま
なんじですか。

B: ホンコン(ほんこん)も　じゅういちじですよ。

Example 2: ペキン(ぺきん) (Beijing)　バンコク(ばんこく) (Bangkok)

A: ペキン(ぺきん)は　いま　なんじですか。

B: じゅういちじですよ。

A: そうですか。じゃあ、バンコク(ばんこく)は　いま
なんじですか。

B: バンコク(ばんこく)は　じゅうじですよ。

1.	シドニー (Sydney) しどに	グアム (Guam) ぐあむ
2.	とうきょう	タイペイ (Taipei) たいぺい
3.	ペキン (Beijing) ぺきん	タイペイ たいぺい
4.	タイペイ たいぺい	ホンコン (Hong Kong) ほんこん
5.	とうきょう	ソウル (Seoul) そうる
6.	ホンコン (Hong Kong) ほんこん	バンコク (Bangkok) ばんこく

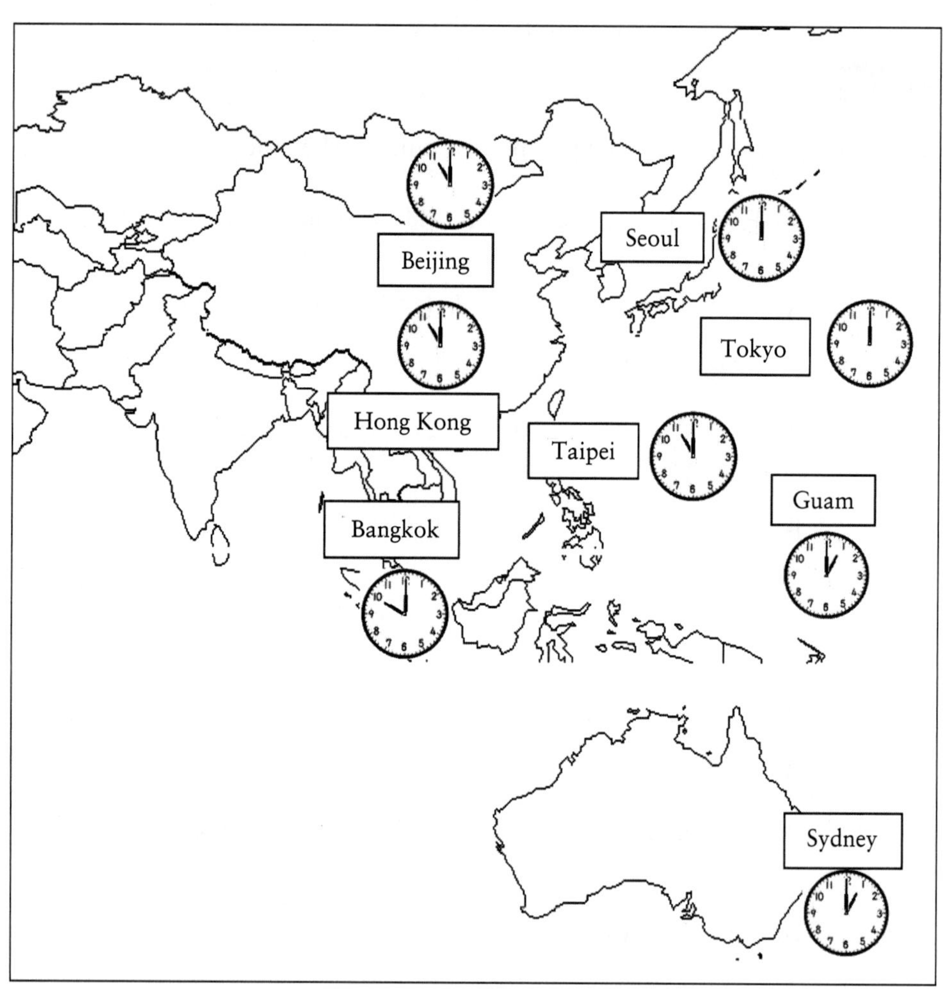

きく　れんしゅう
Listening

じょうずな　ききかた　Listening Strategy

Listening for key words

Listening comprehension passages for this section contain some unknown expressions and words so that you can develop skills to deal with real-life situations in which you may not understand every word. You may be surprised to find that natural speech is very redundant and that it is really not important to understand every single word. Try to focus on key words without worrying too much about the rest. For example, when someone is introduced to you, the most important word to understand is the person's name. Don't worry about the rest; just relax and listen.

きく　まえに　Warm-up

Listen to the dialogue and write the names of the two people who are being introduced

ことばの　リスト(りすと)　Vocabulary

むすめ	(speaker's) daughter
ちち	(speaker's) father
はは	(speaker's) mother

れんしゅう Practice

すずきさんの　むすめさん Mr. Suzuki's daughter

Read the statements below, then listen for the key words in the dialogue. Circle はい or いいえ, according to what you understood.

Situation: Remember that Alice and Mr. Suzuki already met in the main dialogue on page 42. Mr. Suzuki's daughter is standing next to him. He introduces her to Alice.

1. The name of Mr. Suzuki's daughter is Michiko.　はい　いいえ
2. Mr. Suzuki's daughter is a sophomore at Joto University.　はい　いいえ
3. Mr. Suzuki's daughter is majoring in economics.　はい　いいえ
4. Alice's father is Japanese.　はい　いいえ

ききじょうず　はなしじょうず
Communication

Communication Strategy

Using あいづち (attentive feedback) 1

Being a good listener is one of the most important factors in communicating effectively in any language, but the strategies for being a good listener differ considerably between languages. For example, the Japanese tend to avoid frequent or prolonged eye contact, because they do not think that making eye contact indicates a person's interest in the conversation. A Japanese person will tend to feel intimidated or uneasy after prolonged eye contact, so it's a good idea to look away from time to time. Instead of eye contact, Japanese speakers use various other forms of feedback when they are listening. For example, they nod occasionally to show attentiveness. For this reason, Japanese students often nod in the classroom. Another common type of feedback is the frequent use of ええor はい, which both mean *yes*. These expressions do not necessarily indicate agreement. They simply mean that the person is listening to you. If the listener remains silent even though he/she is looking at the speaker, the speaker may consider the listener to be impolite, cold, or even uninterested. In Japanese, feedback given to confirm attentive listening is called あいづち.

Classroom Manners

It is considered inappropriate to eat or drink in the classroom in Japan. Equally inappropriate is putting one's feet or legs up on a chair or desk. Japanese instructors who are not used to such behavior may think these acts show a lack of seriousness or boredom on the part of the student.

れんしゅう Practice

1. Listen to your instructor talk about himself/herself. Sit up straight and nod occasionally to indicate interest while listening.
2. Work with a partner. Tell him/her about a friend. While listening, your partner should nod or say ええ or はい between sentences. Avoid making eye contact.

よむ　れんしゅう
Reading

じょうずな　よみかた　Reading Strategy

Using format as a clue

めいし are generally written in **kanji** and **katakana**, and for a beginning student of Japanese, it may seem impossible to make any sense of them. Nevertheless, it is possible to identify a few facts if you know what to look for, and this is a very important first step in improving your reading skills.

The information provided on めいし typically includes name, position or title, the relevant employer or organization, address, phone and fax numbers, e-mail address, and web address. The information always follows a certain format. For example, the name appears in the center, and the organization and title will be next to or above the name.

よむ　まえに　Pre-reading

1. Look at the horizontally formatted card and circle the telephone number and the name of the organization.
2. Look at the other card. Although it is written vertically, the basic format is the same as that of the first card. The second card is read from right to left. Circle the name of the card owner and the address.

インターネット　ジャパン　Inc.

代表取締役
クリシュナ・カーン

1234 Main Street Suite #100, Portland, OR 87654
TEL: (123) 456-7890 FAX: (123)456-7891

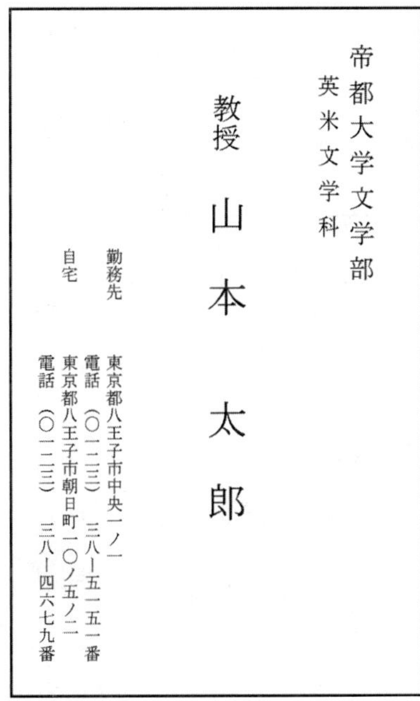

帝都大学文学部
英米文学科
教授
山本　太郎
勤務先　東京都八王子市中央一ノ一
電話（〇一二三）三八ー五一五一番
自宅　東京都八王子市朝日町一〇ノ五ノ一
電話（〇一二三）三八ー四六七九番

れんしゅう Practice

ともだち　ぼしゅう　Looking for a friend

Japanese is usually written in **hiragana, katakana,** and **kanji** as appropriate. Printed Japanese is unlike English in that there are usually no spaces between words. The text in the reading section of this book utilizes all three scripts rather than being limited to **hiragana** and **katakana,** so that you can become familiar with normal written Japanese.

The following are short introductory messages placed on a web page for people who are looking for pen pals. Read the messages and answer the following questions.

ことばの　リスト(りすと) Vocabulary

ネイティブ(ねいてぃぶ)	native (speaker)
～を　さがしています	to be looking for ～

Message 1

はじめまして！ 私(わたし)は東京大学(とうきょうだいがく)の学生(がくせい)です。なまえはけいこです。専攻(せんこう)は英語(えいご)です。今一年生(いまいちねんせい)です。英語(えいご)のネイティブ(ねいてぃぶ)の友達(ともだち)をさがしています。どうぞよろしく。

Message 2

はじめまして。僕(ぼく)はたかしです。千葉大学(ちばだいがく)の三年生(さんねんせい)です。専攻(せんこう)はアジア(あじあ)とアメリカ(あめりか)の歴史(れきし)です。どうぞよろしく。

Message 3

はじめまして。私(わたし)はヤン(やん)・リー(り)と言(い)います。中国(ちゅうごく)から来(き)ました。京都(きょうと)の留学生(りゅうがくせい)です。日本文学(にほんぶんがく)の専攻(せんこう)です。二年生(にねんせい)です。友達(ともだち)をさがしています。よろしく。

Message 4

はじめまして。僕(ぼく)はリチャード(りちゃど)です。オーストラリア(おすとらりあ)のシドニー(しどに)から来(き)ました。今(いま)、大阪大学(おおさかだいがく)の四年生(よねんせい)です。ビジネス(びじねす)の専攻(せんこう)です。よろしく。

よんだ　あとで　Comprehension

1. Complete the following with information about the four people who posted the messages above. Don't worry about writing **kanji** or **katakana**.

Message 1

Name ______________________
School ______________________
Year ______________________
Major ______________________
Hometown/country
(if mentioned) ______________________

Message 2

Name ______________________
School ______________________
Year______________________
Major ______________________
Hometown/country
if mentioned)______________________

Message 3

Name ______________________
School ______________________
Year ______________________
Major ______________________
Hometown/country
(if mentioned) ______________________

Message 4

Name ______________________
School ______________________
Year______________________
Major ______________________
Hometown/country
(if mentioned) ______________________

2. Are there any similarities between you and any of the four people? If there are, describe them.

Example: わたしは　いちねんせいです。 けいこさんも
いちねんせいです。

3. Select one person from the list and write a message to him/her to introduce yourself. If you have yet to decide on a major, write (せんこうは)まだ わかりません, meaning "I don't know my major yet."

そうごう　れんしゅう
Integration

インタビュー Interview
いんたびゅ

1. Ask your classmates about their name, major, year in school, hometown, high school, and country of origin. Write the phrase you will use to greet them, and then make a list of questions to ask. Next, ask the questions, speaking with as many people as you can. Fill in the blanks with the information you gather.

   Greeting phrase: ____________________

   Questions:

   なまえ (name) ____________________

   〜ねんせい (year) ____________________

   せんこう (major) ____________________

   〜から　きました (hometown/country) ____________________

   こうこう (high school) ____________________

2. Based on the answers you get, introduce one of your classmates to another classmate. Write down what is said by each person during the conversation.

   ________ : ____________________

   ________ : ____________________

   ________ : ____________________

   ________ : ____________________

はじめまして。わたし／ぼくは__________といいます。

________は ________から ________きました。

__________だいがくの__________ねんせいです。

せんこうは __________です。 どうぞよろしく。

ロールプレイ Role Play
ろ るぷれい

1. Approach and introduce yourself to the person who is sitting next to you, using the following dialogue as a model.

You： あのう。
Partner：はい。
You： おなまえは　なんですか。　ぼく／わたし、
______って　いいます。どうぞ　よろしく。
Partner：こちらこそ。どうぞ　よろしく。ぼく／わたしの
なまえは______です。
You： ああ、そうですか。ぼく／わたしは______から
きました。
______さんは。
Partner：______です。　ぼく／わたしは
______だいがくの______せい
です。
You： そうですか。　ぼく／わたしも______せい
です。せんこうは　なんですか。
Partner：______です。
You： そうですか。

2. Suppose that you are at an airport to pick up a Japanese person named Yamada whom you have never met. Approach someone and ask if he/she is the person you are looking for using the following dialogue as a starter. Then introduce yourself.

You： あのう、すみませんが。
Partner： はい。
You： やまださんですか。

3. Suppose you have found a Japanese student on campus. Naturally, you want to practice Japanese with him/her. Introduce yourself and strike up a conversation.

カタカナ

Katakana

I. Introduction

In this section, you will learn how to read and write **katakana**. It is important to learn **katakana** because Japanese uses a large number of loan words, many of which are borrowed from English. The following chart shows both print and handwritten styles, with the reading of each **katakana** given in **hiragana**. Note that the use of small **tsu** ッ (つ) for double consonants, the two dots ゛ on the right shoulder to indicate voiced syllables, and the small **ya** ャ (や), **yu** ュ (ゆ), and **yo** ョ (よ) to indicate glides are exactly the same as **hiragana**. A dash ー indicates a long vowel, as explained in Chapter 1.

ン ん	ワ わ	ラ ら	ヤ や	マ ま	ハ は	ナ な	タ た	サ さ	カ か	ア あ
		リ り		ミ み	ヒ ひ	ニ に	チ ち	シ し	キ き	イ い
		ル る	ユ ゆ	ム む	フ ふ	ヌ ぬ	ツ つ	ス す	ク く	ウ う
		レ れ		メ め	ヘ へ	ネ ね	テ て	セ せ	ケ け	エ え
		ロ ろ	ヨ よ	モ も	ホ ほ	ノ の	ト と	ソ そ	コ こ	オ お

II. Katakana ア～ソ

Study the first fifteen **katakana**. Using the mnemonic devices in the right-hand column, practice reading each character. Then practice writing them in your Student Activities Manual following the correct stroke order.

a	ア	ア	ア	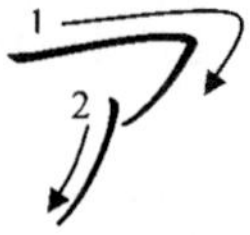  I'd like an *ice*-cream cone.
i	イ	イ	イ	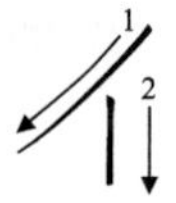  I need an *easel* to draw.
u	ウ	ウ	ウ	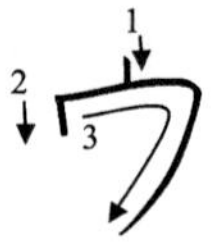  It's a *wick* of a candle.
e	エ	エ	エ	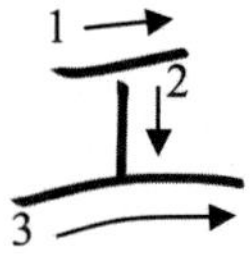  An *egg* is on an egg stand.
o	オ	オ	オ	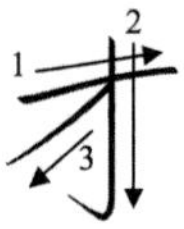  *Oh*, what an odd way to walk.
ka	カ	カ	カ	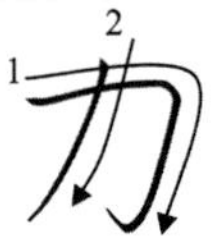  *Karate* kick.
ki	キ	キ	キ	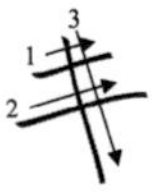  This is a *key*.
ku	ク	ク	ク	  A baby is sleeping in a *cradle*.
ke	ケ	ケ	ケ	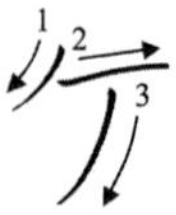  This is a *crooked* K
ko	コ	コ	コ	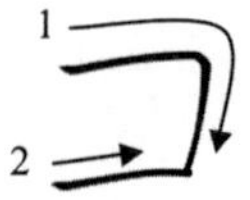 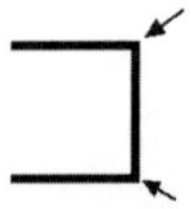 This letter has two *corners*.
sa	サ	サ	サ	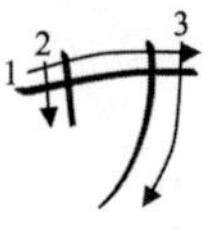  This is a *saddle* on a horse.

shi	シ	シ	シ		*She* (the cat) is sleeping.
su	ス	ス	ス		Here is a *swing set.*
se	セ	セ	セ		Say, isn't that *Señor* García?
so	ソ	ソ	ソ		I'm *sewing* with a needle.

れんしゅう Practice

Read the following words in katakana and guess what they mean.

1. キス **2.** ケーキ **3.** サーカス **4.** ケース **5.** アイス
6. コース **7.** エース **8.** オアシス **9.** シーソー

III. Katakana タ～ホ

Study the following カタカナ. Using the mnemonic devices in the right-hand column, practice reading each character. Then practice writing them in your Student Activities Manual following the correct stroke order.

ta	タ	タ	タ		A crooked *tie.*
chi	チ	チ	チ		A *chick* is trying to fly.
tsu	ツ	ツ	ツ		A cat gets up on her feet.
te	テ	テ	テ		The cat's *tail* is wagging to the left.
to	ト	ト	ト		An Indian *toma-hawk.*

na	ナ	ナ	 ナ		A *knife.*
ni	ニ	ニ	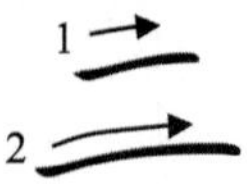 ニ	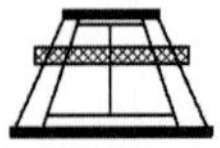	A *neat* tennis court.
nu	ヌ	ヌ	 ヌ		*Noodles* are difficult to eat with chopsticks.
ne	ネ	ネ	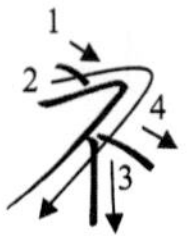 ネ		A *necker-chief* is around my neck.
no	ノ	ノ	 ノ		Someone's *nose.*
ha	ハ	ハ	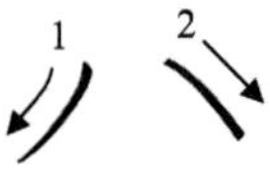 ハ		A *hat.*
hi	ヒ	ヒ	 ヒ		A *heel.*
fu	フ	フ	 フ		A child's *hood.*
he	ヘ	ヘ	 ヘ		I have a bad *head-ache.*
ho	ホ	ホ	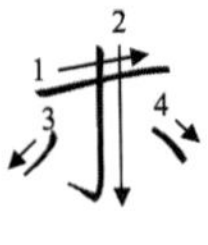 ホ		Two hands *hold* a cross.

れんしゅう Practice

Read the following words in katakana and try to guess what they mean. Remember that the small ッ indicates a double consonant.

1. カタカナ **2.** ネット **3.** セーター **4.** カヌー **5.** ノート

6. エチケット **7.** テキスト **8.** カッター **9.** ホット **10.** ニット **11.** テスト

IV. Katakana マ〜ン
まん

Study the following カタカナ. Using the mnemonic devices in the right-hand column, practice reading each character. Then practice writing them in your Student Activities Manual following the correct stroke order.

ma	マ	マ	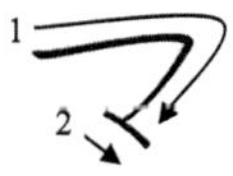 マ		A giant *mush-room*
mi	ミ	ミ	 ミ		Who's three? *Me!*
mu	ム	ム	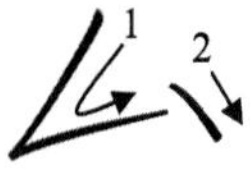 ム		The *moon* is sleep-ing.
me	メ	メ	 メ		The knife is *melting*.
mo	モ	モ	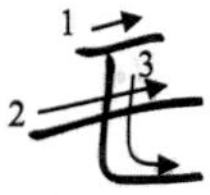 モ		A *monster* appears in Tokyo.
ya	ヤ	ヤ	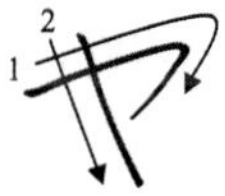 ヤ		A *yacht* in the ocean.
yu	ユ	ユ	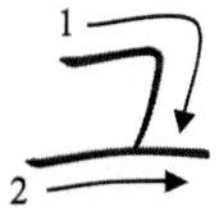 ユ		It's a *U-boat*!
yo	ヨ	ヨ	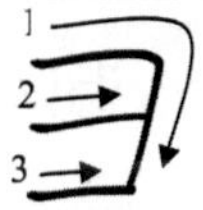 ヨ		*Yoga* is fun.
ra	ラ	ラ	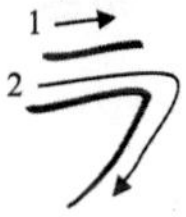 ラ		A *rabbit* with long ears.
ri	リ	リ	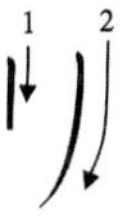 リ		This *rib-bon* has long tails.
ru	ル	ル	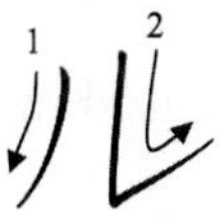 ル		A tree with deep *roots*.

re	レ	レ	レ	*Let's* write a capital L.
ro	ロ	ロ	ロ	A *loaf* of bread.
wa	ワ	ワ	ワ	A *wine* glass.
n	ン	ン	ン	A needle is sharp at the *end*.

れんしゅう **Practice**

Read the following words in katakana and try to guess what they mean.

1. ワシントン
2. ユタ
3. アイオワ
4. オハイオ
5. ノースカロライナ
6. アメリカ
7. イタリア
8. ロシア
9. テキサス
10. オクラホマ
11. ミネソタ
12. アーカンソー
13. サウスカロライナ
14. メキシコ
15. スイス
16. インドネシア
17. モンタナ
18. ミシシッピー
19. イリノイ
20. テネシー
21. メイン
22. オーストラリア
23. フランス

V. Transcribing katakana

A. Rules that apply to transcribing both hiragana and katakana

1. The diacritic marker [゛] indicates a voiced sound, as in ガ [ga] or ギ [gi]. A small circle [゜] indicates the [p] sound as in パ [pa].
2. Small ヤユヨ are used to form sounds such as キャ [kya], シュ [shu], and ミョ [myo].
3. A small ツ indicates a double consonant, as in ホットドッグ *hot dog*.

B. Conventions used in transcribing English words into katakana

1. The English sounds -er, -or, and -ar are heard as [aa] in Japanese. A dash represents the long vowels.

   カーター　　Carter
   ハート　　heart

When **katakana** is written vertically, the long vowel marker (ー) is also written vertically.

ハート
サッカー
リーダー

2. The English [v] is heard in Japanese as [b]. Accordingly, [va], [vi], [vu], [ve] and [vo] become [ba], [bi], [bu], [be] and [bo] in Japanese.

   カバー　cover
   バイオリン　violin

3. The English [l] and [r] are both heard as an [r] in Japanese.

   ライト　right or light
   リーダー　reader or leader
   ロビー　lobby or Robby

4. The English [th] as in *think* and *third* is heard as [s] and the [th] as in *that* or *mother* is heard as [z].

   サンクスギビング　Thanksgiving
   マザーグース　Mother Goose
   サードベース　third base
   バスルーム　bathroom

5. If an English word ends in [k], [g], [m], [f], [v], [l], [s], [z], [th], [p], or [b], the vowel [u] is added in Japanese. The vowel [u] is also added when these sounds are followed immediately by consonants in English.

   ミルク　milk
   リング　ring
   ホテル　hotel
   ミス　Miss
   ジャズ　jazz

6. If an English word contains [t] or [d], the vowel [o] is added in Japanese.

   コスト　cost
   スピード　speed
   ラスト　last
   ベッド　bed

7. The English vowel sounds in *bus* and *cut* or *bath* or *gas* are both heard as [a] in Japanese.

   バス　bus or bath
   カット　cut
   バット　bat
   ガス　gas

8. To approximate as much as possible the pronunciation of people's names and other borrowed sounds, the following combinations are commonly used. Note that these combinations are never used in **hiragana**.

ウィ	[wi]	ウィンストン	Winston	ウィスコンシン	Wisconsin
ウェ	[we]	ウェイン	Wayne	ハイウェイ	highway
ウォ	[wo]	ウォルター	Walter	ウォッカ	vodka
シェ	[she]	シェリル	Sheryl	シェーバー	shaver
ジェ	[je]	ジェーン	Jane	ジェスチャー	gesture
チェ	[che]	チェイス	Chase	チェロ	cello
ティ	[ti]	カーティス	Curtis	アイスティー	iced tea
ディ	[di]	ディーン	Dean	ディズニーランド	Disneyland
デュ	[dju]	デューク	Duke	デュエット	duet
ファ	[fa]	ジェニファー	Jennifer	ファッション	fashion
フィ	[fi]	マーフィー	Murphy	フィンランド	Finland
フェ	[fe]	フェイ	Fay	フェンシング	fencing
フォ	[fo]	フォード	Ford	フォーク	fork

Try writing your name in katakana. Use the above conventions if your name contains any of the sounds listed.

れんしゅう Practice

A. The following words appeared in Chapter 1. Read them and write their meanings in English.

1. アジアけんきゅう ______________________
2. アメリカ ______________________
3. イギリス ______________________
4. オーストラリア ______________________
5. カナダ ______________________
6. スペイン ______________________
7. フランス ______________________
8. メキシコ ______________________

B. Guess what the following words are in English.

1. Food and drinks

1. ハンバーガー 2. ステーキ 3. ホットドッグ 4. カレー
5. スパゲティ 6. サンドイッチ 7. サラダ 8. トマト
9. レタス 10. オレンジ 11. レモン 12. フルーツ
13. バター 14. チーズ 15. ケーキ 16. アイスクリーム
17. チョコレート 18. クッキー 19. ジュース 20. ミルク
21. ポテトチップス 22. ビール 23. コーラ 24. ワイン

2. Sports

1. フットボール 2. バスケットボール 3. テニス 4. サッカー
5. ジョギング 6. スキー 7. スケート 8. バレーボール
9. ラケットボール 10. ゴルフ 11. サーフィン

3. Music

1. ピアノ 2. バイオリン 3. ギター 4. オーケストラ
5. トランペット 6. ジャズ 7. ロック 8. クラシック

4. Household items

1. キッチン 2. リビングルーム 3. ランプ 4. オーブン
5. トースター 6. ラジオ 7. レコード 8. ビデオ
9. カメラ 10. カレンダー

5. Countries

1. ブラジル 2. イギリス 3. ドイツ 4. オランダ
5. イタリア 6. スイス 7. イスラエル 8. ロシア
9. オーストラリア 10. インド 11. タイ 12. ベトナム
13. サウジアラビア

6. Cities

1. ニューヨーク 2. ボストン 3. シカゴ 4. ロサンゼルス
5. サンフランシスコ 6. トロント 7. モントリオール 8. ロンドン
9. パリ 10. ベルリン 11. モスクワ 12. カイロ
13. シドニー 14. バンコク 15. ホンコン

Chapter 3

だいさんか

まいにちの　せいかつ

Daily Routines

Objectives Describing daily routines

Vocabulary Daily activities, numbers, minutes, relative time, days of the week

Japanese Culture College life (1)

Dialogue じゅぎょうが　あります。 *I have a class.*

Grammar

I. Talking about routines, future actions, or events using the polite present form of verbs and the particles に, へ, を, or で

II. Presenting objects or events using 〜が　あります

III. Telling time using the particle に

IV. Using adverbs to express frequency of actions

V. Expressing past actions and events using the polite past form of verbs

Listening Listening for general ideas

Communication Using あいづち (2)

Reading Scanning

たんご
Vocabulary

Nouns

あさ	朝	morning
あさごはん	朝御飯	breakfast
あさって	明後日	the day after tomorrow
あした	明日	tomorrow
うち	家	home
えいが	映画	movie
おととい	一昨日	the day before yesterday
おふろ	お風呂	bath
がっこう	学校	school
かようび	火曜日	Tuesday
きのう	昨日	yesterday
きょう	今日	today
きんようび	金曜日	Friday
クラス (くらす)		class
げつようび	月曜日	Monday
コーヒー (こ ひ)		coffee
ごはん	御飯	meal, cooked rice
こんしゅう	今週	this week
こんばん	今晩	tonight
シャワー (しゃわ)		shower
しゅうまつ	週末	weekend
じゅぎょう	授業	class, course
しゅくだい	宿題	homework
すいようび	水曜日	Wednesday

せいかつ	生活	life, living
せんしゅう	先週	last week
つぎ	次	next
テレビ (てれび)		television, TV
でんわばんごう	電話番号	telephone number
としょかん	図書館	library
どようび	土曜日	Saturday
にちようび	日曜日	Sunday
ばん	晩	night, evening
ばんごはん	晩御飯	supper, dinner
ひる	昼	afternoon
ひるごはん	昼御飯	lunch
べんきょう	勉強	study
ほん	本	book
まいあさ	毎朝	every morning
まいしゅう	毎週	every week
まいにち	毎日	every day
まいばん	毎晩	every night
もくようび	木曜日	Thursday

う -verbs

あります		(to) be held, (to) have; the dictionary form is ある.
いきます	行きます	(to) go; the dictionary form is いく.
かえります	帰ります	(to) return, (to) go home; the dictionary form is かえる.
のみます	飲みます	(to) drink; the dictionary form is のむ.
はいります	入ります	(to) take (a bath), (to) enter; the dictionary form is はいる. おふろに　はいります take a bath
よみます	読みます	(to) read; the dictionary form is よむ.

る-verbs

あびます	浴びます	(to) take (a shower) シャワーを あびます take a shower; the dictionary form is あびる.
おきます	起きます	(to) get up, (to) wake up; the dictionary form is おきる.
たべます	食べます	(to) eat; the dictionary form is たべる.
ねます	寝ます	(to) go to bed; the dictionary form is ねる.
みます	見ます	(to) see, (to) watch; the dictionary form is みる.

Irregular verbs

きます	来ます	(to) come; the dictionary form is くる.
します		(to) do; the dictionary form is する.
べんきょうします	勉強します	(to) study; the dictionary form is べんきょうする.

Question word

いつ		when

Numbers

ゼロ (ぜろ)		zero
れい	零	zero
いち	一	one
に	二	two
さん	三	three
よん、し	四	four
ご	五	five
ろく	六	six
なな、しち	七	seven
はち	八	eight
きゅう、く	九	nine
じゅう	十	ten

Counter

～ふん	～分	～ minute(s), (for) ～ minute(s)

Adverbs

いつも		always
ぜんぜん	全然	not at all (used with negative verb forms)
たいてい		usually
ときどき	時々	sometimes
よく		often; well

Particles

に		at; on; in (point in time) １０じに　ねます。
に		to (goal, activity) クラス(くらす)に　いきます。
で		at; in; on; etc. (location of action or event) としょかんで　べんきょうします。
へ		to (direction) がっこうへ　いきます。
を		direct object marker ほんを　よみます。

Prefixes

こん～	今～	this こんしゅう、こんばん
まい～	毎～	every まいしゅう、まいあさ、まいばん、まいにち

Suffixes

～ようび	～曜日	day (of the week)
～ごろ	～頃	about ～ (used only with time expressions)

たんごの　れんしゅう　Vocabulary Practice

A. まいにちの　せいかつ　Daily activities

おきます

(to) wake up

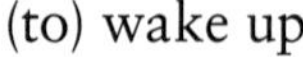

ねます

(to) go to bed

あさごはんを
たべます

(to) eat breakfast

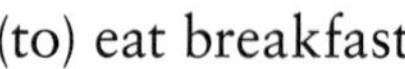

ひるごはん
を たべます

(to) eat lunch

うちで ばんごはんを
たべます

(to) eat dinner at home

べんきょうします／
べんきょうを します

(to) study

としょかんで
べんきょうします。

(to) study at the library

しゅくだいを
します

(to) do homework

ほんを
よみます

(to) read a book

コーヒーを
こ　ひ
のみます

(to) drink coffee

テレビを
て れ び
みます

(to) watch TV

えいがを みます

(to) watch a movie

シャワーを　あびます
し や わ

(to) take a shower

おふろに はいります

(to) take a bath

じゅぎょうが
ありますす

There is / I have a class.

がっこうに／がっこうへ
いきます

(to) go to school

クラス(くらす)に／クラス(くらす)へ
きます

(to) come to the classroom

うちに／うちへ かえります
(to) go home

Activity 1

Say what activities you do in the morning, in the afternoon, and at night.

Example: あさ じゅぎょうが あります (*I have class in the morning.*)

1. あさ (*morning*)
2. ひる (*afternoon*)
3. ばん (*night*)

Activity 2

Work with a partner. Put the activities you have just described in chronological order and tell your partner what your day is like.

B. Relative time expressions

Japanese has a set of words that indicate points in time with respect to the current time. Their English equivalents are words such as today, tomorrow, and yesterday. These words are categorized as relative time expressions because the day we call "yesterday" today will not be "yesterday" tomorrow. On the other hand, time expressions that are fixed, such as 1977, three o'clock, or Friday, are classified as absolute time expressions. Some relative time expressions follow.

いつ	when	きのう	yesterday
あさ	morning	おととい	the day before yesterday
ひる	afternoon	まいにち	every day
ばん	night	まいしゅう	every week
こんばん	tonight	まいあさ	every morning
しゅうまつ	weekend	こんしゅう	this week
きょう	today	まいばん	every night
あした	tomorrow	せんしゅう	last week
あさって	the day after tomorrow		

Activity 3

Answer the following questions.

1. いま、あさですか。ひるですか。ばんですか。
2. 「まいあさ」、「まいにち」、「まいばん」の「まい」って　なんですか。
3. 「まいしゅう」、「こんしゅう」、「せんしゅう」、「しゅうまつ」の「しゅう」って　なんですか。
4. 「こんばん」、「こんしゅう」の「こん」ってなんですか。

Activity 4

For each activity shown on pages a-88–89, create a sentence using the time expressions that apply to your own daily routine. If you want to use きのう (yesterday) or せんしゅう (last week), change the verb form to ～ました instead of ～ます, as in みました (watched) instead of みます (watch).

Example: おきます (to) wake up

あさ、おきます。(*I wake up in the morning.*)

せんしゅう、えいがを　みました。(*I watched a movie last week.*)

C. ～ようび　Days of the week

Note that each day of the week ends with ようび.

Which day of the week?	なんようび
Sunday	にちようび
Monday	げつようび
Tuesday	かようび
Wednesday	すいようび
Thursday	もくようび
Friday	きんようび
Saturday	どようび

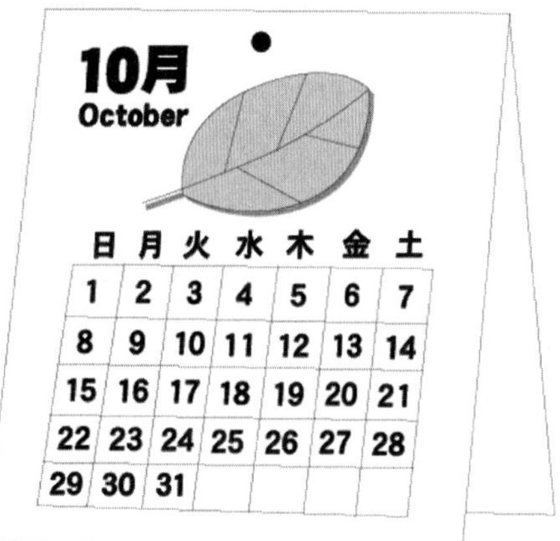

Activity 5

Look at the calendar and give the day of the week for the following dates.

1. 10/16
2. 10/26
3. 10/31
4. 10/1
5. 10/21
6. 10/4
7. 10/27
8. 10/8
9. 10/5
10. 10/7
11. 10/17
12. 10/25

Activity 6

Answer the following questions in Japanese.

1. きょうは　なんようびですか。
2. あしたは　なんようびですか。
3. あさっては　なんようびですか。
4. きのうは　なんようびでしたか。(でした = *was*)
5. おとといは　なんようびでしたか。(でした = was)
6. つぎの　にほんごの　クラス(くらす)は　なんようびですか。

D. すうじ　Numbers

Read the following numbers aloud.

0	ゼロ(ぜろ)、れい	7	なな、しち	20	にじゅう
1	いち	8	はち	30	さんじゅう
2	に	9	きゅう、く	40	よんじゅう
3	さん	10	じゅう	70	ななじゅう、しちじゅう
4	よん、し	11	じゅういち	90	きゅうじゅう
5	ご	12	じゅうに	99	きゅうじゅうきゅう、
6	ろく	13	じゅうさん		きゅうじゅうく

Notes

- Numbers between 11 and 19 are formed by using the number ten followed by the appropriate single digit.

  11 = 10 + 1 じゅういち＝じゅう＋いち
  12 = 10 + 2 じゅうに＝じゅう＋に
  13 = 10 + 3 じゅうさん＝じゅう＋さん

- The numbers 20, 30, 40, 50, 60, 70, 80, and 90 are formed by using the appropriate single digit followed by 10.

  20 = 2 X 10 にじゅう＝に X じゅう
  30 = 3 X 10 さんじゅう＝さん X じゅう
  40 = 4 X 10 よんじゅう＝よん X じゅう

- Numbers like 23 and 35 are formed by combining the tens digit and the ones digit.

  23 = 20 + 3 にじゅうさん ＝ にじゅう＋さん
  35 = 30 + 5 さんじゅうご ＝ さんじゅう＋ご

- The numbers 4, 7, and 9 have two possible pronunciations. The number *40* is usually pronounced よんじゅう. The number *70* can be pronounced either ななじゅう or しちじゅう, and the number *90* is always pronounced きゅうじゅう.

Activity 7

Say the following telephone numbers（でんわばんごう）in Japanese. Use の to indicate a dash.

Example: 123-4567 いちにさんの　よんごろくなな

1. 356-2891
2. 245-6689
3. 8217-0370
4. 03-3986-5772
5. 06-4463-5998
6. 0895-23-5005
7. 090-7244-1456
8. 080-4647-4176

Activity 8

Take turns asking classmates their telephone numbers (でんわばんごう).

Example: A: あのう、でんわばんごうは　なんですか。
B: いちにさんの　よんごろくななです。
A: そうですか。どうもありがとう。

Activity 9

Read the following numbers aloud.

1. 2	6. 11	11. 75
2. 5	7. 17	12. 94
3. 6	8. 20	13. 81
4. 8	9. 49	14. 62
5. 10	10. 53	15. 99

Activity 10

Work in groups of three. One person writes five numbers in Arabic numerals on five separate slips of paper. As he or she shows the numbers, the other two members of the group compete to be the first to call out each number correctly.

E. ～ふん　Minute(s)

Note: * indicates a sound change.

1	* いっぷん	8	* はっぷん／はちふん
2	にふん	9	きゅうふん
3	* さんぷん	10	* じゅっぷん／じっぷん
4	よんふん／よんぷん	11	* じゅういっぷん
5	ごふん	12	じゅうにふん
6	* ろっぷん	20	* にじゅっぷん／にじっぷん
7	しちふん／ななふん	21	* にじゅういっぷん

* なんぷん *how many minutes?*

Activity 11

Say the following times in Japanese.

1. 4:10	5. 12:30	9. 4:17 p.m.	13. 6:55 a.m.
2. 2:25	6. 6:40	10. 9:18 a.m.	14. 9:03 p.m.
3. 7:37	7. 8:09	11. 7:11 p.m.	15. 3:53 p.m.
4. 1:44	8. 1:56	12. 9:02 a.m.	16. 8:30 a.m.

ダイアローグ
だいあろぐ
Dialogue

はじめに Warm-up

Answer the following questions in Japanese.

1. まいにち　じゅぎょうが　ありますか。
2. なんじに　じゅぎゅうが　ありますか。
3. たいてい　どこで　ひるごはんを　たべますか。
4. たいてい　なんじごろ　うちに　かえりますか。
5. きのう　なんじごろ　うちに　かえりましたか。
6. せんしゅうの　しゅうまつ　なにを　しましたか。

じゅぎょうが　あります。 *I have a class.*

It is 9:45 a.m. Ueda is eating a sandwich in front of the foreign language building. Li passes by.

うえだ：　あ、リーさん、おはよう。
リー：　ああ、うえださん。おはよう。　いま、あさごはんですか。
うえだ：　ええ、きょうは　はちじに　じゅぎょうが　ありました。
リー：　そうですか。たいへんですね。
うえだ：　ええ。で、リーさんは？
リー：　ぼくは　としょかんへ　いきます。　あさは　たいてい　としょかんで　しゅくだいを　します。

うえだ：　そうですか。クラス(くらす)は？

リー(り)：　いちじはんに　にほんごの　じゅぎょうが　ありります。
うえださんは？

うえだ：　じゅうじに　れきしの　クラス(くらす)が　あります。

リー(り)：　そうですか。

DIALOGUE PHRASE NOTES

- In the dialogue, the topic particle は follows the time expressions きょう and あさ. In Japanese, a topic does not necessarily have to be the subject of sentence, but it does introduce the item about which the speaker wishes to comment. In the dialogue above, Ueda wants to say something about "today," and Li wants to say the same thing about "mornings." For further discussion of topic particles, refer to the supplementary notes titled "More about the topic particle は" on p. a-106 of this chapter.
- たいへんですね means *that's hard*, in which たいへん means *tough, hard, serious*. ね is an affective particle that commonly appears in conversation to express shared feelings or assumptions. In the dialogue, ね expresses Li's sympathy toward Ueda.
- The で in the phrase で、リー(り)さんは？ is often used in conversation. It can be interpreted as well then, so, or by the way. It is not used in written Japanese.

ダイアローグ(だいあろぐ)の　あとで　Comprehension

A. Read each statement below. Then circle はい if the statement is true and いいえ if it is false.

1. はい　いいえ　　リー(り)さんは　きょうのごご　としょかんで べんきょうします。
2. はい　いいえ　　うえださんは　ごご じゅぎょうが　あります。
3. はい　いいえ　　うえださんは　きょうのあさ　じゅぎょうが ありました。

B. Answer the following questions in Japanese.

1. うえださんは　なんじごろ　あさごはんを　たべましたか。
2. にほんごの　じゅぎょうは　なんじに　ありますか。
3. じゅうじに　なにが　ありますか。

にほんの　ぶんか
Japanese Culture

The academic year in Japan

Japanese colleges and universities usually begin the academic year in April. Summer vacation starts at the end of July. The fall semester, or session, runs from September or October through January or February. The winter break is usually short, from the end of December through the beginning of January.

College classes

The usual class period in Japanese colleges is 90 or 100 minutes. Apart from seminars and some science classes, most classes are straight lectures, and little interaction takes place between students and professors. Many classes meet once a week for a full academic year, resuming after summer vacation and winter break. Major examinations are usually held only once, at the end of the academic year, and the exam period lasts a couple of weeks.

College housing

The majority of Japanese colleges are commuter schools, and few have dormitories. Those dormitories that do exist are rarely found on campus. Most Japanese college students live at home or in an apartment. Their average commute is about an hour but may be as long as two hours in large cities.

Financial aid

Many parents pay for their children's college education in Japan. Although there are scholarships available from various sources, student loans do not exist.

According to a recent study by a student support organization (**Gakusei Engoka**) over 80 percent of students have part-time jobs or アルバイト（あるばいと）／バイト（ばいと） (from the German "arbeiten," meaning *work*). Common jobs for students include convenience store or supermarket clerk, かていきょうし (private tutor for junior and senior high school students), and waiter or waitress.

ぶんぽう
Grammar

I. Talking about routines, future actions, or events using the polite present form of verbs and the particles に, へ, を, or で

Chapter 2 (see p. a-46) introduced the copula verb です and the topic particle は. This chapter deals with regular verbs and four additional particles.

A. Polite present form of verbs

Unlike English, all Japanese verbs have a polite form and a plain form. The polite form is used with acquaintances, people of different age groups, strangers in public places, on TV and radio broadcasts, and in letters. The plain form is used among family members, young children, close friends of the same age, and in newspapers and magazine articles. You will first learn the basics of Japanese verbs using the polite form in this book.

Verb tenses

Japanese verbs have only two tenses: past and non-past. The non-past tense indicates both present and future actions or states.

Question			
		Verb	
がっこう	に	いきます	か。

Do you go to school? / Are you going to school?

Answer	
	Verb
いいえ、	いきません。

No, I don't. / No, I'm not.

In the above example, いきます can indicate either the habitual action of going to school or future action. The meaning must be taken from the context.

Verb classes

There are three classes of Japanese verbs: う-verbs, る-verbs, and irregular verbs. Japanese has only two irregular verbs: きます and します. (します can be combined with certain nouns to produce irregular compound verbs, as noted below.) These verb classes will become more useful as you learn different forms of inflection in Chapter 7 (see pp. b-19–20).

	Polite affirmative form	Polite negative form	Verb class
to go	いきます	いきません	う -verb
to go home	かえります	かえりません	う -verb
to read	よみます	よみません	う -verb
to get up	おきます	おきません	る -verb
to go to bed	ねます	ねません	る -verb
to eat	たべます	たべません	る -verb
to come	きます	きません	Irregular
to do	します	しません	Irregular
to study	べんきょうします	べんきょうしません	Irregular

Note that べんきょうします is considered an irregular verb because it is a compound verb consisting of べんきょう and します. You will learn more compound verbs (noun +します) in later chapters.

B. Direct object particle, を

The particle を marks a direct object. The direct object receives the action of the verb. For example, in the sentence "John buys a car," car is the direct object. In English, the direct object is understood by its location (it generally appears immediately after the verb), but in Japanese it is followed by を, as in the following examples. The particle を was once pronounced *wo*, but is now pronounced *o*.

Topic	Direct object		Verb (action)
	Noun	Particle	
わたしは	ひるごはん	を	たべます。

I eat lunch. / I will eat lunch.

スミス（すみす）： しゅうまつ、よく　なにを　しますか。
What do you often do on weekends?

たなか： テレビ（てれび）を　みます。
I watch TV.

スミス（すみす）： そうですか。わたしも　よく　テレビ（てれび）を　みます。
Is that so? I often watch TV, too.

Notes

- べんきょうします consists of the noun べんきょう, which means *study*, and the verb します. Thus, it can be paraphrased as べんきょうを　します, which literally means *do the study*. In the latter sentence, use の to indicate what is being studied.

  にほんごを　べんきょうします。
  I study Japanese.

  にほんごの　べんきょうを　します。
  I study Japanese. (literally, *I do the study of Japanese.*)

- を may be omitted when the meaning can easily be inferred from the context of the conversation. However, it is not easy to determine exactly when to delete を. In this textbook you will sometimes see instances in which particles have been omitted.

C. Destination or goal particles に and へ

The particle に indicates a goal, a destination, or a point of arrival or contact. It is similar to the English prepositions to, into, or onto. The particle へ indicates a direction toward which something or someone moves. When used as a particle, the pronuciation of へ is exactly the same as that of え [e]. When used in other contexts, it is pronounced like the English word *hay*. Like を, the particles に and へ may be omitted when the meaning can be inferred easily from the context.

Destination/Goal		Verb
Place noun	Particle	
うち	に／へ	かえります

I will go home. / I am going home.

スミス(すみす)：　どこに　いきますか。　*Where are you going?*
たなか：　がっこうへ　いきます。　*I am going to school.*

へ can replace に in verbs of motion such as いきます, きます, and かえります, but these particles are not interchangeable with other types of verbs.

がっこうに／へ　いきます。
I will go to school. / I go to school.

だいがくに／へ　きます。
I will come to the university. / I come to the university.

おふろに　はいります。
I will take a bath. / I take a bath.

かばん (*bag*) に　ほんを　いれます (*put*)。
I will put a book in the bag. / I put a book in the bag.

D. Place of action and event, で

The particle で indicates the place at which an action or event takes place. It is translated as *in*, *at*, or *on* in English.

Place of action		Verb phrase (action)
Noun	Particle	
としょかん	で	えいがを　みます。

I see a movie at the library. / I am going to see a movie at the library.

スミス(すみす)：　どこで　べんきょうしますか。
Where do you (will you) study?

たなか：　としょかんで　します。
I study (will study) at the library.

はなして みましょう　Conversation Practice

Activity 1

Complete each sentence using the appropriate particles.

Example: しゅくだい　／　します
しゅくだいを　します。

1. ほん　／　よみます
2. おふろ　／　はいります
3. うち　／　ねます
4. テレビ(てれび)　／　みます
5. クラス(くらす)　／　きます
6. としょかん　／　いきます
7. シャワー(しゃわ)　／　あびます
8. がっこう　／　ひるごはん　／　たべます
9. うち　／　かえります

Activity 2

Answer the following questions.

Example: よく　としょかんに　いきますか。
ええ、いきます。 or いいえ、いきません。

1. あさごはんを　たべますか。
2. まいあさ　コーヒー(こひ)を　のみますか。
3. よく　テレビ(てれび)を　みますか。
4. よく　えいがに　いきますか。
5. こんばん　としょかんで　べんきょうしますか。

Activity 3

Work with a partner. In the column headed わたし below, write はい if you are thinking of doing the stated activity today, and いいえ if you are not. Then ask your partner whether he/she is planning to do these activities. Start your questions with the phrase あとで (later). Switch roles after you reach the bottom of the list.

Example: A: あとで、ほんを　よみますか。

B: ええ、よみます。 or いいえ、よみません。

	わたし	パートナー (ぱ と な)
	はい／いいえ	はい／いいえ
ほん／よみます		
ほかの (another) じゅぎょう／いきます		
おふろ／はいります		
シャワー (しゃ わ)／あびます		
えいが／みます		
にほんごの　しゅくだい／します		
テレビ (て れ び)／みます		
ごはん／たべます		
うち／かえります		

II. Presenting objects or events using ～が　あります

The phrase X が　あります means *there is X*. This phrase is used to describe an object, event, or activity. Depending on the context, ～が　あります can also be used to express possession.

ほんが　あります。
There is a book. / I have a book.

えいがが　あります。
There is a movie.

しゅくだいが　あります。
There is homework. / I have homework.

スミス（すみす）：　しゅうまつ　なにを　しますか。
What are you going to do this weekend?

たなか：　がっこうに　いきます。
I am going to school.

スミス（すみす）：　え、どうしてですか。
Really, why?

たなか：　としょかんで　にほんの　えいがが　あります。
There is a Japanese movie (playing) at the library.

スミス（すみす）：　あ、そうですか。
Oh, I see.

Notes

- Use the particle で to describe where an event will take place, as in the dialogue above.

  としょかんで　えいがが　あります。
  There is a movie at the library.

- When ～が　あります expresses possession, use ～は to indicate the possessor.

  ぼくは　じゅぎょうが　あります。
  I have a class.

  やまださんは　テレビ（てれび）が　ありません。
  Yamada-san does not have a TV.

はなして みましょう Conversation Practice

Activity 1

Work with a partner. You have the following event listing for Tokyo Disney Resort. Tell your friend about various shows and locations.

Example: ワールド・バザールで　ドローイング・クラスが　あります。

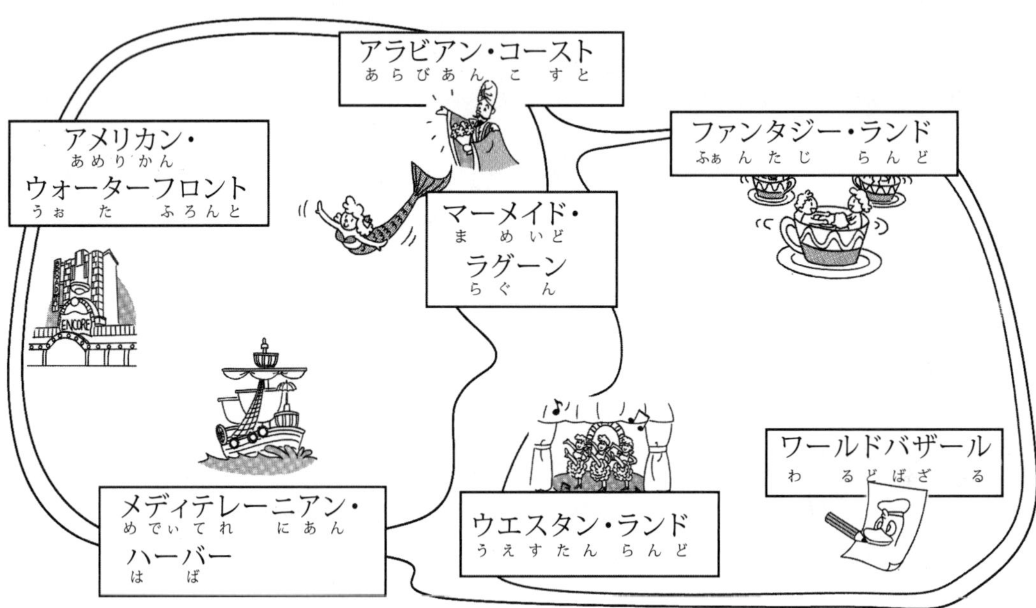

Tokyo Disney Resort Theme Park	Special Events
ワールド・バザール	ドローイング・クラス
ファンタジー・ランド	アリスのティーパーティ
ウエスタン・ランド	フロンティア・レビュー
アメリカン・ウォーターフロント	ミュージカル「アンコール」
メディテレーニアン・ハーバー	ウォーター・カーニバル
マーメイド・ラグーン	ミュージカル「アンダー・ザ・シー」
アラビアン・コースト	マジック・ショー

Activity 2

Work with the class. Ask at least three classmates if they have a class after Japanese class, and if they do, find out what and where it is. Then fill in the chart with the classmate's name, class and location.

Example: A: このあと (*after this class*) じゅぎょうが　ありますか。

B: ええ、ぶんがくの　じゅぎょうが　あります。

A: そうですか。どこで　ありますか。

B: スミス・ホール(すみす　ほる) (*Smith Hall*) で　あります。

or

A: このあと (*after this class*) じゅぎょうが　ありますか。

B: いいえ、ありません。～さんは？

A: わたしは　えいごの　じゅぎょうが　あります。

なまえ	じゅぎょう	ばしょ (location)

III. Telling time using the particle に

The particle に with a time expression indicates a specific point in time. This use of に corresponds to the English prepositions at, in, or on. It may be used to express clock times, days of the week, months, or years. For example:

ごじ<u>に</u>	<u>at</u> 5 o'clock	げつようび<u>に</u>	<u>on</u> Monday
ごがつ<u>に</u>	<u>in</u> May	１９９６ねん<u>に</u>	<u>in</u> 1996

The particle に is never used with the words きょう, いま, あさ, ばん, いつ, まい～ (every ～), こん～ (this ～), らい～ (next ～).

Point in time		
Time	Particle	
ろくじはん	に	おきます。

スミス（すみす）：うえださんは　きょう　きますか。
Is Ms. Ueda coming today?

たなか：ええ、ごじに　きますよ。
Yes, she is coming around 5 o'clock.

スミス（すみす）：リー（り）さんも　きますか。
Is Mr. Li coming, too?

たなか：いいえ、リー（り）さんは　どようびに　きます。
No, he is coming on Saturday.

たなか：すみません。いま　なんじですか。
Excuse me. What time is it now?

スミス（すみす）：じゅうじ　よんじゅうさんぷんです。
It's 10:43.

たなか：どうも　ありがとう。
Thank you very much.

スミス（すみす）：いいえ。
Not at all.

Notes

- For the pronunciation of numbers and number +ふん, refer to vocabulary sections D and E, pages a-91–93.
- The pronunciation of some numbers may change, depending on the counters being used. For example:

  よん → よじ　よんふん
  いち → いちじ　いっぷん

- We have seen the use of はん meaning "half past the hour." Another way to say this is the more literal さんじゅっぷん. For example: さんじさんじゅっぷん／さんじはん = 3:30.
- When two or more time expressions are used together, list them from the largest to the smallest unit (for example, day and time), and connect them with の. A few words like まいにち do not take の. For example,

  どようびの　さんじに　きます。
  I am coming at 3: 00 o'clock on Saturday.
  まいにち　はちじに　おきます。
  I wake up at 8 o'clock every day.

- Use 〜ごろ or ごろ（に） to express an approximate time. For example,

  たなか：　きょう　なんじごろ（に）　かえりますか。
  About what time are you going to go home today?
  スミス（すみす）：　よじごろ　かえります
  I will go home around 4 o'clock.

はなして みましょう Conversation Practice

Activity 1

Work with a partner. A Japanese film festival is going on all week at the student union. Look at the following schedule and ask each other what time the various screenings begin.

Example: A: となりの トトロ(ととろ)は いつ ありますか。
B: げつようびの ごぜん じゅういちじに あります。

Movie titles	Date and Time
となりの トトロ(ととろ)	Monday 11:00 A.M. Wednesday 5:35 P.M. Friday 8:30 P.M.
たんぽぽ	Tuesday 10:50 A.M. Thursday 12:05 P.M. Saturday 3:15 P.M.
フラガール(ふらがーる)	Wednesday 10:00 A.M. Friday 10:55 A.M. Sunday 7:45 P.M.
ゴジラ(ごじら)	Monday 9:40 P.M. Thursday 10:20 A.M. Saturday 12:00 P.M.
リング(りんぐ)	Tuesday 4:25 P.M. Friday 6:08 P.M. Sunday 10:25 A.M.
シャル・ウイ・ダンス(しゃる・うい・だんす)	Wednesday 9:10 P.M. Thursday 12:00 P.M. Saturday 9:30 A.M.
手紙(てがみ) (*Letter*)	Monday 2:33 P.M. Tuesday 11:10 A.M. Sunday 11:44 A.M.

Activity 2

Combine the following phrases to form complete sentences. Use whatever particles are necessary.

Example: ごじ／かえります
<u>ごじに かえります。</u>

1. まいあさ／コーヒー(こーひー)／のみます
2. あした／ばん／とうきょう／いきます
3. げつようび／じゅういちじごろ／かえります

4. らいしゅう／どようび／えいが／みます
5. まいにち／しちじごろ／おふろ／はいります
6. いま／クラス（くらす）／あります

Activity 3

Work with your classmates. Following the model in Box 1 of the chart below, fill in all the blanks with the appropriate particles. Use an X to indicate that no particle is required. Then ask your classmates はい／いいえ questions based on the statements in the chart. If someone answers はい , write his or her name in the box. Try to fill one row or column with different names.

Example: A: スミス（すみす）さんは　まいにち　ほんを　よみますか。
B: はい、よみます。

Write スミス（すみす）さん in Box 1.

①________さん まいにち_X_ ほん_を_ よみます。	②________さん がっこう____ しゅくだい____ します。	③________さん きょう____ コーヒー（こひ）____ のみます。	④________さん まいしゅう____ げつようび____ としょかん___ いきます。
⑤________さん もくようび____ じゅぎょう____ あります。	⑥________さん としょかん____ べんきょう____ します。	⑦________さん こんばん____ しゅくだい____ します。	⑧________さん うち____ ひるごはん____ たべます。
⑨________さん あさはちじごろ ____ ごはん____ たべます。	⑩________さん じゅうにじはん ____ じゅぎょう____ おわります。	⑪________さん まいあさ____ テレビ（てれび）____ みます。	⑫________さん にちようび____ がっこう____ きます。
⑬________さん まいばん____ おふろ____ はいります。	⑭________さん さんじごろ____ うち____ かえります。	⑮________さん こんばん____ はちじ____ テレビ（てれび）____ みます。	⑯________さん まいあさ____ しちじ____ シャワー（しゃわ）____ あびます。

Activity 4

Ask a partner about his or her class schedule for the week to complete the following chart. Then switch roles.

Example: A: げつようびは　じゅぎょうが　ありますか。
B: ええ、ありますよ。
A: そうですか。　いつですか。
B: ごぜんはちじに　にほんごの　じゅぎょうが　あります。
そして、くじに　ぶんがくの　じゅぎょうが　あります。

～ようび	じゅぎょう
げつようび	8 A.M.- にほんご　9 A.M.- ぶんがく
かようび	
すいようび	
もくようび	
きんようび	

IV. Using adverbs to express frequency of actions

Japanese has a variety of adverbs that express how often one does something, as shown in the following illustration.

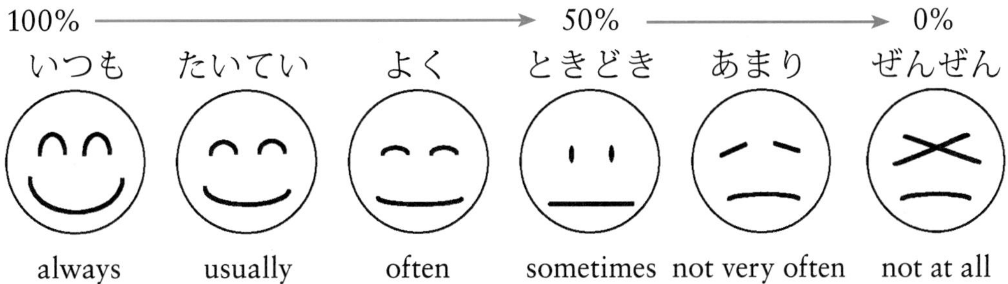

Sentences containing いつも, たいてい, よく or ときどき end with an affirmative verb form.

わたしは いつも あさ コーヒー（こ ひ）を のみます。
I always drink coffee in the morning.

わたしは たいてい じゅういちじに ねます。
I usually go to bed at eleven o'clock.

わたしは よく としょかんに いきます。
I often go to the library.

わたしは ときどき じゅうじごろ おきます。
I sometimes get up about 10:00.

The adverbs あまり and ぜんぜん must always be used with the negative form of the verb.

わたしは あまり ほんを よみません。
I don't read books very much.

わたしは ぜんぜん あさごはんを たべません。
I don't eat breakfast at all.

スミス（すみす）：よく あさごはんを たべますか。
Do you always eat breakfast?

たなか：いいえ、ぜんぜん たべません。
No, I never eat it.
スミス（すみす）さんは？
How about you, Mr. Smith?

スミス（すみす）：わたしは たいてい たべますよ。
I usually do.

たなか：そうですか。
I see.

Notes

- とても may be used before よく in order to express very frequent actions.

    たなかさんは　とても　よく　としょかんに　いきます。
    Mr. Tanaka goes to the library very often.

- The position of an adverb of frequency in a sentence is relatively flexible. These adverbs usually appear immediately before the verb, but may appear before the direct object without any significant change in meaning.

    わたしは　としょかんに　あまり　いきません
    I don't go to the library very often.

    わたしは　あまり　としょかんに　いきません。
    I don't go to the library very often.

はなして　みましょう　Conversation Practice

Activity 1

Complete the sentences below with an adverb of frequency that best describes your own habits. Choose from いつも, たいてい, よく, ときどき, あまり, or ぜんぜん.

Example: うちで　あさごはんを　たべます。
うちで　あさごはんを　あまり　たべません。

1. りゅうがくせいセンター(せんた) (*International Student Center*) に　いきます。
2. としょかんで　べんきょうします。
3. シャワー(しゃわ)を　あびます。
4. うちで　しゅくだいを　します。
5. おふろに　はいります。
6. あさ　ほんを　よみます。

Activity 2

Ask a partner whether he or she does something often. Then fill in the chart with activities that he or she does and does not do frequently.

Example: A: ～さんは　ほんを　よく　よみますか。

B: いいえ、あまり　よみません。

	パートナー (ぱとな)	わたし
いつも		
よく		
ときどき		
あまり		
ぜんぜん		

Activity 3

Work with members of your class. Write down what you do or don't do frequently in the chart in Activity 2. Tell individual classmates what you do and ask whether he or she has similar habits. Find a classmate who shares your interests.

Example: A: わたしは　ときどき　としょかんに　いきます。
～さんは　よく　としょかんに　いきますか。

B: はい、　わたしも　ときどき　としょかんに　いきます。

or　はい、　よく　いきます。

or　いいえ、　わたしは　あまり　いきません。

or　いいえ、　わたしは　ぜんぜん　いきません。

V. Expressing past action and events using the polite past forms of verbs

Forming the polite past form of a verb is quite easy. All you need to do is to use ました instead of ます for an affirmative sentence, and ませんでした instead of ません for a negative sentence.

Question	
	Verb (past)
あさごはんを	たべましたか。

Did you eat breakfast?

Answer	
	Verb (past)
いいえ、	たべませんでした。

No, I didn't.

スミス（すみす）：きのう　しゅくだいが　ありましたか。
Was there an assignment yesterday?

たなか：いいえ、ありませんでしたよ。
No, there wasn't.

スミス（すみす）：そうですか。どうも。
I see. Thank you.

	Polite affirmative form		Polite negative form		Verb class
	present	past	present	past	
	～ます	～ました	～ません	～ませんでした	
to go	いきます	いきました	いきません	いきませんでした	う -verb
to eat	たべます	たべました	たべません	たべませんでした	る -verb
to come	きます	きました	きません	きませんでした	Irregular
to do	します	しました	しません	しませんでした	Irregular

はなして　みましょう　Conversation Practice

Activity 1

The chart below lists everything Mr. Smith did yesterday. Looking at the chart, describe each of his activities.

Example: スミス（すみす）さんは　しちじに　おきました。

7:00 A.M.	Wake up	1:30 P.M.	English class
7:10 A.M.	Shower	2:30 P.M.	Study at the library
8:00 A.M.	Breakfast	4:30 P.M.	Go home
8:45 A.M.	Go to school	6:00 P.M.	Dinner
9:00 A.M.	Japanese class	7:30 P.M.	Watch TV
10:00 A.M.	Literature class	9:00 P.M.	Do homework
12:00 M.	Lunch at school	12:00 A.M.	Go to bed

Activity 2

Answer the following questions, based on Mr. Smith's chart in Activity 1.

Example: A: スミス(すみす)さんは　きのう　はちじに　おきましたか。

B: いいえ、おきませんでした。

1. スミス(すみす)さんは　きのう　おふろに　はいりましたか。
2. スミス(すみす)さんは　きのう　がっこうで　ひるごはんを　たべましたか。
3. スミス(すみす)さんは　きのう　れきしの　じゅぎょうが　ありましたか。
4. スミス(すみす)さんは　きのうのばん　シャワー(しゃわ)を　あびましたか。
5. スミス(すみす)さんは　きのう　としょかんへ　いきましたか。
6. スミス(すみす)さんは　うちで　しゅくだいを　しましたか。
7. スミス(すみす)さんは　じゅういちじごろ　ねましたか。

Activity 3

Work with a partner. Fill in the table below with as much detail as possible describing what you did yesterday. Your partner will have a blank table and will ask you questions to figure out what you did. Compare the two tables when you are done.

Example: A: きのう　なんじに　おきましたか。

B: はちじごろ　おきました。～さんは？

A: わたしは　しちじに　おきました。

B: そうですか。あさごはんは　たべましたか。

A: いいえ、たべませんでした。でも、コーヒー(こひ)を　のみました。

5 A.M.		4 P.M.	
6 A.M.		5 P.M.	
7 A.M.		6 P.M.	
8 A.M.		7 P.M.	
9 A.M.		8 P.M.	
10 A.M.		9 P.M.	
11 A.M.		10 P.M.	
12 P.M.		11 P.M.	
1 P.M.		12 A.M.	
2 P.M.		1 A.M.	
3 P.M.			

More about the topic particle は

In Chapter 2 (see pages 46–47), the topic of the sentence was also the subject of the sentence as in わたしは　がくせいです (*I am a student*). As you learned in the Dialogue section of this chapter, the subject serves often as the topic, but not always. The function of the topic is to present something the speaker wishes to comment on, so topics can include time expressions, direct objects, goals, locations, and other words. Understanding how the topic works in Japanese conversation and learning how to use topics can be quite difficult, and more explanations follow later in this book. Do not be surprised if the topic particle は appears when you don't expect any particle, as in きょうは (*today*) or where you expect a different particle, as in しゅくだいは (*homework*) instead of しゅくだいを .

しゅくだいは　あした　します。
I will do the homework tomorrow.
(literally, *Speaking of homework, I will do it tomorrow.*)

あしたは　じゅぎょうが　あります。
There is a class tomorrow.
(literally, *Speaking of tomorrow, there is a class.*)

A: よく　えいがを　みますか。
Do you watch movies often?

B: ええ。
Yes.

A: じゃあ、テレビは？
てれび
Well, how about TV?

B: テレビは　みませんね。
てれび
No, I don't watch TV.

A: しゅうまつは　なにを　しますか。
What will you do this weekend?

B: えいがを　みます。にほんの　えいがですよ。
I'm going to a movie. A Japanese film.

A: そうですか。いいですね。
Is that so? That sounds good.

きく　れんしゅう
Listening

じょうずな　ききかた　Listening Strategy

Listening for general ideas

Conversations are often full of redundancy and unimportant details, and it is not necessary to understand every single spoken word. It is more important to pick up a few key words and to get a general idea of what the conversation is about. If you need to know specific details or information, you can always ask questions about them for clarification.

みっつの　ライフスタイル(らいふすたいる)　Three different lifestyles

Think about your lifestyle and write down some of the words and phrases that describe it. Then listen to three people talking about their daily lives. Decide which person's life is most like yours. Try to explain the reasons for your choice. There will be some conversational fillers and unknown words in what you hear, but don't worry about them. Try to pick out a few words at a time, write them down, and get the gist of each monologue. Then, try to guess which one of the following people fits in each description.

1. ______________________________

2. ______________________________

3. ______________________________

ききじょうず　はなしじょうず
Communication

Communication Strategy

Using あいづち　(attentive feedback) 2

In Chapter 2 (p. a-66), you learned that the Japanese give feedback, or あいづち, in several ways during a conversation, and that はい and ええ do not necessarily indicate agreement. In addition to indicating that the listener is following the conversation, the use of はい and ええ can mean that the listener sympathizes with the speaker, or that the listener agrees with the speaker's opinion. It is not easy for people unfamiliar with this use of あいづち to interpret correctly which meaning of はい and ええ is intended in many cases. A classic example is that of an American businessperson who reports that a negotiation seemed to be going well because his or her Japanese counterpart appeared to be agreeing with what was being said, but that the deal ultimately fell through, leaving the American bewildered.

The words はい and いいえ are used between phrases as well as between sentences. In the following example, speaker B constantly interrupts speaker A so that A never finishes a sentence.

A: きのう えいがが　あって ...	A: *There was a movie yesterday, and . . .*
B: ええ、	B: *Yeah/Yes.*
A: おもしろいって いうから いってみたんですが ...	A: *I went because I heard it would be interesting, but . . .*
B: ええ、ええ	B: *Yeah, yeah.*
A: ぜんぜん おもしろくなくて ...	A: *It was not interesting at all, and . . .*

Although this might appear rude according to Western standards, by Japanese standards B is not being rude, because A expects constant feedback from B. Indeed, A would feel uncomfortable if B waited for him or her to finish the sentence. In fact, this type of interruption can be seen in many types of conversational feedback in Japanese.

れんしゅう　Practice

Work with a partner. Imagine that both of you are in front of the library and your partner is pointing out different buildings on campus. Say はい or ええ between phrases and sentences to indicate that you understand what he or she is saying.

よむ　れんしゅう
Reading

じょうずな　よみかた　Reading Strategy

Scanning

There are many ways to read a text. Reading style depends on the reader's purpose. For example, if you are looking for certain information, such as the title of a movie, a date, or a topic, you may scan for a specific word or phrase. If you are looking for a reference article, you might skim the abstracts of papers. If you are writing a critique of an article, you will read it in detail. In this chapter, we will discuss the scanning process.

Scanning is a technique used to located specific information or facts quickly. People scan a text to look up a word in a dictionary or a name in the telephone directory, or to search for an answer to a comprehension question. In order to scan, a reader must know what he/she is looking for to be able to search for specific words or phrases.

Scanning is also an effective pre-reading tool when reading numerous texts. The reader may scan the text to assess its relevance, then skim it to get the gist, and if necessary, go back to the text yet again for more detailed reading. When scanning is used as a pre-reading tool, it is a good idea to look for items that signal text organization, such as numbers, steps, or words such as first and second. Also, words that appear in boldface, italics, a larger font size, or a different color may also indicate key information.

れんしゅう　Practice

A. Your friend asks you when you are available to go out for lunch next week. You check your appointment book, which is shown on the next page. Use the information there to answer the following:
   1. What kind of information you look for in an appointment book in cases like this.
   2. The day of the week and time that is most convenient for you. Use the phrase ～ようびの　～じは　どうですか (*How about ～?*).

   Example: げつようびの　じゅうにじは　どうですか。
   How about 12 o'clock Monday?

B. Another friend asks you to play tennis with him. Check your appointments in the table below to let him know the day of the week and time that you can play. Use the phrase ～ようびの　～じは　どうですか (*How about ～?*)

10/1 〜 10/7			
10/1 月	9時〜12時 クラス 1時半〜2時 クラス 3時半〜10時 アルバイト	10/5 金	9時〜12時 クラス 1時半〜2時 クラス
10/2 火	9時〜10時 クラス 10時半〜12時 クラス 1時〜2時 田中先生 4時〜6時 クラス	10/6 土	9時〜5時 アルバイト
10/3 水	9時〜12時 クラス 1時半〜2時 クラス 4時半〜7時半 クラス	10/7 日	デート
10/4 木	9時〜10時 クラス 10時半〜12時 クラス 4時〜6時 テスト	**NOTES**	

ジョンソンさんの一日 Ms. Johnson's Daily Routine

よむ まえに Pre-reading

A. Write five Japanese sentences about your daily routine.

B. Read the question below and identify the words or phrases to scan for in order to find out the answer quickly.

ジョンソンさんは　まいにち　じゅぎょうが　ありますか。

When you are done, scan the passage on the following page. Give your answer to the instructor as soon as you find it.

ことばの リスト Vocabulary

そして	and, then
その後	after that
ですから	so, therefore
でも	but
学生会館	Student Union Building

私の一日

キム・ジョンソン

私は毎日七時半に起きます。そして、シャワーを浴びます。たいてい八時ごろ朝ご飯を食べます。そして、八時半ごろ大学へ行きます。日本語の授業は毎朝九時にあります。その後、よく図書館で勉強します。昨日も図書館でテストの勉強をしました。

昼ご飯はたいてい学生会館で食べます。でも、昨日は食べませんでした。月曜日と水曜日と金曜日の午後は英語と文学の授業があります。火曜日と木曜日の午後は授業がありません。たいてい五時半ごろ家に帰ります。六時ごろ晩ご飯を食べます。そして、宿題をします。テレビはあまり見ません。いつも十一時半に寝ます。

よんだ　あとで　Comprehension

Answer these questions in Japanese.

1. ジョンソンさんは　なんじごろ　おきますか。
2. ジョンソンさんは　いつ　ねますか。
3. げつようびは　なんの　じゅぎょうが　ありますか。
4. ジョンソンさんは　がくせいかいかんへ　よく　いきますか。
5. ジョンソンさんは　きのう　なにを　しましたか。
6. ジョンソンさんは　よく　テレビを　みますか。

そうごう　れんしゅう
Integration

すずきさんの　まいにち

Form a group of three people. There should be three types of groups: A, B, and C. Your instructor will tell you which group you are in. Listen to an interview with Suzuki-san, and take notes on the schedule sheet below. Discuss the interview with your partners and make sure that your information is correct. Then form a different group of three. All of the members in this group should come from different groups, one from Group A, another from Group B, and the other from Group C. Exchange information with the others to discover if there are discrepancies in your information.

～ようび	なにを　しますか。
にちようび	
げつようび	
かようび	
すいようび	
もくようび	
きんようび	
どようび	

ロールプレイ (ろ るぷれい)　Role Play

Imagine that you are talking to a Japanese friend. Explain to him or her how a typical American college student might spend a week.

Chapter 4

第四課（だいよんか）

にほんの　まち

Japanese Cities

Objectives	Asking about places and indicating location
Vocabulary	Buildings, landmarks, adjectives
Dialogue	このへんに　ぎんこうが　ありますか。 *Is there a bank around here?*
Japanese Culture	Geography and demographics of Japan
Grammar	I. Referring to things using これ, それ, あれ, どれ
	II. Asking for and giving locations using ～は　～に　あります／います and ここ, そこ, あそこ
	III. Describing people and things using adjectives + noun, and polite present forms of adjectives
	IV. Describing people, things, and their locations using ～に　～が　あります／います
	V. Using よ and ね
Listening	Using redundancy in speech
Communication	Getting someone's attention (1)
Kanji	Introduction to **kanji**　大　学　校　先　生
Reading	Using script types as clues to word boundaries

単語
たんご
Vocabulary

Nouns

アパート		apartment
えき	駅	station
えんぴつ	鉛筆	pencil
かばん	鞄	luggage, bag
カフェ		coffee shop, café (recent term)
きっさてん	喫茶店	coffee shop (traditional term)
きょうかしょ	教科書	textbook
ぎんこう	銀行	bank
けしゴム	消しゴム	eraser
こうえん	公園	park
こうばん	交番	police box
このへん	この辺	this area
コンビニ		convenience store
じしょ	辞書	dictionary
スーパー		supermarket
たてもの	建物	building, structure
テスト		test
デパート		department store
ノート		notebook
ビル		building
びょういん	病院	hospital
ペン		pen
ボールペン		ballpoint pen

ほんや	本屋	bookstore
まち	町	town
ゆうびんきょく	郵便局	post office
りょう	寮	dormitory
レストラン		restaurant

る -verbs

います	to be; to exist (used for an animate beings). The dictionary form is いる.

Demonstrative words

ここ	here, this place
これ	this object, this
そこ	there, that place (close to the listener or slightly removed from both speaker and listener)
それ	that object, that (close to the listener or slightly removed from both speaker and listener)
あそこ	over there, that place (far away from both speaker and listener)
あれ	that, that object over there

い -adjectives

あおい	青い	blue
あかい	赤い	red
あたらしい	新しい	new
いい		good
おおきい	大きい	big
きいろい	黄色い	yellow
くろい	黒い	black
しろい	白い	white
たかい	高い	tall, high
ちいさい	小さい	small

ちゃいろい	茶色い	brown
ふるい	古い	old

な -adjectives

きれい(な)		clean, pretty, neat
ゆうめい(な)	有名(な)	famous
りっぱ(な)	立派(な)	fine, splendid, nice

Question words

だれ		who
どれ		which one
どんな		what kind of

Adverbs

あまり		very (always used with a negative form)
とても		very (always used with an affirmative form)
どうも		very どうも　ありがとう　Thank you very much どうも　すみません　I'm very sorry

Suffix

～や	～屋	store (for example, ほんや　bookstore)

単語の練習 Vocabulary Practice

A. まち Towns

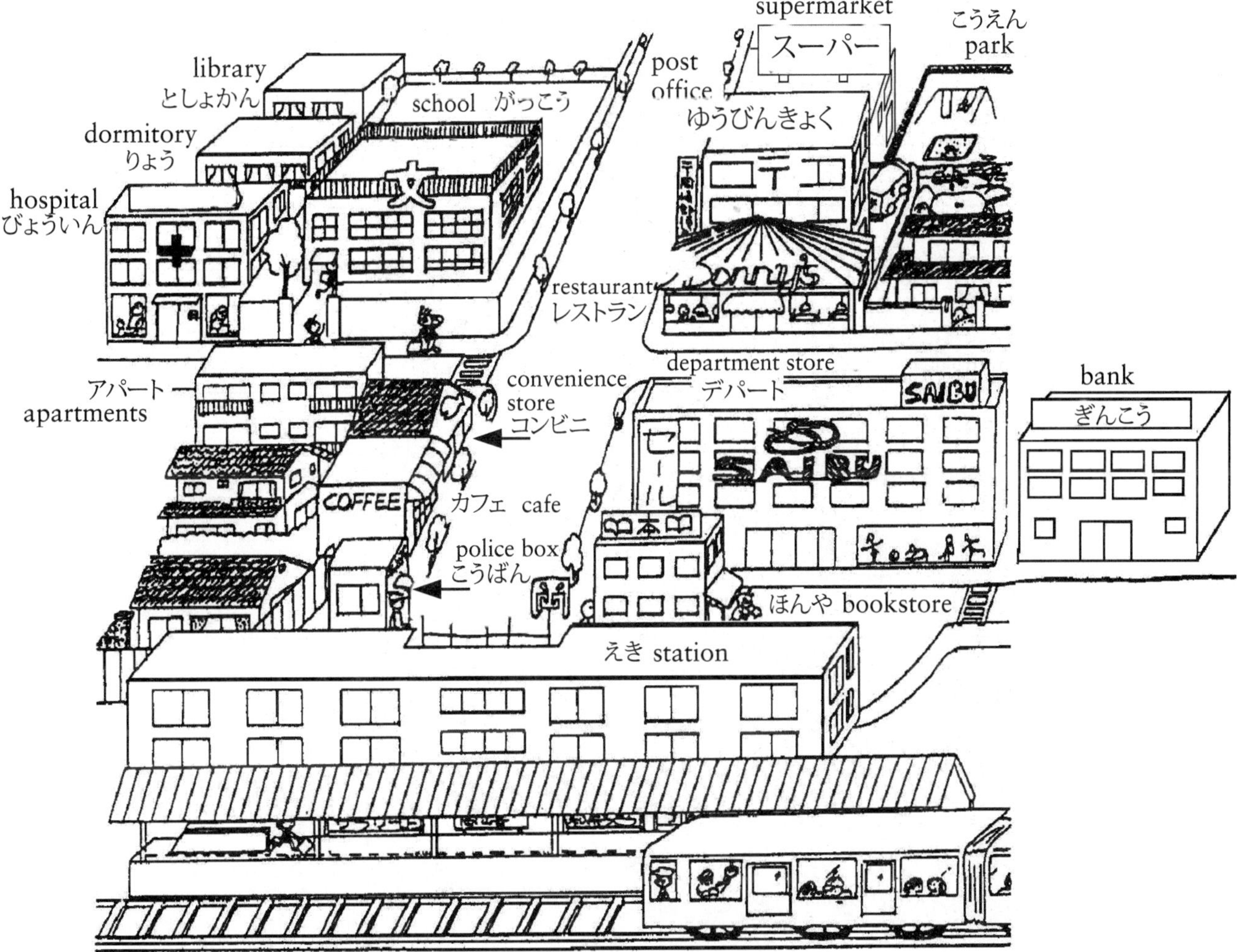

Activity 1

Complete the chart with the Japanese word for each symbol.

Location	Map Symbol	Japanese
station		
bank		
post office		
supermarket	S	
school	文 ⊗	
hospital		
restaurant		
coffee shop		
police box	X	
department store	D	
convenience store	7	

Activity 2

Answer these questions in Japanese.

1. よく　カフェに　いきますか。
2. よく　コンビニに　いきますか。
3. なんじごろ　うちに　かえりますか。
4. ～さんは　うちに　すんでいますか。アパートに　すんでいますか。りょうに　すんでいますか。（すんでいます *to live*）
5. せんしゅう　スーパーに　いきましたか。
6. しゅうまつは　ときどき　デパートに　いきますか。
7. よく　どこで　べんきょうしますか。
8. レストランで　よく　なにを　たべますか。

B. Adjectives

あたらしい new
大(おお)きい big
たかい tall, high
ちいさい small
ふるい old
きれい(な) clean, pretty, neat
ゆうめい(な) famous
りっぱ(な) nice, fine, splendid

あおい blue
あかい red
きいろい yellow
くろい black
しろい white
ちゃいろい brown

Activity 3

Write an antonym for each of the following words. Follow the example.

Example: きたない (dirty) → きれい

大(おお)きい	
あたらしい	
しろい	
あかい	
むめい (unknown)	

Activity 4

Create as many sentences as you can using 〜は　adjectives です and the adjectives in the above list.

Example: わたしの　学校(がっこう)は　大(おお)きいです。

C. School supplies

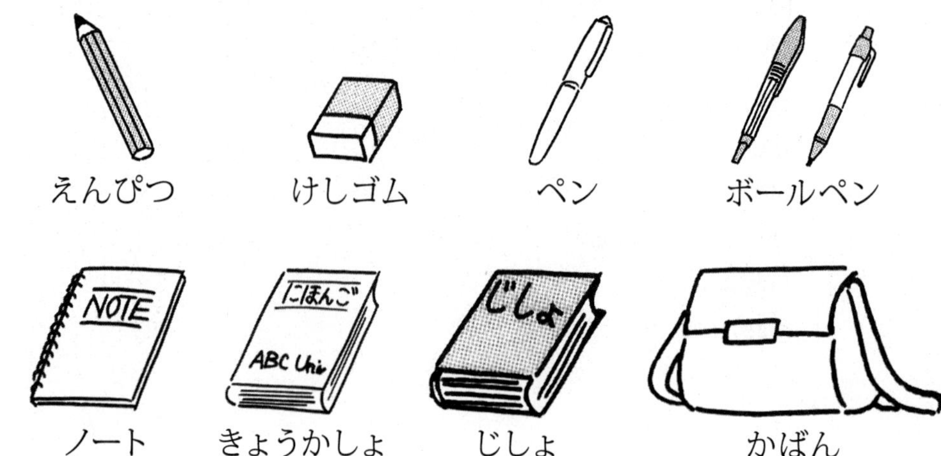

Activity 5

Create sentences describing the color(s) and/or size for each of the items above that you own.

Example: わたしの　かばんは　ちゃいろいです。じしょは　しろいです。

ダイアローグ
Dialogue

はじめに Warm-up

The Shibuya/Harajuku District is a popular hangout for young Japanese. Look at the map of Shibuya and Harajuku below and try to identify some of the landmarks in the area.

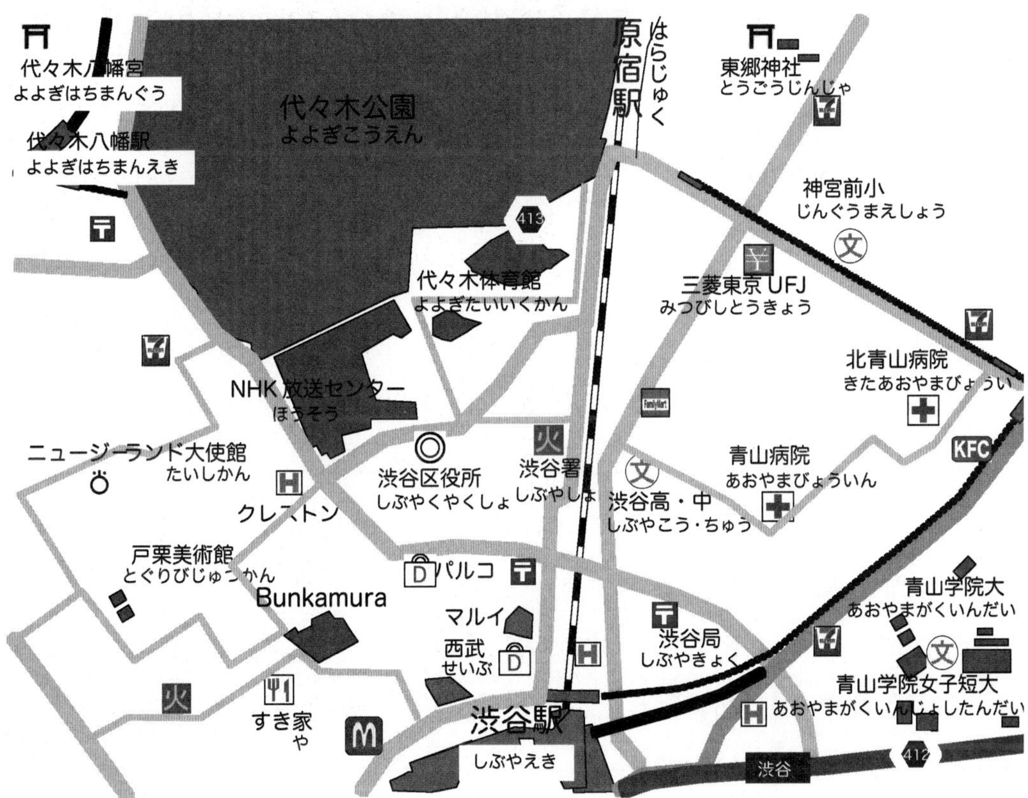

Shibuya and Harajuku

このへんに　ぎんこうが　ありますか。*Is there a bank around here?*

Ueda is meeting a friend in Shibuya. She has just gotten off the train, and realizes that she needs to withdraw some cash. She approaches a passerby (つうこうにん) in front of Shibuya Station (しぶやえき).

うえだ：　あのう、すみませんが。

つうこうにんA：　はい。

うえだ：　このへんに　ぎんこうが　ありますか。

つうこうにんA：　ええ、ありますよ。あそこに　たかい　ビルが　ありますね。

うえだ：　ええ。

つうこうにんA：　あれですよ。

うえだ：　あ、そうですか。どうも　ありがとう　ございます。

つうこうにんA：　いいえ。

In the building:

うえだ：　あのう、すみません。

つうこうにんB：　はい。

うえだ：　ぎんこうは　どこに　ありますか。

つうこうにんB：　あ、ぎんこうは　それですよ。

うえだ：　ああ、どうも。

つうこうにんB：　いいえ。

At the entrance of the bank:

うえだ： あのう、すみませんが、ATM は　どこですか。
こういん (*clerk*)： そこに　ございます。
うえだ： ああ、どうも。

Dialogue Phrase Notes

- When someone thanks you, it is common to say いいえ. In this case, いいえ means *Don't mention it*, or *You're welcome.*
- Like English, Japanese uses a variety of expressions, such as あ (*Ah / Oh*), ああ (*Oh / OK*), へえ〜(*Hmm / Oh*) to indicate understanding or surprise.
- どうも is an abbreviation of phrases such asどうも　ありがとう and どうも　すみません. It is very common to use only どうも in conversation.
- ございます is the polite form of あります. In this dialogue, the bank clerk uses it when speaking with Ueda.

ダイアローグの　後(あと)で　Comprehension

Answer the following questions in Japanese.

1. うえださんは　どこに　いきますか。
2. それは　しぶやえきに　ありますか。
3. どんな　たてものですか。

日本の文化
にほん ぶんか
Japanese Culture

Geography and demographics of Japan

Japan is an island nation consisting of about 3,000 islands. Among them, Honshu, Hokkaido, Kyushu, and Shikoku are the four major islands. Japan lies east of

北海道
ほっかいどう
本州
ほんしゅう
九州
きゅうしゅう
四国
しこく

Korea, Russia, and China and is separated from continental Asia by the Sea of Japan. The country is comparable in size to the state of California, with a climate that varies from cool temperate in the north to subtropical in the south.

Mountains cover nearly three quarters of Japan. Since so little flat area exists, many hills and mountainsides are cultivated all the way to the top. There are many volcanoes in Japan because the country lies in an area where several continental plates meet. The most famous volcano is Mt. Fuji, which is the highest point of Japan, with an elevation of 3,776m (12,388 feet). Considered to be one of the most beautiful mountains in the world, Fuji-san, as the Japanese call it, is held sacred and can be seen from Tokyo when the weather is clear.

As Japan is situated in a volcanic zone along the Pacific deeps, frequent low-intensity earth tremors and occasional volcanic activity are felt throughout the islands. Destructive earthquakes occur several times a century. Hot springs are numerous and have been developed as resorts.

The population of Japan is about 125,000,000. While nearly the entire population is Japanese, more than half of the non-Japanese population is Korean. Several smaller minorities from other parts of Asia, India, Latin America, and the Mideast live mostly in Tokyo and other large cities.

Japanese neighborhoods

Japanese neighborhoods tend to develop around a train station. Surrounding a station are various stores, restaurants, banks, post offices, bus terminals, and other buildings. It is also common to find a police box (こうばん) in front of a station. A police box usually has a couple of officers on duty around the clock. People often ask officers for directions.

Police boxes in Tokyo are designed to match the atmosphere of the neighborhood. Many of them include artistic architectural detail, with "KOBAN" signs written in romanized text instead of the characters 交番 (こうばん), to appear more friendly and modern.

Map symbols

In Japan, streets are not usually laid out with a north-south or east-west orientation, and many are designated only by number, so being able to read a Japanese map and keeping one handy is essential to getting around in Japan. If you happen to be in a car, GPS navigation systems are common, and some cell phones have a feature to access maps online. For a chart of Japanese map symbols and their meanings, visit the Nakama 1 student website.

カフェ vs きっさてん

Around the turn of the last century, the term カフェ came into use in Japan. Until then きっさてん had been the only word for *coffee shop*. These words now refer to different types of coffee shops. A カフェ usually has a modern interior and hip urban feel, and serves food and coffee intended to appeal to women and younger consumers. (for example, Starbucks, or スタバ as the Japanese tend to call it.) The term きっさてん refers to a more traditional coffee shop and tends to imply a less sophisticated atmosphere. Many きっさてん allow smoking inside, so they are often considered resting spots for smokers, especially businessmen.

文法
ぶんぽう
Grammar

I. Referring to things, using これ, それ, あれ,どれ

In Chapter 1, you learned the Japanese words to ask about objects around you, using これ／それ／あれは　にほんごで　なんと　いいますか. This chapter introduces the general use of これ, それ, あれ and どれ. これ, それ, あれ and どれ are nouns that refer to things.

A. これ means *this* or *this thing*. It refers to something that is close to the speaker.

これは　わたしの　えんぴつです。
This is my pencil.

B. それ means *that* or *that thing*. It refers to something that is closer to the listener than the speaker or somewhat away from both of them.

それは　わたしの　えんぴつです。
That is my pencil.

C. あれ means *that* or *that thing over there*. It refers to something away from both of them.

あれは　わたしの　えんぴつです。
That one over there is my pencil.

D. どれ means *which* or *which thing*. It is a question word that asks for a choice between two or more items.

スミス：　たなかさん、それは　なんですか。
Ms. Tanaka, what is that?

たなか：　これは　にほんごの　きょうかしょです。
This is a Japanese textbook.

スミス：　あ、そうですか。じゃあ、あれも　にほんごの　きょうかしょですか。
I see. Then, is that one over there a Japanese textbook, too?

たなか：　いいえ、あれは　にほんごの　じしょです。
No, that's a Japanese dictionary.

スミス：　それは　たなかさんの　ほんですか。
Is that one your book?

たなか：　いいえ、ちがいます。
No, it isn't.

スミス：　じゃあ、たなかさんの　ほんは　どれですか。
Which one is your book, Ms. Tanaka?

たなか：　あれです。
That one over there.

スミス：　あれは　だれの　ノートですか。
Whose notebook is that over there?

たなか：　あれですか。キムさんの　ノートです。
That one over there? It's Ms. Kim's.

スミス：　そうですか。
Is that so?

Notes

- これ, それ, あれ and どれ are pronouns and cannot be followed by another noun.
- It is rude to refer to people using これ, それ, あれ, どれ because they refer to things. However, you can use them to refer to a person in a picture because he/she is not considered a person.
- Actual distances that these words indicate vary depending on context. それ would imply much greater distance when it is used to point out a building than when it is used to point to an item in a room. In the picture below, これ refers to the building in front of the speaker and the listener, あれ refers to the house far away from them, and それ refers to the one that is somewhat away from them but not quite far enough for them to call it あれ.
- だれ means *who,* but it also means *whose* if followed by the particle の.

  だれが　きますか。　*Who is coming?*
  これは　だれの　ほんですか。　*Whose book is this?*

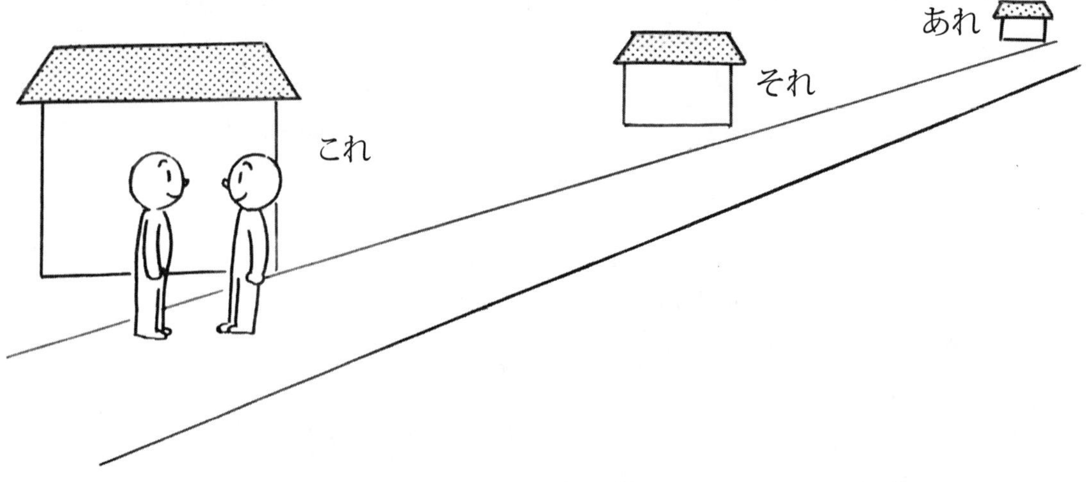

話(はな)して　みましょう　Conversation Practice

Activity 1

Look at the following drawing of a room. Smith is asking Kimura the Japanese words for various objects in the room. Complete the following conversations using これ, それ and あれ.

Example: スミス：　<u>これ</u>は　にほんごで　なんと　いいますか。
きむら：　けしゴムと　いいます。

1. スミス：　__________は　にほんごで　なんと　いいますか。
   きむら：　けしゴムと　いいます。
2. スミス：　__________は　にほんごで　なんと　いいますか。
   きむら：　じしょと　いいます。
3. スミス：　__________は　にほんごで　なんと　いいますか。
   きむら：　えんぴつと　いいます。
4. スミス：　__________は　にほんごで　なんと　いいますか。
   きむら：　ノートと　いいます。
5. スミス：　__________は　にほんごで　なんと　いいますか。
   きむら：　かばんと　いいます。

Activity 2

Work with a partner. Look at the following drawing. Pretend you are person A, and your partner is person B. Some erasers, pencils, books, and dictionaries are scattered around the room. First, let your partner decide who among the following people owns each item and mark it on the drawing.

たなか先生(せんせい)　きむらさん　アリスさん　キムさん　スミスさん　リンさん

Then ask who owns each item and write it under the owner's name. After you finish, have your partner check your answers.

Example: A: これ／それ／あれは　だれの　ほんですか。

B: きむらさんの　ほんです。

Activity 3

Work with a partner. Looking at the map below, ask a classmate to locate certain buildings using これ, それ and あれ. Assume that both of you are standing in front of the police box.

Example: A: これ／それ／あれは　＿＿＿＿＿＿＿＿ですか。

B: はい、そうです。 or いいえ、そうじゃありません。

Activity 4

Work with a partner. Look at the following town maps. Imagine that your partner is a new student and you are showing him/her the campus. First, decide where you and your partner are among the locations numbered 1 through 4. Then, describe the buildings around you, using これ, それ, あれ, どれ.

Example: A: これ／それ／あれは________________です。

B: そうですか。じゃあ、これ／それ／あれは　なんですか。

A: ______________です。

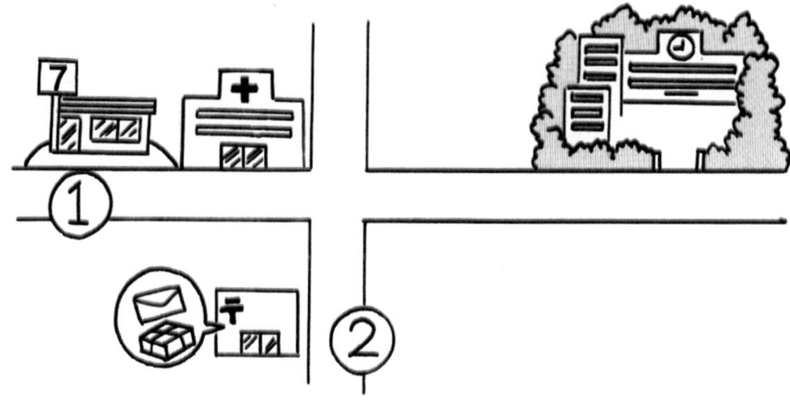

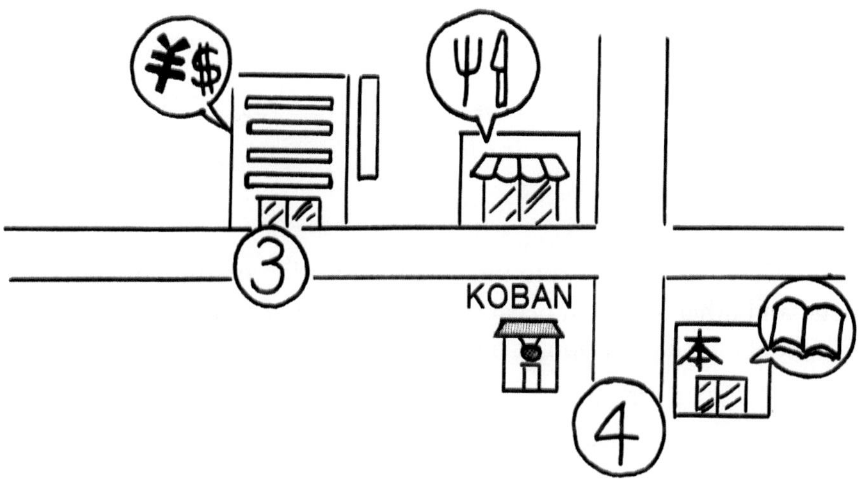

II. Asking for and giving locations using ～は　～に　あります／います and ここ, そこ, あそこ

A. ここ、そこ、あそこ、どこ

The words これ，それ，あれ，どれ refer to objects. When these words are used to point out a building, the speaker is viewing the building as an object rather than as a location. However, buildings and facilities are also considered places or locations. In order to refer to the location, you need to use ここ，そこ，あそこ，どこ instead.

ここ means *here* or *this place*, and refers to the area close to the speaker.

そこ means *there* or *that place,* and refers to the area close to the listener but away from the speaker, or between, or some distance from both of them.

あそこ means *that place over there*, and refers to the area far away from both the speaker and the listener.

どこ means *where.*

B. ～は　～に　あります

In Chapter 3 (p. a-103), you learned that the verb あります (*there is X*) is used to describe the existence of an object or event. It is commonly used to ask or identify the location of objects such as pens, books, and buildings. To ask about location, use ～は　どこに　ありますか. Here に is a particle that indicates the location of an object.

じしょは　どこに　ありますか。　*Where is the dictionary?*

りょうは　どこに　ありますか。　*Where is the dormitory?*

The answer to these questions might be: Location に　あります.

ここに　あります　*It's here.*

あそこに　あります。　*It's over there.*

The word あります is never used to indicate the location of animate objects such as people, pets, and other animals, because it is used only for lifeless objects. Use います to talk about the location of living beings.

キム：まもるさんは　どこに　いますか。　*Where is Mamoru?*

スー：ここに　います。　*He is here.*

スミス：あのう、すみませんが、ゆうびんきょくは　どこに　ありますか。
Um, excuse me, but where is the post office?

たなか：そこに　あります。
It's there.

スミス：あ、そうですか。どうも。
I see. Thanks.

(The teacher is taking attendance, but he doesn't see Ms. Kim.)

先生(せんせい)：　キムさんは　どこに　いますか。
Where is Ms. Kim?

ブラウン：　先生(せんせい)、いま　としょかんに　います。
Professor, she is in the library now.

先生(せんせい)：　あ、そうですか。じゅぎょうに　きますか。
I see. Is she coming to class?

ブラウン：　さあ、よくわかりません。
Well, I am not sure.

Notes

- Location に　あります／います can be abbreviated as Location です.

  なかがわ：　スミスさんの　りょうは　どこですか。
  Where is Mr. Smith's dormitory?
  スミス：　あそこです。
  Over there.

  先生(せんせい)：　キムさんは　どこに　いますか。
  Where is Ms. Kim?
  ジョンソン：　としょかんです。
  In the library.

- You cannot use the particle で in this structure because で indicates a location at which an event or activity takes place. When you are merely asking or indicating the location of a building or object, no activity is implied.

  スミス：　どこで　えいがが　ありますか。
  Where is the movie?
  なかがわ：　あそこで　あります。
  It will be over there.

  キム：　こうえんは　どこに　ありますか。
  Where is the park?
  やまだ：　あそこに　あります。
  It's over there.

話してみましょう Conversation Practice

Activity 1

Work with a partner. Look at the drawing of a room. One person asks questions about the location of the objects and people, ～は どこに　あります／いますか and the other person responds using ここ／そこ／あそこ and ～に　あります／います or ～です. Follow the model.

Example: A: ノートは　どこに　ありますか。
B: ここに　あります。／ここです。

1. けしゴム
2. やまださん
3. にほんごの　じしょ
4. スミスさん
5. ボールペン
6. きょうかしょ

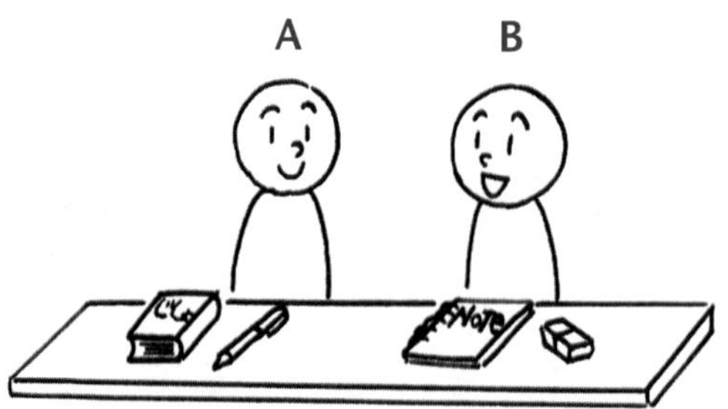

Activity 2

Look at the following drawing of a street. Your partner will ask you where the following buildings are. Answer his/her questions based on the picture.

Example: A: あのう、としょかんは　どこに　ありますか。
B: そこに　あります。
A: ああ、そこですね。どうも。

1. こうえん
2. こうばん
3. ゆうびんきょく
4. ほんや
5. としょかん

III. Describing people and things using adjectives + noun, and polite present forms of adjectives

There are two types of adjectives in Japanese. Both of them modify nouns directly and can be used at the end of sentence to describe a noun. One is called an い -adjective because it ends in い before a noun, as in 大(おお)きい　うち (*big house*) and ちいさい　うち (*small house*). The other type is called a な -adjective, because the adjective takes な before a noun as in りっぱな　うち (*fine house*) and きれいな　うち (*pretty house*).

A. Describing people and things, using adjectives and adverbs + noun

りょうは　ふるい　たてものです。
The dormitory is in an old building.

えきビルは　ゆうめいな　たてものです。
The station building is a famous building.

The formation of adjective + noun is the following. Note that the dictionary form is the form in which dictionaries list adjectives and verbs.

い -adjectives

Dictionary form　大(おお)きい
大(おお)きい　+　うち　→　大(おお)きい　うち

な -adjectives

Dictionary form:　きれい
きれいな　+　うち　→　きれいな　うち

やまなか：あれは　わたしの うちです。
That one over there is my house.

スミス：へえ、大(おお)きい　うちですね。
Wow, it's a large house, isn't it?

ジョンソン：ゆうびんきょくは　どこに　ありますか。
Where is the post office?

ほんだ：ゆうびんきょくですか。あそこです。
The post office? Over there.

ジョンソン：ああ、りっぱな　たてものですね。
I see, it's a nice building.

B. Describing and commenting on places using adjectives (polite affirmative and negative forms), and とても and あまり.

Polite affirmative form

わたしの　かばんは　あかいです。
My bag is red.

おがわさんのりょうは　とても　ちいさいです。
Mr. Ogawa's dorm is very small.

びょういんは　とても　きれいです。
The hospital is very clean.

Polite negative form

わたしの　かばんは　くろくありません。
My bag is not black.

わたしの　かばんは　くろくないです。
My bag is not black.

びょういんは　あまり　大(おお)きくありません。
The hospital is not very big.

びょういんは　あまり　大(おお)きくないです。
The hospital is not very big.

すずきさんのりょうは　あまり　りっぱじゃありません。
Mr. Suzuki's dorm is not very nice.

すずきさんのりょうは　あまり　りっぱじゃないです。
Mr. Suzuki's dorm is not very nice.

The following charts show the formation of polite forms and adjective + noun for い- and な-adjectives.

い -adjectives

Dictionary form	Polite affirmative form	Polite negative form	adjective + noun
大(おお)きい (large)	大(おお)きいです	大(おお)きくありません 大(おお)きくないです	大(おお)きいうち
いい * (good)	いいです	よくありません よくないです	いいうち

* い -Adjective いい, meaning *good*, has an irregular negative form.

な -adjectives

Dictionary form	Polite affirmative form	Polite negative form	Adjective + noun
ゆうめい (famous)	ゆうめいです	ゆうめいじゃありません ゆうめいじゃないです	ゆうめいな うち

ジョンソン：ほんださんの　うちは　どこですか。
Where is your house, Mr. Honda?

ほんだ：それです。
It's there.

ジョンソン：ああ、とても　きれいな　うちですね。
Wow, it's a very nice house, isn't it.

ほんだ：ありがとう。でも、あまり　大(おお)きくありませんよ。／大(おお)きくないですよ。
Thank you, but it is not very big.

NOTES

- The alternative negative form, ～ないです, is considered colloquial and only used in spoken language.
- Note that the negative form of a な-adjective is the same as that of a noun + です.

  Negative of noun + です　　大学生(だいがくせい)じゃありません。

  Negative of な -adjective　　きれいじゃありません。

  りょうは　とても　きれいです。
  The dormitory is very nice/clean.

  りょうは　あまり　きれいじゃありません。
  The domitory is not very nice /clean.

- The adverbs とても and あまり are often used with adjectives, and both may be translated as *very* in English. とても occurs with an affirmative form, and あまり occurs with a negative form. The combination of あまり　～ません／ないです means *not very.*
- Use どんな (*what kind of* ～) to ask about characteristics of people and objects.

  イー：どんな　たてものですか。
  What kind of building is it?

  ホン：くろい　たてものです。
  It is a black building

話(はな)してみましょう Conversation Practice

Activity 1

Describe buildings, objects, and people using the boxed adjectives and the phrases listed below.

Example: わたしの　りょう／たてもの

わたしの　りょうは　ふるい　たてものです。

大(おお)きい	ちいさい	あたらしい	ふるい	たかい	
あかい	あおい	しろい	くろい	きいろい	いい
きれい	りっぱ	ゆうめい	ちゃいろい		

1. わたしの　大学(だいがく)／大学(だいがく)
2. わたしの　うち／たてもの
3. わたしの　かばん／かばん
4. にほんごの　先生(せんせい)／ひと (person)
5. びょういん／たてもの
6. 先生(せんせい)の　ペン／ペン

Activity 2

Work with a partner. Ask your classmates what kinds of places they prefer for doing one of the following activities:

Example: うちを　かいます。 (*to buy*)

A: どんな　うちが　いいですか。

B: ふるい　うちが　いいですね。

1. 大学院(だいがくいん)に　はいります。
2. カフェで　べんきょうします。
3. びょういんに　いきます。
4. りょこうに　いきます。 (*to go on a trip*)
5. レストランで　ごはんを　たべます。

Activity 3

Look at the chart describing various buildings, and answer the following questions, paying attention to はい, いいえ, とても and あまり.

Examples: A: ゆうびんきょくは　大(おお)きいですか。

B: いいえ、大(おお)きくありません。

or いいえ、大(おお)きくないです。

A: ぎんこうは　大(おお)きいですか。

B: はい、とても　大(おお)きいです。

	ゆうびんきょく	ぎんこう	スーパー	びょういん
大(おお)きい	いいえ	とても	あまり	はい
あたらしい	とても	いいえ	はい	あまり
いい	あまり	いいえ	とても	とても
きれい	はい	いいえ	はい	はい
ゆうめい	いいえ	あまり	いいえ	はい
りっぱ	あまり	とても	いいえ	はい

1. スーパーは　いいですか。
2. ゆうびんきょくは　あたらしいですか。
3. びょういんは　きれいですか。
4. びょういんは　あたらしいですか。
5. ゆうびんきょくは　いいですか。
6. ぎんこうは　りっぱですか。
7. ぎんこうは　ゆうめいですか。

Activity 4

Work with a partner. Using the adjectives you have just learned, tell your partner about your home and belongings. Then ask your partner whether his/her place and belongings also share these characteristics. Follow the model.

Example: A: わたしの　アパートは　あたらしいです。

～さんの　アパートも　あたらしいですか。

B: ええ、とても　あたらしいです。／

いいえ、あまり　あたらしくありません。

IV. Describing people, things, and their locations using 〜に　〜が　あります／います

The phrase 〜に　〜が　あります／います *means there is a person/object in a certain location*. It uses the same verbs and the location particle に like 〜は　〜に　あります／います, but their usage is different. Whereas 〜は　〜に　あります/います is used to ask for or tell the location of something or someone, 〜に　〜が　あります／います is used to describe a scene in which someone or something exists in a given location or to ask what is in that location.

あ、ここ<u>に</u>	ねこ<u>が</u>	います。	*Oh, there is a cat right here.*
ほら、あそこ<u>に</u>	すずきさん<u>が</u>	います。	*Look! I see Mr. Suzuki over there.*
大学(だいがく)<u>に</u>	ほんや<u>が</u>	あります。	*There is a bookstore in the university.*
えき<u>に</u>	ゆうびんきょく<u>が</u>	あります。	*There is a post office in the station.*

ブラウン：そこに　ほんが　ありますか。
Is there a book there (near you)?

おがわ：ええ、ありますよ。ブラウンさんの　ほんですか。
Yes, there is. It that yours?

ブラウン：ええ、そうです。ありがとう。
Yes, it is. Thank you.

たなか：このへんに　なにが　ありますか。
What is in this area?

スミス：とても ゆうめいな　こうえんが あります。
There is a very famous park.

うえだ：すみません、このへんに　スーパーが　ありますか。
Excuse me. Is there a supermarket around here?

つうこうにん (*passerby*)：ええ、ありますよ。
Yes, there is.

うえだ：そうですか。どこに　ありますか。
I see. Where is it?

つうこうにん (*passerby*)：あそこですよ。
It is over there.

Notes

- The location may be marked by には instead of just に, if the location is the topic of a sentence.

  Example: にほんには　ふじさんが　あります。
  As for Japan, Mt. Fuji is there.

- ～に　～が　あります cannot be replaced with ～は　～です.

話(はな)してみましょう Conversation Practice

Activity 1

The box below represents a room. You are at location A. Decide where to place the objects listed in the chart and fill in blanks 2 through 8 accordingly. Then, assuming you are talking with a person at location B, complete the chart with the location number and correct location noun (ここ, そこ or あそこ). Finally, create sentences describing the location of each object, following the example.

Example: ここに　くろい　ペンが　あります。

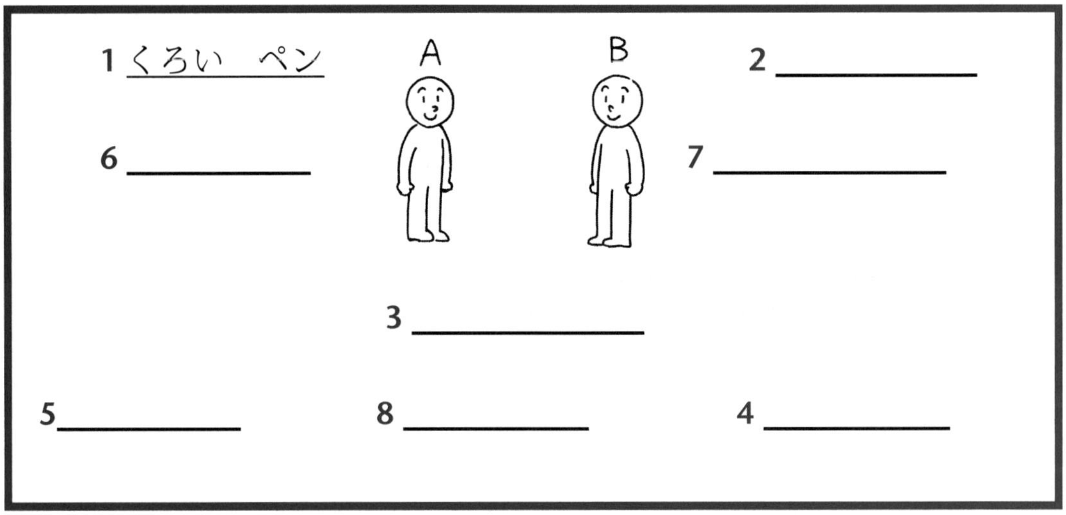

1 くろい　ペン　　A　　B　　2 ________

6 ________　　7 ________

3 ________

5 ________　　8 ________　　4 ________

Location 1–8	ここ／そこ／あそこ	Object
1	ここ	くろい　ペン
		あかい　ボールペン
		ふるい　かばん
		しろい　かばん
		きいろい　ノート
		ちゃいろい　えんぴつ
		ふるい　じしょ
		きれいな　きょうかしょ

Activity 2

Work with a partner. Ask your partner where the objects in Activity 1 are located on his/her map for the same exercise, and write in the name of the objects in the correct location below. Use the location number to specify the exact location.

Example: A: 1に　なにが　ありますか。
B: くろい　ペンが　あります。

1 くろい　ペン
6 ________
A
B
2 ________
7 ________
3 ________
5 ________
8 ________
4 ________

Activity 3

Work with a new partner. Ask your partner about buildings in his/her neighborhood. Then write a description of the neighborhood using adjectives you have just learned.

Example: A: このへんに　どんな　たてものが　ありますか。

B: ぎんこうが　あります。

A: どんな　たてものですか。

B: たかい　たてものです。でも、あまり きれいじゃありません。

Activity 4

Work in a group of four. One person will think of a famous city or a country. Try to guess the name of the city or the country by asking who lives there or what landmarks are found there. Use そこ to refer to the target city or country.

Examples: A: そこに　なにが　ありますか。

B: ビッグベン (Big Ben) が　あります。

A: ロンドンですか。

B: はい、そうです。

V. Using よ and ね

Japanese employs a variety of sentence final particles to indicate the speaker's assumption, intention, and other subtle nuances. Two of the most common particles used in conversation are ね and よ.

A. The particle ね

The particle ね can be translated as 〜*isn't it?/right?/correct?* in English. It indicates that the speaker thinks the listener shares the same information, opinions, or feelings. ね is used when the speaker is seeking the listener's agreement, or confirming a fact, or to create a sense of togetherness between the speakers. For example, in the following exchange, Li is confirming that a **kanji** quiz is scheduled for today.

リー：きょう　かんじの　テストが　ありますね。
We have a kanji test today, right?

キム：ええ。
Yes.

In the following sentence, Li thinks that Yoyogi Park is pretty and assumes Kim thinks the same. So, he is seeking her agreement.

リー：代々木公園(よよぎこうえん)は　きれいですね。
Yoyogi Park is pretty, isn't it?

キム：ええ、ほんとうに　きれいですね。
Yes, it is indeed pretty.

In the following sentence, John does not necessarily assume that Yamashita shares the same opinion about the park. Instead, he invites Yamashita to share his opinion by using ね. The speaker uses ね in this way to create a sense of togetherness or familiarity with the listener.

やました：こうえんは　あそこです。
The park is over there.

ジョン：ああ、りっぱな　こうえんですね。
Wow, it is a nice park, isn't it?

B. The particle よ

The particle よ can be translated as *I tell you* or *you know* in English. よ indicates the speaker's assumption that the listener does not share the speaker's opinion or information. Therefore, it is used when the speaker wishes to emphasize to the listener that he/she is imparting completely new information, and can sound authoritative. When overused or used improperly, よ sounds pushy and overly aggressive.

リー：　先生(せんせい)、あした　テストが　ありますか。
Are we going to have a test tomorrow?

先生(せんせい)：　いいえ。テストは　あさってですよ。
No, it will be the day after tomorrow.

ブラウン：　このへんに　ぎんこうが　ありますか。
Is there a bank around here?

つうこうにん (*passerby*)：　ええ、そこに　ありますよ。
Yes, it is there.

ブラウン：　あ、あかいたてものですね。
Ah, the red building, right?

つうこうにん (*passerby*)：　ええ、そうです。
Yes, it is.

話(はな)してみましょう　Conversation Practice

Activity 1

Complete the following conversations by choosing ね or よ.

Example: A: あのう、このへんに　コンビニが　ありますか。
B: ええ、 あります（ね／よ）。あそこです。
A: あ、あれです（ね／よ）。どうも　ありがとう　ございます。

1. A: すみません、いま　なんじですか。
B: ３じはんです（ね／よ）。
A: そうですか。どうも　ありがとう。

2. A: きょう　なんじに　かえりますか。
B: ６じごろ　かえります。
A: ６じごろです（ね／よ）。じゃあ、６じはんに　いきます。

3. A: あの、これは　スミスさんの　じしょですか。
B: いいえ、それは、うえださんの　じしょです（ね／よ）。
A: あ、そうですか。どうも。

4. A: あの、先生(せんせい)、テストはあしたです（ね／よ）。
B: ええ、そうです。

5. A: あの、先生(せんせい)、らいしゅうの　かようびは　やすみです（ね／よ）。
B: いいえ、かようびは　じゅぎょうが　あります。
やすみは　すいようびです（ね／よ）。

6: A: すみません。ゆうびんきょくは　どこですか。
B: あそこに　たかいビルが　あります(ね/よ)。
A: ええ。
B: ゆうびんきょくは　あそこに　あります。
A: ああ、そうですか。どうも。
B: いいえ。

Activity 2

Work with a partner. The following conversations sound slightly unnatural because they are missing the particle ね or よ. Revise the conversation using ね or よ where appropriate.

Example: A: あのう、すみませんが、やまだびょういんは　どこですか。
B: やまだびょういんですか。あそこです。
A: あ、あれです<u>ね</u>。どうも　ありがとう　ございます。
B: いいえ。

1. A: あのう、このへんに　びょういんが　ありますか。
B: いいえ、ありません。びょういんは　とおい (*far away*) です。
A: そうですか。どうも。

2. A: そこに　しろい　たてものが　あります。
B: ええ。
A: それは　なんですか。
B: それは　ほんやです。

3. A: これは　なんですか。
B: なっとうです。
A: え、なっとう?　なっとうって　なんですか。
B: Fermented soy beans です。

4. A: あれは　デパートですか。
B: いいえ、スーパーです。
A: とても　りっぱな　スーパーです。
B: そうです。

聞く　練習
き　れんしゅう
Listening

上手な　聞き方　Listening Strategy
じょうず　き　かた

Using redundancy in speech

In Chapters 2 and 3 (see p. a-67 and p. a-117), you learned that it is not necessary to understand every single word in order to understand a conversation, and that it is important to pick up only a few key words. In face-to-face conversations, there are many clues as to what a person is saying, such as facial expressions, gestures, and intonation. Context and general knowledge will also help you guess words you may have missed.

学生街　Campus Town
がくせいがい

聞く　前に　Warm-up
き　まえ

Listen to the following conversations. They take place on a busy street that runs near Joto University. Since there is a lot of background noise, some of the words in the conversations cannot be heard. Try to guess the missing words and write them down.

1. ______________________________
2. ______________________________
3. ______________________________

聞いた　後で　Comprehension
き　あと

Based on the conversation you have just heard, complete the following sentences with the correct building names.

1. しろい　たてものは__________です。
2. __________は　ほんやの　ちかくに　あります。
3. そのちゃいろい　たてものは__________です。

聞き上手 話し上手
きじょうず はなじょうず
Communication

Communication Strategy

Getting someone's attention (1)

In Chapter 1 (p. a-18), you learned the phrase, あのう、すみません (*Excuse me*) as a way of getting someone's attention. In this chapter, you will learn more about すみません along with other phrases commonly used in this context.

In current Japanese, すみません has three separate functions: to apologize, to get someone's attention, or to thank. すみません is probably the phrase most commonly used to get someone's attention. It is often preceded by あのう (*ah . . .*) or ちょっと (*well . . .*) and followed by が (but), as in あのう　すみませんが, ちょっと　すみませんが, and あのう　ちょっと　すみませんが.

あのう by itself may also be used to get someone's attention. For example, if someone wants to initiate a conversation at a meeting or a party, the person can say あのう and wait for the listener to respond. あのう is also used as a conversation filler when one cannot think of the right word. If you want to ask someone a personal question, first say しつれいですが or あのう　しつれいですが (literally, *I am being rude, but . . .*). For instance, あのう　しつれいですが、にほんの　かたですか is a polite way of asking someone whether he/she is Japanese.

Finally, along with あのう or すみません，おねがいします (literally, *I am requesting*) may also be used to get the attention of someone who provides a service, such as a store clerk.

練習 Practice
れんしゅう

A. Listen to three dialogues and identify the phrase used to approach the listener in each dialogue.

B. You are looking for a certain building or facility, and your classmates are all strangers. Ask for its location using the appropriate expression.

漢字(かんじ) Kanji

漢字(かんじ) Introduction to Kanji

In addition to **hiragana** and **katakana**, the Japanese writing system makes extensive use of **kanji**, which are characters borrowed from Chinese. When the Japanese adopted **kanji**, they also adopted the Chinese way of reading them. At the same time, the Japanese gave the Chinese characters Japanese readings for existing Japanese words. Consequently, a **kanji** character has two or sometimes more readings. The Chinese reading of a **kanji** is called the **on** reading, and the Japanese reading is called the **kun** reading. For example, the **on** reading for the **kanji** 大 (*big*) is だい as in 大学(だいがく). Its **kun** reading is おお as in 大(おお)きい. Chinese words incorporated into Japanese are usually given **on** readings, as in 大学(だいがく), 学生(がくせい) and 先生(せんせい).

A **kanji** can be used only for its specific meaning. Thus, even if 五 (*five*) is read ご, one may not use it to replace the **hiragana** ご in おはようございます or あさごはん.

Kanji originated as pictographs and some of the characters still retain their pictorial qualities. For example, 川 (*river*) developed from the picture, 大 (*big*) from 大 (a man extending arms and legs), and 生 (*life*) from 生 (picture of a plant coming out). The exact number of existing **kanji** has never been clear, but it is estimated to be more than 40,000. Approximately 3,000 **kanji** are commonly used in Japan. The Japanese Ministry of Education has designated 1,945 for use in publications such as newspapers and magazines.

Learning **kanji** can be a laborious process. However, once a certain number of **kanji** have been learned, it becomes easier because **kanji** can be associated on the basis of their components. In dictionaries, **kanji** are classified according to 214 basic component shapes, or radicals, each of which has a unique meaning. The following **kanji,** which share the common radical 言, have something to do with language: 訳 (*translation*), 話 (*talk*), 語 (*language*), and 読 (*reading*).

A **kanji** is written according to a fixed stroke order. The general rule is to write from top to bottom, and left to right. Also, a horizontal line is usually drawn before a vertical one.

In Japanese, **kanji** are used mostly for nouns and stems of verbs, adjectives, and adverbs. Grammatical markers, such as particles and inflectional endings, are not written in **kanji**. For example, in the following sentence, the nouns わたし and さかな are written with the **kanji** 私 and 魚, and the verb stem た of たべます is written with the **kanji** 食. The particles は and を as well as the verb ending べます are written in **hiragana**.

私は魚を食べます。(わたしは　さかなを　たべます。*I eat fish.*)

Note the following format for the **kanji** charts used in this book The charts will contain the typeset version of the character, a handwritten version, and stroke order. The **on** readings are in **katakana** and the **kun** readings are in **hiragana**.

学	学	to study, learn まな(ぶ)　ガク・ガッ　学校(がっこう)　大学(だいがく)	丶 丶丶 丶丶丿 ⺍ 𭕄 学 学 学

How to write kanji: Stroke order

Stroke order is very important not only in writing but also in reading, especially when reading handwritten **kanji**. In the handwritten style, lines are often connected and some strokes are simplified. The following are the basic rules for writing **kanji**.

1. Write from left to right. 二 川
2. Write from top to bottom. 川 三
3. Write 冂 as shown. 冂
4. When enclosing a square, write the bottom line last. 冂 冂 田 田

   It is also important to distinguish the following three types of strokes:

   stop 生

   release 大

   hook 学

大	大	big, large おお(きい) ダイ 大学生(だいがくせい)	一 ナ 大
学	学	to study, learn まな(ぶ) ガク・ガッ 学校(がっこう) 大学(だいがく)	学 (8 strokes)
校	校	school コウ 学校(がっこう)	校 (10 strokes)
先	先	ahead; previous さき セン 先生(せんせい)	ノ ㇒ 牛 生 ⺧ 先
生	生	life, to live なま・う(まれる) セイ 学生(がくせい) 先生(せんせい)	ノ ㇒ 牛 牛 生

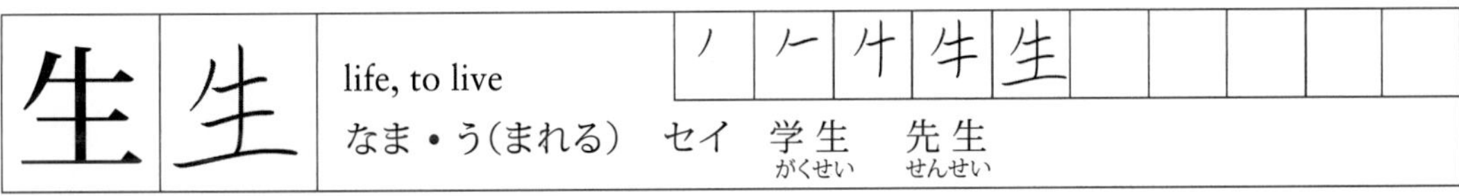

練習(れんしゅう) Practice

Read the following sentences.

1. スミスさんはニューヨーク大学の学生です。
2. ジョンソンさんは学校の先生です。
3. 学生：「やまだ先生、おはようございます。」
   先生：「あっ、きむらさん、おはよう。」

読む 練習
よ れんしゅう
Reading

上手な 読み方 Reading Strategy
じょうず よ かた

Using script types as clues to word boundaries

Unlike English, Japanese words are not separated by spaces. However, there are certain ways of identifying word and phrase boundaries. For example, **katakana** and **kanji** are always used for content words such as nouns, verbs, and adjectives. If a series of **katakana** appears within a sentence, it usually indicates a word or name. **Hiragana** is always used for particles like は, が, の and に and for the endings of verbs and adjectives. Other content words are written in **hiragana** as well. When several **hiragana** appear in the middle of a sentence, you should read them carefully because they may contain more than one word.

練習 Practice
れんしゅう

Read the following sentences and try to identify word boundaries using script types as a clue. In this exercise, each noun should be grouped with its particle as one word. Then insert a slash between the words. Don't worry about understanding the meaning of the sentences completely, and don't be overwhelmed at the sight of **kanji** you don't know the readings for.

私はアメリカのウエストサイド大学の三年生です。
専攻は歴史とフランス語です。でも、日本語も勉強しています。

城東(じょうとう)大学 Joto University

Scan the following reading and circle the words you don't know. Then read the passage and try to guess from context what the unknown words mean.

城東(じょうとう)大学は東京(とうきょう)にあります。学生は三万人(さんまんにん)ぐらいいますが、教授(きょうじゅ)は千人(せんにん)ぐらいです。とても古(ふる)い大学です。キャンパスはあまり大きくありませんが、きれいな建物(たてもの)がたくさんあります。公園(こうえん)もあります。それから、大学の図書館(としょかん)はとても有名(ゆうめい)です。城東(じょうとう)大学には経済学部(けいざいがくぶ)と文学部(ぶんがくぶ)と商学部(しょうがくぶ)と法学部(ほうがくぶ)があります。留(りゅう)学生センターもあります。アメリカとオーストラリアからたくさん留(りゅう)学生が来(き)ます。

読(よ)んだ　後(あと)で　Comprehension

Answer these questions in Japanese.

1. 城東(じょうとう)大学は　どこに　ありますか。
2. 城東(じょうとう)大学は　あたらしい　大学ですか。
3. 城東(じょうとう)大学の　キャンパスは　どんな　キャンパスですか。
4. 城東(じょうとう)大学には　ゆうめいな　たてものが　ありますか。
5. 城東(じょうとう)大学には　どんな　学生が　たくさん　いますか。

総合練習
そうごうれんしゅう
Integration

学校しょうかい School introductions

Form groups of three or four. Have each person create one or two sentences about your school such as its location, size, things you see on campus, famous buildings, etc. Then work together to write a brief paragraph describing your school to students in Japan who are interested in studying abroad.

ロールプレイ Role Play

With a partner, act out each of the following scenarios, then switch roles.

1. You want to go to a hospital. You see a white building in the distance as you pass a police box. Ask the police officer if it is a hospital.
2. You are looking for a bank. Approach a passerby and ask if there is a bank in the neighborhood.
3. You have invited a Japanese friend to your neighborhood. Show your friend around your house.

Chapter 5

第五課（だいごか）

日本（にほん）の　うち
Japanese Homes

Objectives	Asking about places; stating location and distance
Vocabulary	Campus facilities, objects in the room and classroom, nature, more adjectives
Dialogue	リーさんの　アパート Mr. Li's apartment
Japanese Culture	Japanese houses
Grammar	I. Referring to people, places, and things using この, その, あの, どの II. Using location nouns: 中（なか）, そと, となり, よこ, ちかく, うしろ, まえ, 上（うえ）, 下（した）, みぎ, ひだり III. Referring to things mentioned immediately before, using noun/adjective + の (pronoun) IV. Expressing distance and duration using the particles から, まで, and で and the suffix ～ぐらい V. More about the topic marker は and the similarity marker も (double particles and は vs. が)
Listening	Distinguishing sounds in words and phrases
Communication	Getting someone's attention (2)
Kanji	**Kanji** derived from pictures and symbols (1) 山 川 田 人 上 中 下 小 日 本
Reading	Using visual clues

単語(たんご) Vocabulary

Location nouns

うえ	上	on, above, over
うしろ	後ろ	behind, in back of
した	下	under, beneath
そと	外	outside
ちかく	近く	near, in the vicinity of
となり	隣	next to
なか	中	in, inside
ひだり	左	to the left, left side
まえ	前	in front of, in the front
みぎ	右	to the right
よこ	横	next to, at the side of

Nouns

いす	椅子	chair
いぬ	犬	dog
え	絵	picture
おしいれ	押し入れ	Japanese-style closet, storage space
がくしょく	学食	school cafeteria (a shortened form of 学生しょくどう)
がくせいかいかん	学生会館	student union
かわ	川	river
き	木	tree
きょうしつ	教室	classroom
くるま	車	car
こくばん	黒板	chalkboard
コンピュータ		computer
じてんしゃ	自転車	bicycle

しゃしん	写真	photograph
ソファ		sofa
たいいくかん	体育館	gym
たんす	箪笥	chest, drawers
つくえ	机	desk
テーブル		table
でんわ	電話	telephone
ドア		door
トイレ		toilet, restroom
とけい	時計	clock, watch
ところ	所	place
ねこ	猫	cat
バス		bus
ビデオ		video
ひと	人	person
ふとん	布団	futon
ベッド		bed
へや	部屋	room
ほんだな	本棚	bookshelf
まど	窓	window
もの	物	thing (tangible)
やま	山	mountain
ラボ		laboratory

う -verb

かかります	to take (time), it costs; the dictionary form is かかる .

Demonstrative words

この	this [+ noun]
その	that [+ noun]
あの	that [+ noun] over there
どの	which [+ noun]?

い -adjectives

あかるい	明るい	bright
くらい	暗い	dark
せまい	狭い	cramped, narrow
はやい	速い	fast, quick
ひろい	広い	spacious, wide

な -adjective

しずか (な)	静か (な)	quiet

Particles

から		from
で		by means of, by, with
まで		until, to

Suffixes

～ぐらい／くらい		about ～ (duration or quantity)
～じかん		～ hours

Expressions

あがってください	上がって下さい	Please come in.
あるいて	歩いて	on foot
いらっしゃい		Welcome! Come in.
おじゃまします	お邪魔します	Thank you. (literally, *I will intrude on you.*) (said before going inside someone's house or apartment)
ごめんください	御免下さい	Excuse me, Anyone home?

Question word

どのぐらい／どのくらい		how long, how much, how many

単語の練習(たんご れんしゅう) Vocabulary Practice

A. キャンパス College campus

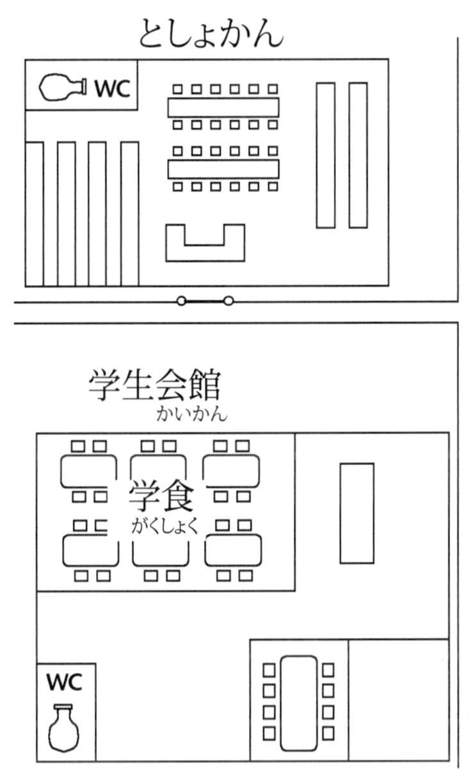

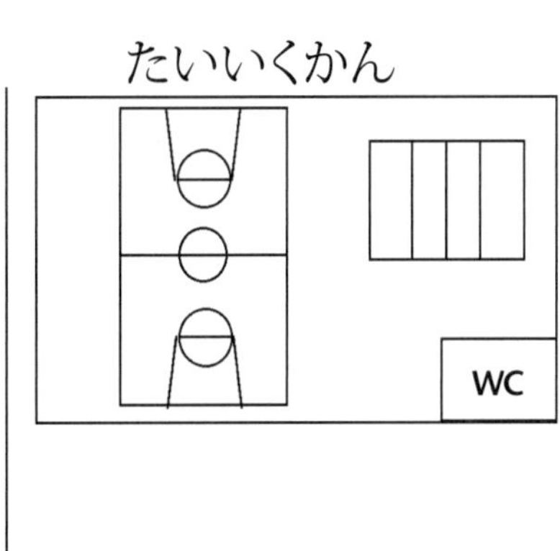

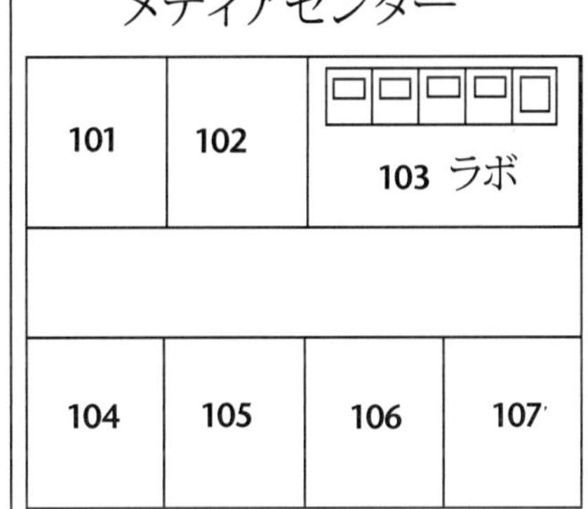

学生会館(かいかん)	student union	たいいくかん	gym
学食(がくしょく)	school cafeteria	ラボ	laboratory
きょうしつ	classroom	トイレ	restroom
メディアセンター	media center		

Activity 1

しつもんに　こたえて下(くだ)さい。 Answer these questions in Japanese.

1. ラボで　なにを　べんきょうしますか。
2. コンピュータのラボは　どこに　ありますか。
3. 学生会館(かいかん)に　どんなものが　ありますか。
4. たいいくかんは　どこに　ありますか。
5. 学生会館(かいかん)に　学食(がくしょく)が　ありますか。
6. よく　学食(がくしょく)で　べんきょうしますか。
7. 学生会館(かいかん)に　きょうしつが　ありますか。
8. トイレは　どこに　ありますか。

B. へやと きょうしつ Rooms and classrooms

ドア	door
まど	window
おしいれ	Japanese-style closet
いぬ	dog
ねこ	cat
つくえ	desk
いす	chair
ソファ	sofa
テーブル	table
本棚（ほんだな）	bookshelf
ふとん	futon
たんす	chest, drawers
ビデオ	video
コンピュータ	computer
でんわ	telephone
とけい	clock, watch
え	picture
しゃしん	photograph
こくばん	chalkboard
ベッド	bed

Activity 2

Look at the pictures on page a-170 and name all the objects you see.

Example: ドアが　あります。

Activity 3

しつもんに　こたえて下(くだ)さい。Answer these questions in Japanese.

1. きょうしつに　どんな　ものが　ありますか。
2. ～さんの　へやに　どんな　ものが　ありますか。
3. としょかんに　どんな　ものが　ありますか。
4. ラボに　どんな　ものが　ありますか。

C. しぜん　Nature

Activity 4

しつもんに　こたえて下(くだ)さい。Answer these questions in Japanese.

1. このへん (*this area*) に　山(やま)が　ありますか。
2. このへん (*this area*) に　川(かわ)が　ありますか。
3. 大学の　キャンパスに　川(かわ)が　ありますか。山(やま)が　ありますか。
4. キャンパスに　大きい　きが　ありますか。どこに　ありますか。

D. のりもの　Transportation

くるま
car

じてんしゃ
bicycle

バス
bus

Activity 5

In small groups, guess who owns a car or a bicycle and write the number in the column, YOUR GUESS. Then ask each person in your group whether he/she has a car or a bicycle, and write the correct total in the ANSWER (こたえ) column.

Example: A: 〜さんは　くるまが　ありますか。
B: ええ、あります。〜さんも　くるまが　ありますか。
or いいえ、ありません。〜さんは　くるまが　ありますか。
A: ええ、あります。
or いいえ、ありません。
B: そうですか。

	YOUR GUESS	ANSWER (こたえ)
くるま		
じてんしゃ		

E. Describing buildings and rooms

あかるい　bright
くらい　dark
しずか　quiet
ひろい　spacious, wide
せまい　cramped, narrow

Activity 6

Work with the entire class. Ask each other what kinds of rooms your classmates have.

Example: A: 〜さんの　アパートは　どんなところですか。
B: あまり　ひろくありません。でも、あかるいです。

ダイアローグ
Dialogue

はじめに　Warm-up

しつもんに　こたえて下(くだ)さい。 Answer these questions in Japanese.

1. 今　どんなところに　すんでいます (*to live*) か。アパートですか。りょうですか。うちですか。（〜にすんでいます = *to reside in* 〜）
2. 〜さんのへやは　どんな　へやですか。
3. 〜さんのへやに　どんな　ものが　ありますか。

リーさんの　アパート　*Mr. Li's apartment*

Ueda pays a visit to Li's apartment.

上田(うえだ)：　ごめん下(くだ)さい。

リー：　あ、上田(うえだ)さん。いらっしゃい。どうぞ　あがって下(くだ)さい。

上田(うえだ)：　おじゃまします。

上田(うえだ)：　わあ、とても　あかるいですね。

リー：　ええ。この　アパートは　たかい　ところに　ありますから。

上田(うえだ)：　あそこに　りっぱな　たてものが　ありますね。あれは大学　ですか。

リー： ええ、あれは　じょうとう大学の　たいいくかんですよ。

上田(うえだ)： え、じゃあ、たいいくかんの　となりの　ちゃいろい　ビルは　なんですか。

リー： あれは　としょかんです。そして、その　まえのが　学生会館(かいかん)です。

上田(うえだ)： そうですか。ここから　大学まで　どのくらい　かかりますか。

リー： バスで　にじゅっぷんぐらい　かかります。
でも、ぼくは　たいてい　じてんしゃで　いきますよ。

上田(うえだ)： そうですか。じてんしゃでは　どのくらい　かかりますか。

リー： じゅうごふんぐらいです。

上田(うえだ)： へえ、はやいですね。

Dialogue Phrase Notes

- ごめん下(くだ)さい means *Is anyone home?* It is used when you have arrived at the entrance of someone's residence and need to get his or her attention.
- いらっしゃい means *welcome.* あがって下(くだ)さい means *please enter.* Both are common expressions to invite someone inside.
- おじゃまします means *thank you* and is used when you enter someone's house or room.
- Sentence + から means *It's because* ～.

  このアパートは　たかいところに　ありますから。
  It's because this apartment is high up (on a hill).
- へえ means, *Is that so?* or *Really?* へえ indicates the speaker's mild surprise about what has just been said. はやい means *fast.* Ueda expresses her surprise about how fast Li can get to school by saying へえ、はやいですね (*Really, that fast?*).

ダイアローグの後(あと)で Comprehension

Answer the following questions in Japanese.

1. リーさんの　アパートは　どんな　ところですか。
2. リーさんの　アパートから　大学まで　じてんしゃで　どのくらい かかりますか。
3. たいいくかんは　どんな　たてものですか。
4. としょかんは　どこに　ありますか。

日本の文化
にほん　ぶんか
Japanese Culture

Japanese houses

A traditional Japanese house is made of wood with heavy ceramic tiles, or かわら. Although it is being replaced with more modern western-style houses or a combination of Japanese and western-style houses, the traditional Japanese house can still be found in many parts of Japan, especially in rural areas.

Some elements of traditional houses have been incorporated into western-styles houses as well.

For example, both traditional and contemporary houses have a mudroom, or げんかん, where you must take off your shoes inside the entrance. Typically, this area is lower than the main portion of the house.

After taking off your shoes, it is polite to put them down facing the door. A host or hostess of the house usually invites people in by saying あがって下(くだ)さい (*please come in*) or its polite form, おあがり下(くだ)さい. These phrases literally mean *please come up*, because the main portion of the house is above the area where the shoes are left.

Many contemporary homes contain one or more traditional Japanese rooms as well. These rooms are divided by a sliding door, ふすま , or by a paper screen, しょうじ . The flooring consists of straw mats called たたみ . The room may have an area (とこのま) where a flower arrangement is placed and a scroll is hung.

Traditional Japanese rooms also contain a large closet, called おしいれ , to store ふとん (Japanese bedding). ふとん are spread on the たたみ mats at bedtime, then folded and put away in the morning, so that the room can be used for multiple purposes. A futon sofa is an American invention.

Most contemporary rooms have wood floors. Carpet is not a popular choice because the high level of humidity in summer poses a potential hazard for bacteria and germs. The door to a room, whether Japanese or Western style, is almost always closed. A closed door doesn't necessarily mean *don't disturb*, so knock to find out if anyone is in the room. Still, don't be surprised if a Japanese person comes into your room without knocking. It happens often among family members.

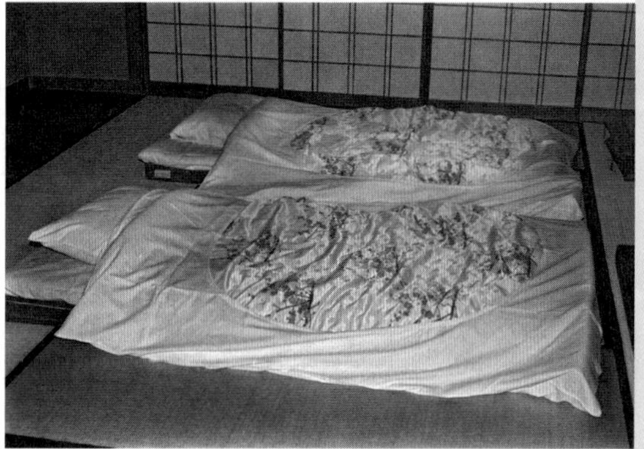

Japanese bathrooms

Most Japanese people prefer to take a bath every night, instead of taking a shower in the morning. The Japanese bathroom, or おふろ, is a room only for bathing. The toilet is in a separate room. The bathroom has a tiled area for washing and rinsing prior to entering the tub. The water is usually very hot (about 110°F/41–42°C). Cold water may be added from the faucet if it is too hot, but overdoing it means that the water won't be warm for the rest of the family, who will use the same hot water. When finished, instead of draining the tub, the cover is replaced to retain the heat. Although Japanese-style toilets are still used in Japan, western-style toilets are now more common in private homes, and often come equipped with a cleansing device called a Washlet® (ウォシュレット). These operate similarly to bidets, but offer a range of high-tech features. Most models have seat-warming controls, and some even have sensors to raise and lower the toilet lid automatically.

A pair of slippers is usually placed inside the restroom. Be careful not to walk out with these slippers on! The door to a restroom, public or private, should be kept closed at all times. Always knock on the door to see if the room is occupied, and do not forget to close the door afterward.

Public restrooms are often marked W.C. (water closet) or with the Japanese term お手(て)洗(あら)い / 御(お)手(て)洗(あら)い (literally, *handwashing*). The sign for the men's room is usually indicated by a male icon or the character for man (男(おとこ)). A female icon or the character for woman (女(おんな)) indicates the women's room. In some women's restrooms, an electronic device called 音姫(おとひめ) ® conveniently provides the white noise of running water or air. While it's sometimes necessary to press a button, most 音姫(おとひめ) ® are sensor-activated.

文法(ぶんぽう)
Grammar

I. Referring to people, places, and things using この, その, あの, どの

The words この, その, あの, どの constitute another series of demonstrative words that indicate the location of an object in relation to the speaker and listener, but they are adjectives that must modify nouns and cannot be used by themselves. In contrast, これ, それ, あれ, どれ and ここ, そこ, あそこ, どこ are nouns that must be used alone.

この + **Noun**	this [Noun] (close to the speaker)
その + **Noun**	that [Noun] (away from the speaker and close to the listener, or somewhat away from both the speaker or the listener.)
あの + **Noun**	that [Noun] over there (far away from both the speaker and the listener.)

	Noun		
この	へや	は	あかるいですね。

This room is bright, isn't it?

	Noun		
その	人(ひと)	は	田中(たなか)さんですか。

Is that person Mr./Ms. Tanaka?

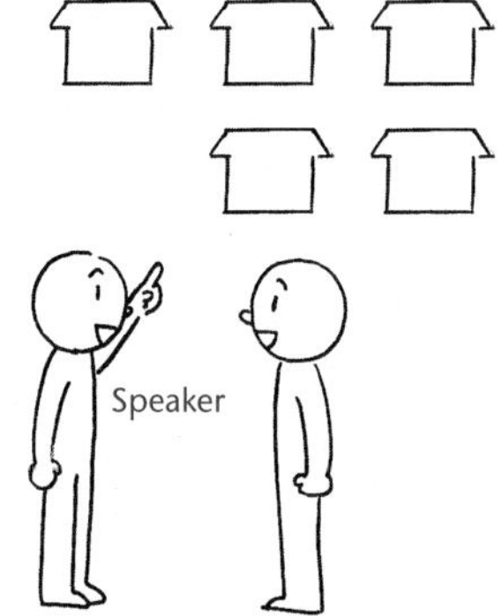

	Adjective	Noun	
すずきさんの　うちは	どの	たてもの	ですか。

Which building is your house, Ms. Suzuki?

	Noun	
あの	うち	です。

It's that house over there.

山中(やまなか)：本田(ほんだ)さんの　うちは　どの　うちですか。
Which house is your house, Mr. Honda?

本田(ほんだ)：それです。
It's that one.

山中(やまなか)：りっぱな　うちですね。
Oh, it's splendid, isn't it!

本田(ほんだ)：いいえ。
Not at all.

Notes

- これ, それ, あれ, どれ are not used to refer to people unless you are discussing people in a photo or drawing, but この, その, あの, どの can be used to refer to people without being impolite, such as この人(ひと), その人(ひと), あの人(ひと), どの人(ひと).
- A more polite way to refer to people is to say このかた, そのかた, あのかた, どのかた instead of この人(ひと), その人(ひと), あの人(ひと), どの人(ひと). Use かた to refer to someone you don't know well, whom you want to treat politely.
- その can be used to refer to something previously mentioned.

  山中(やまなか)：上田(うえだ)さんは　ウエストサイド大学の　学生です。
  Ms. Ueda is a student at Westside University.

  チョイ：<u>その</u>　人(ひと)は　日本人(ひほんじん)ですか。
  Is she (literally, *that person) a Japanese?*

話(はな)してみましょう Conversation Practice

Activity 1

Look at the drawing of the bedroom. 上田(うえだ)さん is standing on the left side of the room (A), and you are at location B. You are making comments about the room to 上田(うえだ)さん. Change the following sentences into your comments addressed to 上田(うえだ)さん, using この, その, あの, どの.

Example: いい ベッドですね → <u>その ベッドは</u> いいですね。

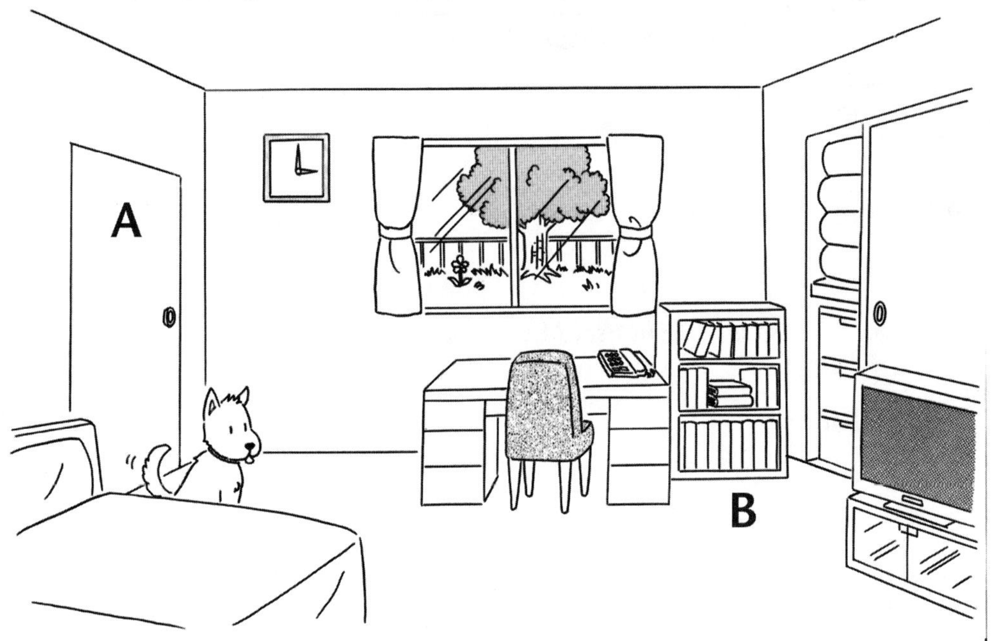

1. あかるい へやですね。
2. 大きい きですね。
3. ひろい つくえですね。
4. りっぱな テレビですね。
5. ふるい とけいですね。
6. 大きい いぬですね。

Activity 2

Work with a partner. Look at the drawing of the living room. You are sitting on the sofa (location A) and your partner is at location B. Your partner will name some items. Create statements about each item using この, その, あの.

Example: Your partner: ソファ

You: <u>この</u> ソファは きれいですね。

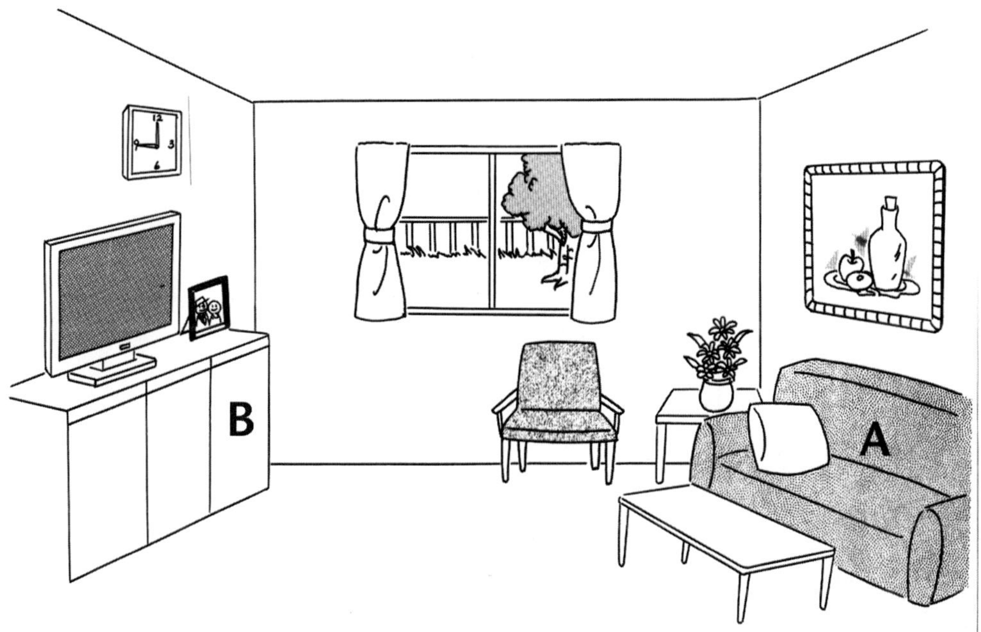

II. Using location nouns: 中(なか), そと, となり, よこ, ちかく, うしろ, まえ, 上(うえ), 下(した), みぎ, ひだり

Location nouns such as まえ (*front*) and うしろ (*back*) are used to describe the location of an object relative to another object, such as *X is in front of Y* and *Z is behind Y.*

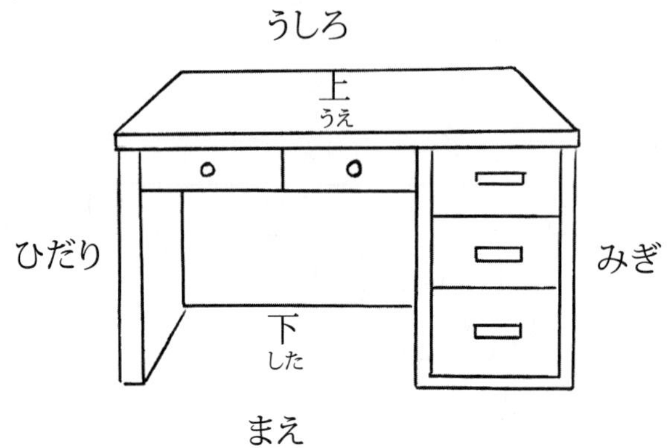

ちかく

つくえの	まえ	in front of	the desk
つくえの	うしろ	behind	the desk
つくえの	上(うえ)	on/above	the desk
つくえの	下(した)	below/under	the desk
つくえの	みぎ	to the right of	the desk
つくえの	ひだり	to the left of	the desk
つくえの	ちかく	close to	the desk

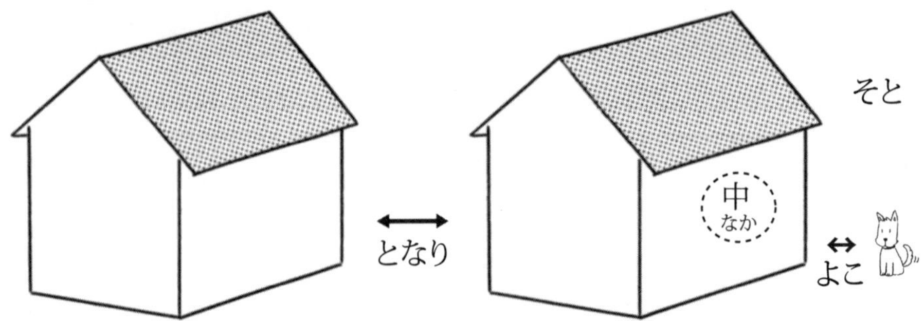

うちの	中(なか)	inside	the house
うちの	そと	outside	the house
うちの	となり	next to	the house
うちの	よこ	next to/adjacent to	the house

Both となり and よこ mean *next to*. Use となり if two things next to each other are of the same type, such as two houses or two desks. Use よこ if two things belong to different categories such as a dog next to a house.

わたしは　こくばんの　まえに／へ　いきました。
I went to the chalkboard. (literally, *I went to the front of the chalkboard*)

ドアの　まえまで　きました。
I came to the door. (literally, *I came to the front of the door*)

チョイ：どこで　ひるごはんを　たべますか。
Where do you eat lunch?

高田(たかだ)：わたしは　よく　その　きの　下(した)で　たべます。
I usually eat it under that tree.

ブラウン：山田(やまだ)さんは　どこですか。
Where is Mr. Yamada?

大川：たいいくかんの　ちかくで　みましたよ。
I saw him near the gym.

中山(なかやま)：そこに　いぬが　いますか。
Is there a dog there?

ジョンソン：ええ、つくえの　下(した)に　いますよ。
Yes, it is under the desk.

アリソン：学食(がくしょく)は　どこですか。
Where is the school cafeteria?

山本(やまもと)：学生会館(かいかん)の　中(なか)です。
It's inside the student union.

NOTES

- Expression with location nouns can be used with any place particles, such as に, へ, で.
- Location nouns can be used with the Noun の Noun construction. For example:

うちの　うしろの　山(やま)	*the mountain behind my house*
うちの　まえの　川(かわ)	*the river in front of my house*
となりの　うち	*the house next door*
となりの　人(ひと)	*a person next to me, my next-door neighbor*
上(うえ)の　アパート	*the apartment above my floor*

話(はな)してみましょう Conversation Practice

Activity 1

Look at the drawing of a classroom. Answer the following questions, using location nouns and ～は ～に　あります／います.

Example: こくばんは　どこに　ありますか。／こくばんは　どこですか。
先生の　うしろに　あります。／先生の　うしろです。

1. コンピュータは　どこに　ありますか。
2. いぬは　どこに　いますか。
3. 先生の　かばんは　どこに　ありますか。
4. ノートは　どこに　ありますか。
5. まどは　どこに　ありますか。
6. テレビは　どこに　ありますか。
7. えんぴつは　どこに　ありますか。
8. けしゴムは　どこに　ありますか。

Activity 2

Look at the drawing of the room. Some objects are missing and their locations are indicated with question marks. Ask your partner what is in each location, then write in the names of the objects in the appropriate locations. Your partner will answer the questions using the drawing on page a-180.

Example: A: つくえの 上(うえ)に なにが ありますか。
B: でんわが あります。

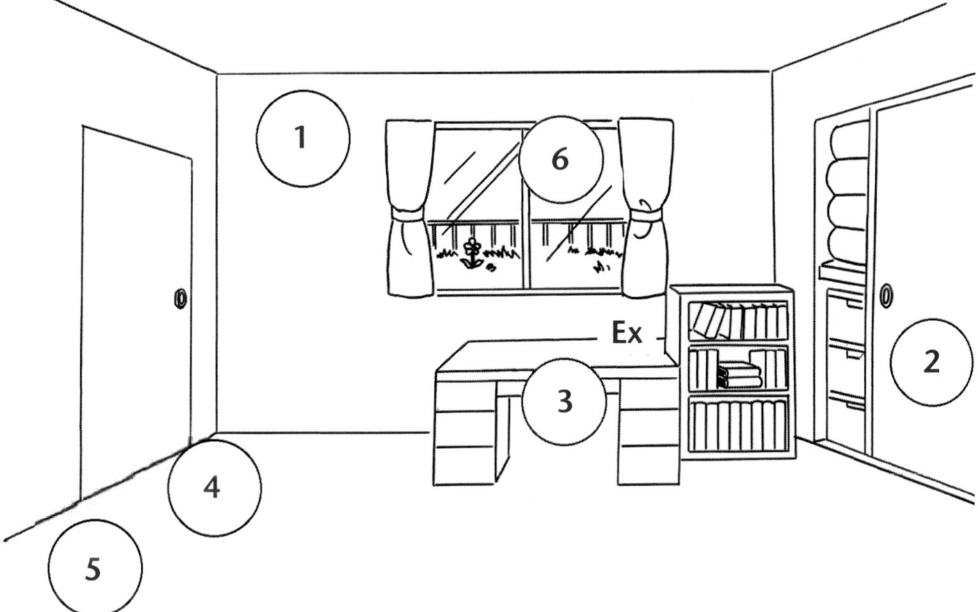

Activity 3

Work with a partner. Have your partner draw the following objects in the picture. As you ask your partner about their locations, write the items in your own copy of the house. When you are done, check your drawing with your partner's.

Example: A: じてんしゃは　どこに　ありますか。／じてんしゃは　どこですか。

B: ドアの　みぎに　あります。

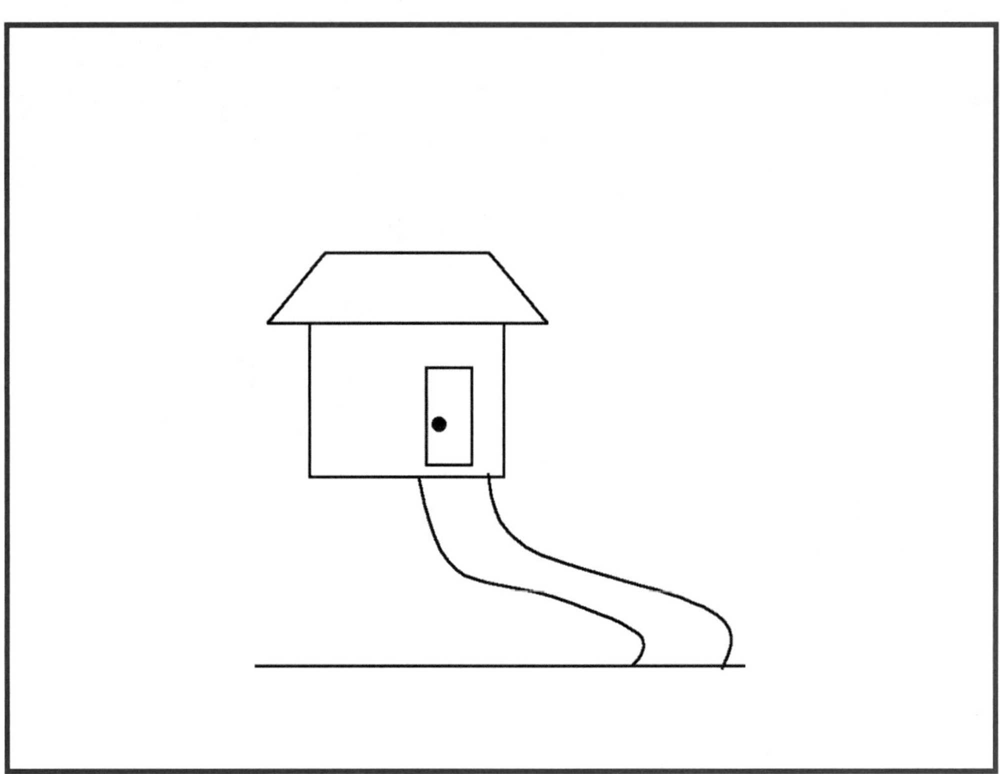

1. まど
2. ドア
3. 山（やま）
4. 川（かわ）
5. き
6. くるま
7. いぬ
8. ねこ
9. じてんしゃ

Activity 4

Look at the drawing of the campus. Your partner will ask you where the following buildings are. Answer his/her questions based on the picture.

Example: A: あのう、すみません。学生会館(かいかん)は　どこですか。

B: その　大きい　きの　うしろに　あります。

A: そうですか。どうも　ありがとう　ございます。

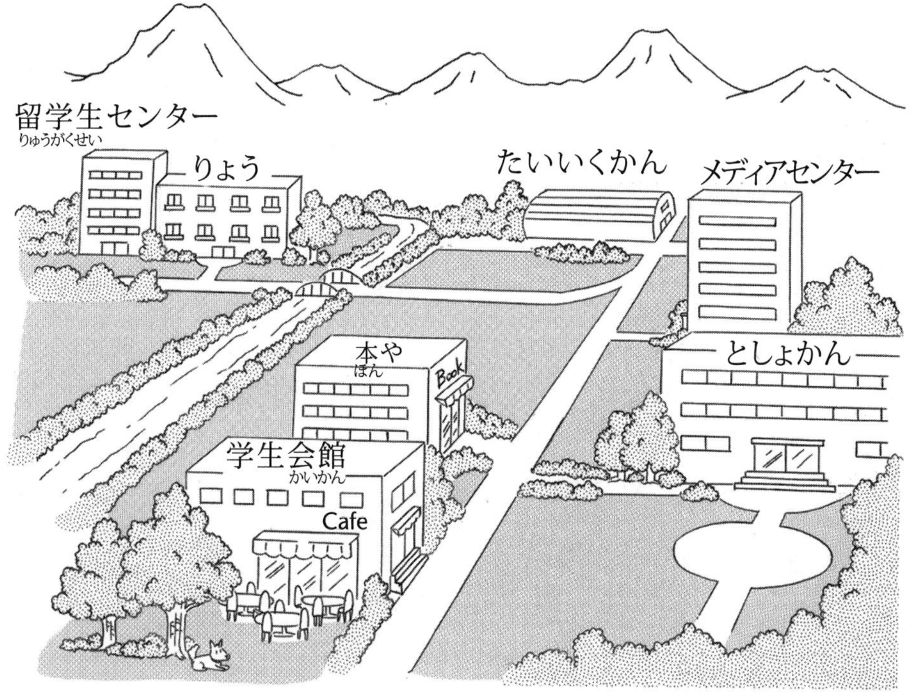

1. 留(りゅう)学生センター
2. たいいくかん
3. コンピュータのラボ
4. 学食(がくしょく)
5. としょかん

Activity 5

Ask a partner about the location of various buildings on your campus. Take notes, then check your partner's answers against a campus map.

Example: A: あのう、すみません。

ラボは　どこに　ありますか。／ラボは　どこですか。

B: この　ビルの　中(なか)に　あります。／この　ビルの　中(なか)です。

A: あ、そうですか。どうも　ありがとう　ございます。

III. Referring to things mentioned immediately before, using noun/adjective + の (pronoun)

The pronoun の means *one* or *ones* in English, as in "red one" and "big one." の usually refers for things and is rarely used for people. It must be directly preceded by an adjective or a noun.

い -adjective +	の	ちゃいろいの	*brown one*
な -adjective +	の	きれいなの	*pretty one*
Noun +	の	スミスさんの	*Mr. Smith's*

イアン：この　りっぱな　かばんは　だれのですか。
Whose is this nice bag?

中本(なかもと)：その　大きいのですか。
That big one?

それは　田中(たなか)さんの　かばんですよ。
It's Mr. Tanaka's.

石川(いしかわ)：この　あかい　ソファは　きれいですね。
This red sofa is pretty.

中田(なかだ)：ええ、でも、あのくろいのも　いいですよ。
Yes, but that black one over there is nice, too.

石川(いしかわ)：あの　大きいのですか。
Do you mean, that big one over there?

中田(なかだ)：ええ。
Yes.

石川(いしかわ)：ああ、あれも　いいですね。
Oh, that one is nice, too.

Note that the pronoun の cannot be used with the particle の or with この, その, あの or どの.

話(はな)してみましょう Conversation Practice

Activity 1

Use の to state what belongs to whom. Follow the model. Start your sentences with この or あの .

Example: スミスさんの りっぱな かばん／わたしの 小(ちい)さい かばん
この りっぱな かばんは スミスさんのです。
あの 小(ちい)さいのは わたしのです。

1. スミスさんの ふるい つくえ ／ 田中(たなか)さんの あたらしい つくえ
2. わたしの あおい ボールペン ／ 先生の あかい ボールペン
3. すずきさんの ひろい へや ／ わたしの せまい へや
4. 上田(うえだ)さんの しろい とけい ／ キムさんの くろい とけい
5. リーさんの あかるい へや／ スミスさんの くらい へや

Activity 2

Work with the class. Look around at various belongings in the classroom. Ask who owns what to complete the chart below.

Example: A: あのう、すみません、この あかい ボールペンは だれのですか。
B: 先生のですよ。
A: あ、そうですか。どうも。

Item	Owner
あかい ボールペン	先生

IV. Expressing distance and duration using the particles から, まで and で and the suffix 〜ぐらい／くらい

The particles から (*from*) and まで (*until, to*) express starting and end points in time and space. The particle で specifies a tool or means such as transportation, craft tools, and kitchen utensils. The suffix ぐらい／くらい (*about, approximately*) indicates approximate distance, duration of time, or amount. These expressions are often used to talk about how long someone does something or how long it takes to get from one place to another. Note that くらい and ぐらい are interchangeable.

A. 〜から (*from*), 〜まで (*to, until*)

アパートから	学生会館(かいかん)まで	いきました。	*I went from the apartment to the student union.*
ここから	あの川(かわ)まで	１０ぷん かかります。	*It will take ten minutes from here to the river.*
月曜日(げつようび)から	金曜日(きんようび)まで	じゅぎょうが あります。	*I have a class from Monday through Friday.*
５じから	６じまで	やすみです。	*I have a break from 5 o'clock to 6 o'clock.*

B. で (*by means of, with, by*)

なんで	きましたか。	*How* (literally, *by what means*) *did you come?*
バスで	かえります。	*I go home by bus.*
テレビで	みました。	*I saw it on TV.*
えんぴつで	かきます。	*I write with a pencil.*

Note that the particle で cannot be used to express on foot. Use あるいて instead.

あるいて	いきます。	*I go on foot. / I walk.*

C. 〜ぐらい (*about, approximately*)

８じかんぐらい／くらい	ねました。	*I slept about eight hours.*
どのぐらい／くらい	かかりますか。	*How long does it take?*
３０ぷんぐらい／くらい	かかります。	*It will take about 30 minutes.*

山本(やまもと)：ここから 小川(おがわ)さんの うちまで どのぐらい かかりますか。
How long does it take from here to your house, Mr. Ogawa?

小川(おがわ)：じてんしゃで ５ふんぐらい かかります。
It's about five minutes by bicycle.

山本(やまもと)：そうですか。はやいですね。
I see. That's fast.

Notes

- 〜じ as in いちじ, にじ means *o'clock*. To indicate duration, use 〜じかん.

  いちじかん (*for one hour*) にじかん (*for two hours*) にじかんはん (*for two and a half hours*)
- 〜ふん can be used to indicate both a specific time as in いちじ じゅっぷん (*1:10*) and duration, as in じゅっぷん (*for ten minutes*).
- Omit ぐらい／くらい if you want to talk about precise duration of time:

  大学から　えきまで　バスで　２３ぷん　かかります。
  It takes 23 minutes by bus from the university to the station.

  たいいくかんまで　あるいて　５ふん　かかります。
  It takes five minutes to get to the gym on foot.

話(はな)してみましょう　Conversation Practice

Activity 1

State how long it takes to get to each destination in the chart below. Follow the model.

Example: うち　学校　じてんしゃ　about 5 minutes
うちから　学校まで　じてんしゃで　ごふんぐらいかかります。

Starting point	Destination	Transportation	Time
うち	学校	じてんしゃ	5 minutes
ここ	としょかん	あるいて	About 10 minutes
としょかん	びょういん	くるま	15 min
ボストン	ニューヨーク	バス	4.5 hours
ボストン	ニューヨーク	くるま	About 4 hours

Activity 2

Working with a partner, ask how long it takes to get from location A to B and fill out the information.

Example: A: うちから　学校まで　あるいて　どのぐらい／くらい かかりますか。

B: 20 ぷんぐらい／くらい　かかります。

A: そうですか。

Location A	Location B	あるいて	じてんしゃ	バス	くるま
うち	学校				
としょかん	たいいくかん				
うち	びょういん				
このまち	となりのまち				

Activity 3

Ask your partner what he/she is planning to do after class today. Use から〜まで〜 as well as the time expressions and daily routine vocabulary that you have learned in earlier chapters.

Example: A: 今日(きょう)は　これから　なにを　しますか。

B: そうですね。3じから　4じまで　じゅぎょうが ありります。そして、5じごろ　かえります。

A: そうですか。

B: 〜さんは？

A: わたしは　うちに　かえります。

そして、ばんごはんまで　べんきょうします。

V. More about the topic marker は and the similarity marker も (double particles and は vs. が)

As explained in the supplementary note in Chapter 2, the particle は specifies the topic. Because it is the part of a sentence about which the speaker wishes to make some statement, it usually appears at the beginning of the sentence. The particle は can be used to mark any type of noun as the topic of a sentence, including the subject or direct object, a location, or a time expression.

This section introduces more uses of は in relation to particles that have some related characteristics, such as the similarity marker も and the subject marker が.

A. Double particles with the topic marker は and the similarity marker も

Both は and も may replace を (direct object) or が (subject) but they must follow after other particles.

Subject	わたしは　学生です。 上田(うえだ)さんも　学生です。	I am a student. Ms. Ueda is a student, too.
Direct Object	コーヒーは　あさ　のみます。 ジュースも　あさ　のみます。	I drink coffee in the morning. I drink juice in the morning, too.
Place of action で	としょかんでは　べんきょうしました。 ラボでも　べんきょうしました。	I studied in the library I studied in the lab, too.
Place of existence に	いすの　下(した)には　ねこが　います。 いすの　上(うえ)にも　います。	There is a cat under the chair. There is one on the chair, too.
Starting point から	先生からは　でんわが　ありました。 ともだちからも　でんわが　ありました。	I got a phone call from the teacher. I got one from my friend, too.

Occasionally, some particles such as に (point in time) and に／へ (goal) may be deleted if they are easily recoverable from the context. For example, the time particle に is often deleted when the noun indicates a day of the week.

Time に	火曜日(かようび)（に）は　クラスが　あります。 木曜日(もくようび)（に）も　あります。	I have a class on Tuesday. I have one on Thursday, too.
Goal に／へ	びょういん（に／へ）は　明日(あした)　いきます。 ぎんこう（に／へ）も　いきます。	I will go to the hospital tomorrow. I will go to the bank, too.

ペギー：しゅうまつは　なにを　しましたか。
What did you do on the weekend?

下田（しもだ）：山（やま）に／へ　いきました。
I went to the mountains.

ペギー：いいですね。山（やま）（に／へ）は　よく　いきますか。
That's nice. Do you go to the mountains often?

下田（しもだ）：ええ、らいしゅうの　土曜日（どようび）（に）も　いきます。
Yes, I am going there next Saturday, too.

アリソン：大学までは　あるいて　どのぐらい　かかりますか。
How long does it take to get to school on foot?

川中（かわなか）：１じかんぐらい　かかります。
It takes about an hour.

アリソン：え、そうなんですか。毎日（まいにち）　あるいて　きますか。
Is that so? Do you walk to school every day?

川中（かわなか）：いいえ、バスで　きます。
No, I come to school by bus.

Note: Relative time expressions such as 今日（きょう） and 明日（あした） do not take a particle. は and も follow the noun directly.

今日（きょう）は　びょういんに　いきます。　明日（あした）も　いきます。
I will go to the hospital today. I will go tomorrow as well.

B. は vs. が

The particle は cannot be used with a question word, because は specifies the topic of a sentence, which is information already known to the speaker. Use は when there is a question word in the comment (the part of the sentence that follows the topic).

学生会館（かいかん）は	どこですか	*Where is the student union?*
山田（やまだ）さんは	どの人（ひと）ですか。	*Which person is Mr. Yamada?*
たいいくかんは	どこに　ありますか。	*Where is the gym?*
チョイさんは	どこへ　いきましたか。	*Where did Ms. Choi go?*

The particle が marks the grammatical subject of a sentence. Always use が when the subject is, or contains, a question word.

どの人(ひと)が　先生ですか。　*Which person is the teacher?*

そこに　なにが　ありますか。　*What is there?*

だれが　いきますか。　*Who will go?*

Also use が when information about a subject is important or situationally new to the listener and/or the speaker. This use of が generally occurs when the speaker introduces a situation or scene he/she has just noticed.

あ、あそこに　ねこが　いますよ。　*Look, there is a cat over there!*

あ、中本(なかもと)さんが　きました。　*Ah, Ms. Nakamoto has just arrived.*

Once a subject noun has been mentioned, は is often used when referring to the same subject in subsequent sentences. For example:

本田(ほんだ)：　あそこに　いぬが　いますね。
There is a dog over there.

小川(おがわ)：　ええ、あれは　わたしの　いぬです。
Yes, that's my dog.

Note: それ can also be used to refer to something mentioned previously. In this usage, それ means *it* in English. Likewise, その～ and そこ can be used in the same way.

あそこに　かばんが　あります。
There is a bag over there.

それ／そのかばんは　田中(たなか)さんのです。
It is Mr./Ms. Tanaka's.

学生会館(かいかん)に　学食(がくしょく)が　あります。
There is a cafeteria in the student union.

そこは　とても　きれいです。
It (that place) is very clean/nice.

話(はな)してみましょう Conversation Practice

Activity 1

First circle the question words, then complete the following sentences with が or は .

Example: (だれ) が 学生ですか。

1. リーさん________どの　人(ひと)ですか。
2. どれ________びょういんですか。
3. どの　コンピュータ________あたらしいですか。
4. 学食(がくしょく)________どこですか。
5. アリスさん________どんな　人(ひと)ですか。
6. だれ________いますか。
7. デパート________どこに　ありますか。
8. すずきさん________どちらから　きましたか。
9. あの　きれいな　たてもの________なんですか。

Activity 2

Create two sentences based on each sentence below. One should express a similarity with the first sentence; the other should contrast with the first sentence.

Example: あさごはんを　たべます。
ばんごはんも　たべます。でも、ひるごはんは　たべません。

1. バスは　じゅうじに　きました。
2. 山田(やまだ)さんと　いきます。
3. バスで　大学に　いきます。
4. 昨日(きのう)　おふろに　はいりました。
5. 昨日(きのう)の　ばん　シャワーを　あびました。

Activity 3

Work with a partner. Ask your partner a question using the words supplied in column A. Your partner will answer the question using the words in column B to create a topic from the subject of the question (underlined in the example).

Example: **A** **B**

いつ／コーヒーを　のみます。　あさ

A: いつ　コーヒーを　のみますか。

B: コーヒーですか。コーヒーは　あさ　のみますね。

	A	B
1.	どこ／その　本(ほん)を　みました。	大学の　本(ほん)や
2.	なに／びょういんに　いきました。	くるま
3.	いつ／その　えいがを　みました。	昨日(きのう)
4.	どこ／ジョンソンさんと　いきました。	きっさてん
5.	なに／えきから　いきました。	バス
6.	だれ／いました。	先生
7.	いつ／しゅくだいを　します。	しゅうまつ
8.	どんな　くるま／きました。	トヨタ

Activity 4

Work with a partner. Choose two cities with which you're both familiar and write their names in the following chart. First discuss, then list, the aspects they share in common. Think of as many things as you can.

Example: とうきょう, シカゴ

A: とうきょうには　いい　レストランが　ありますよ。

B: そうですか。シカゴにも　たくさん　ありますよ。

A: そうですか。日本(にほん)の　レストランも　ありますか。

B: ええ、たくさん　ありますよ。

Similarity	City 1:__________	City 2:__________

Interrogative Expressions

You have learned a lot of question words. Here is a summary of Japanese interrogative expressions.

だれ	who	だれの へやですか。 *Whose room is it?*
なに／なん	what	おなまえは なんですか。 *What is your name?* なんねんせいですか。 *What year are you in school?* いま なんじですか。 *What time is it now?*
いつ	when	山田(やまだ)さんは いつ きますか。 *When will Mr. Yamada come?*
どこ	where	山田(やまだ)さんは どこに いますか。 *Where is Mr. Yamada?*
どの + noun	which	山田(やまだ)さんは どの 人(ひと)ですか。 *Which person is Mr. Yamada?* 山田(やまだ)さんの りょうは どの たてもの ですか。 *Which building is Mr. Yamada's dormitory?*
どれ	which one	山田(やまだ)さんのりょうは どれですか。 *Which one is Mr. Yamada's dormitory?*
どんな + noun	what kind of	山田(やまだ)さんの へやは どんな ところ ですか。 *What kind of place is your room, Mr. Yamada?*

聞く 練習
きれんしゅう
Listening

上手な聞き方 Listening Strategy
じょうずきかた

Distinguishing sounds in words and phrases

Listening to conversations in Japanese can seem like reading long sentences without **kanji** or other clues to distinguish word boundaries. It takes practice to be able to distinguish words and phrases from a succession of sounds. Listening for repeated words, familiar words, intonation, and pauses can help you to identify word boundaries. If you are listening to an announcement, anticipate what to expect and try to listen for important information.

ひっこしを　てつだう **(Helping a friend move into a new apartment)**

Useful Expressions

おきます　　to place
おいて下さい（くだ）　　please place/put

聞く 前に Warm-up
きまえ

When you're moving into a new place, what kinds of words do you expect to use? Circle the terms you are most likely to use.

き　　まえ　　ベッド　　山（やま）　　バス　　よこ　　テレビ

たいいくかん　　ぎんこう　　いす　　みぎ　　ひだり　　ちかく

Now listen to the conversation and write down words you hear repeatedly.

1. ______________________
2. ______________________
3. ______________________
4. ______________________
5. ______________________
6. ______________________

聞(き)いた後(あと)で Comprehension

Listen to the conversation again. Then verify the layout of the apartment. Are all the objects in the room properly described?

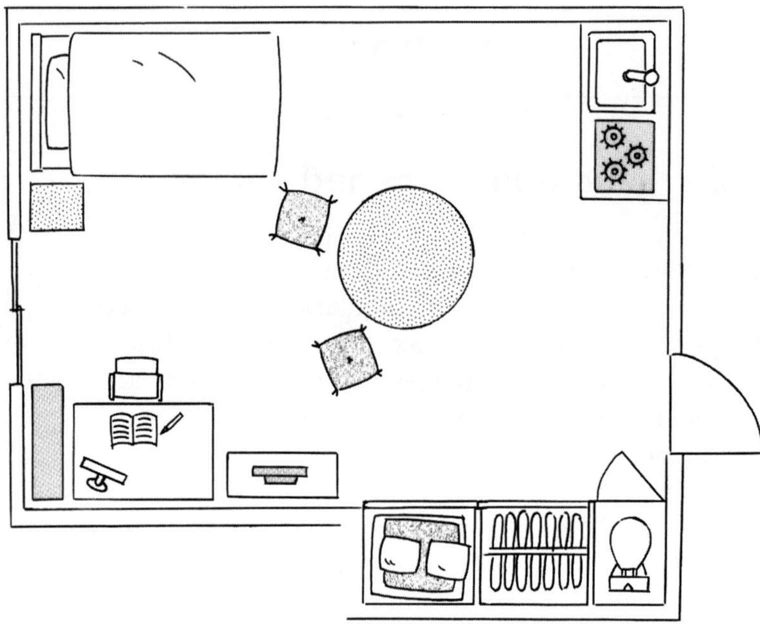

Describe each object in the room as thoroughly as you can, using different location nouns.

Now describe the place where you live in a few sentences.

聞き上手　話し上手
きじょうず　はなじょうず
Communication

Communication Strategy

Getting someone's attention (2)

Talking to someone in your non-native language can be a strain, especially if the person is a stranger. This is certainly true in Japan as well, where people tend to be less open with strangers. One explanation for this is that Japan was isolated from the Western world for over 250 years under the government's seclusion policy, from the seventeenth to the mid-nineteenth century. During that period Japan virtually remained a relatively homogeneous nation. Moreover, under the feudal order, a strong sense of hierarchy was developed. The sense of hierarchy and distinction between in-group and out-group remains strong in modern Japan. In-group refers to one's family, people at one's place of work, classmates, etc. The Japanese are very aware of the difference in intimacy that should be maintained between those in the in-group and out-group, and act accordingly. Any non-Japanese by definition belongs to the out-group, and thus, along with the fear of not being able to communicate, a Japanese person might deliberately avoid contact with a non-Japanese, even at the risk of appearing indifferent. This of course is a generalization, and there is a great deal of variation in individual behavior. It is important, however, to understand this background, and to use the appropriate phrases in approaching a stranger or someone you don't know well. The following is a summary of some useful expressions and other strategies you can employ.

Approaching people:

あのう（ちょっと）
すみませんが／しつれいですが。
あのう　すみませんが／しつれいですが。
ちょっと　すみませんが／しつれいですが。
あのう　ちょっと　すみませんが／しつれいですが。
おねがいします。　(used to get the attention of someone who provides services, such as a store clerk)

Thanking someone:

すみません。
ありがとう　ございます。

Giving feedback as a listener:

Nodding
Avoiding prolonged eye contact
ええ／いいえ

練習 Practice
れんしゅう

A. Imagine that you are in Japan and want to ask someone the time. Approach the person to get attention. Ask the time. Thank him/her. Try to act out the scene with a partner.

B. Imagine that you are at a party on a college campus and want to meet someone from Japan. There are many Asian students at the party, but you are not sure if they are Japanese. Approach someone and find out if he/she is Japanese. If the person is from Japan, introduce yourself.

漢字
かんじ
Kanji

Kanji derived from pictures and symbols (1)

Kanji derived from pictures

The number of **kanji** derived from pictures and symbols totals to only about 200, but these characters tend to represent basic or core meanings. Many of them also appear in more complex characters. Therefore, it is important to become familiar with their shapes and meaning.

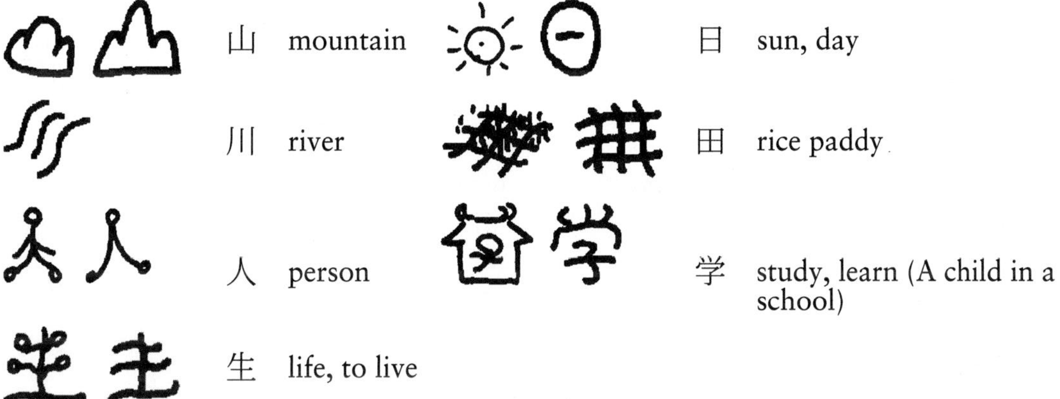

Some **kanji** that represent abstract ideas have been created from symbols.

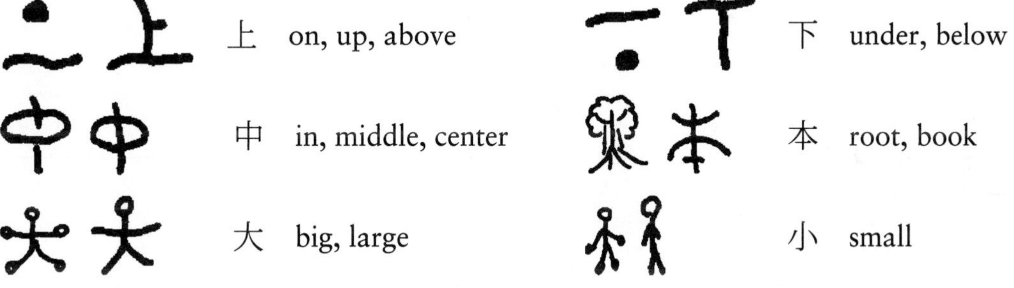

山	山	mountain	やま　サン・ザン	山川(やまかわ)さん　富士山(ふじさん)　山(やま)の上(うえ)
川	川	river	かわ・がわ　セン	小川(おがわ)さん　川中(かわなか)さん　ミシシッピー川(がわ)
田	田	rice paddy	た　デン	上田(うえだ)さん　田中(たなか)さん
人	人	person	ひと　ジン・ニン	日本人(にほんじん)
上	上	on, up, above	うえ　ジョウ・カミ	テーブルの上(うえ)
中	中	in, middle, center	なか　チュウ	へやの中(なか)　中国(ちゅうごく)
下	下	under, below	した　くだ(さい)　カ・ゲ	まどの下(した)　いって下(くだ)さい
小	小	small	ちい(さい)　ショウ	小(ちい)さいへや
日	日	sun, day	ひ・び　ニチ・ニ・ジツ・カ	日本(にほん)　昨日(きのう)*　今日(きょう)*　明日(あした)*
本	本	root, book	もと　ホン・ボン・ポン	山田(やまだ)さんの本(ほん)　日本(にほん)

An asterisk (*) indicates an irregular reading.

よめるようになったかんじ (**kanji** and compounds you can now read)

山　川　田中　日本人　上　下　中　小さい　日本　本　本棚(だな)　本屋(や)
毎(まい)日　中国(ごく)　今日(きょう)　明日(あした)　明後日(あさって)　昨日(きのう)　一昨日(おととい)　日曜(よう)日　上(あ)がって下(くだ)さい

日本人のなまえ (Japanese family names): 山川(やまかわ)　田中(たなか)　中田(なかだ)　川中(かわなか)　山中(やまなか)
上田(うえだ)　本田(ほんだ)　小川(おがわ)　大川(おおかわ)　中川(なかがわ)　小田(おだ)　下田(しもだ)　中本(なかもと)　山本(やまもと)

練習(れんしゅう) Practice

Read the following sentences.

1. 山田先生は日本大学の先生です。
2. 「上田」は日本語(ご)のなまえですが、上田さんはアメリカ人です。
3. きょうしつの中に小さいとけいがあります。
4. ふとんの下にねこがいます。
5. 日本にはきれいな山と川がたくさんあります。
6. なまえをかいて下さい。

読む 練習 (よ れんしゅう)
Reading

上手な読み方 (じょうず よ かた) Reading Strategy

Using visual clues

Photos, illustrations, and graphs can often help you understand what you read. For example, it's much easier to understand a description of a room or a house while looking at a floor plan. Such visuals not only help create context for a text, but they may also provide additional information not included in the text.

読む 前に (よ まえ) Pre-reading

Look at the picture of an office, and determine what kinds of information it conveys.

田中先生の研究室(けんきゅうしつ) Professor Tanaka's Office

Vocabulary

奥(おく)	the inner part of a building, room, etc.
手前(てまえ)	this side (side closer to the speaker)
鉢植(はちうえ)	potted plant
たくさん	many, a lot

田中先生の研究室(けんきゅうしつ)はとても広(ひろ)いです。部屋(へや)の右(みぎ)には大きい本棚(ほんだな)があります。本棚(ほんだな)には本(ほん)がたくさんあります。本棚(ほんだな)の横(よこ)には窓(まど)があります。窓(まど)は部屋(へや)の右(みぎ)にあります。窓(まど)の外(そと)には小さい鉢植(はちうえ)があります。そして、窓(まど)の近(ちか)くには先生の机(つくえ)があります。机(つくえ)の上には本がたくさんあります。机(つくえ)は部屋(へや)の左側(ひだりがわ)にあります。机(つくえ)の上にはコンピュータと電話(でんわ)があります。部屋(へや)の手前(てまえ)には小さいソファがあります。ソファの上にも本がたくさんあります。ソファの横(よこ)に小さい椅子(いす)があります。ソファの下にねこがいます。

読(よ)んだ後(あと)で Comprehension

Identify four discrepancies between the text and the drawing, and write them on the lines below.

1. ____________________
2. ____________________
3. ____________________
4. ____________________

総合練習
そうごうれんしゅう
Integration

アパートさがし Looking for an apartment

1. You are a Tokyo real estate agent. Bring to class or draw a floor plan of an apartment indicating the location of the door, windows, bedrooms, kitchen (キッチン), bathroom, and any other rooms. Then complete the information below.

Number of bedrooms__________________________________

Apartment location __________________________________

Distance from campus__________________________________

Facilities near the apartment ____________________________

2. Your instructor will divide the class into two groups. Half of the class will act as real estate agents, and the other half will try to rent an apartment. Prospective tenants should talk to as many agents as possible, take notes on each rental property, and decide which apartment to rent.

ロールプレイ Role Play

1. You are showing around a visitor from Japan who doesn't speak English. Tell the visitor about your campus as he/she asks you questions.

2. Your host family asks you what kind of place you live in. Describe your dorm or apartment.

Chapter 6

第六課（だいろっか）

休（やす）みの 日

Leisure Time

Objectives Describing routine and leisure activities

Vocabulary Routine activities (2), leisure activities, adjectives of emotion and condition

Dialogue 週末（しゅうまつ）は どうでしたか。*What did you do over the weekend?*

Japanese Culture Japanese colleges and college life

Grammar

I. Using the particles と and に

II. Commenting about the past, using polite past adjectives and the copula verb です

III. Connecting verb and adjective phrases and sentences using the て-form of verbs; making requests using the て-form

IV. Connecting phrases, using the て-forms of verbs and adjectives

V. Extending an invitation using ませんか

Listening Making sense of missing pronouns

Communication Using そうですか and そうですね

Kanji **Kanji** derived from pictures and symbols (2)
今 私 月 火 水 木 金 土 曜 何 週 末 休

Reading Identifying missing nouns

単語
たんご
Vocabulary

Nouns

アルバイト		part-time job
うんどう	運動	exercises うんどう （を） します to exercise (を is commonly deleted)
おんがく	音楽	music
かいもの	買い物	shopping
ゲーム		game
コンサート		concert
こんど	今度	next time
ざっし	雑誌	magazine
さんぽ	散歩	walk, stroll さんぽ （を） します to take a walk
しごと	仕事	job
しつもん	質問	question しつもん （を） します (to) ask a question
ジョギング		jogging
しんぶん	新聞	newspaper
せんたく	洗濯	laundry
そうじ	掃除	cleaning
てがみ	手紙	letter
テニス		tennis テニスを します to play tennis
ともだち	友達	friend
パーティ		party
ピクニック		picnic

プール		pool
メール		e-mail
やすみ	休み	rest, absence, a day off
やすみのひ	休みの日	a day off, holiday
りょうしん	両親	parents
りょうり	料理	cooking, cuisine りょうり （を） します to fix a meal

う -verbs

あいます	会います	(to) meet; the dictionary form is あう .
あそびます	遊びます	(to) play; the dictionary form is あそぶ .
あるきます	歩きます	(to) walk, ～まで あるきます (to) walk (up) towards; the dictionary form is あるく .
いいます	言います	(to) say; the dictionary form is いう .
およぎます	泳ぎます	(to) swim; the dictionary form is およぐ .
かきます	書きます	(to) write; the dictionary form is かく .
ききます	聞きます / 聴きます	(to) ask (聞きます, (to) listen to(聴きます); the dictionary form is きく .
はなします	話します	(to) talk; the dictionary form is はなす.
まちます	待ちます	(to) wait; the dictionary form is まつ .
よびます	呼びます	(to) call (someone), (to) invite; the dictionary form is よぶ .

る -verbs

かけます		(to) make (a phone call); the dictionary for is かける . でんわを かけます
でかけます	出かけます	(to) go out; the dictionary form is でかける .

い -adjectives

いそがしい	忙しい	busy
うれしい	嬉しい	happy
おもしろい	面白い	interesting

かなしい	悲しい	sad
さびしい	寂しい	lonely
たのしい	楽しい	fun
つまらない		boring
むずかしい	難しい	difficult
やさしい	易しい、優しい	easy (易しい), kind (優しい)

な-adjectives

げんき (な)	元気 (な)	healthy, cheerful, lively (person)
ざんねん (な)	残念 (な)	sorry, regrettable
だいじょうぶ (な)	大丈夫 (な)	all right, no problem
たいへん (な)	大変 (な)	tough
にぎやか (な)	賑やか (な)	lively (place or event)
ひま (な)	暇 (な)	free, idle, unscheduled

Adverbs

いっしょに	一緒に	together
ぜひ	是非	By all means. / I'd love to.
ゆっくり		slowly, ゆっくりします, to relax, to take it easy

Particles

と		with, together with (association)
と		and (exhaustive listing)
に		in order to, for (purpose)
に		to (goal, receiver)

Expressions

ちょっと つごうが わるくて	ちょっと都合が悪くて	I'm a little busy. (*literally,* Sorry, it's a little inconvenient.)
ちょっと ようじが あって	ちょっと用事があって	Sorry, I have some errands/business to attend to.

単語(たんご)の練習(れんしゅう) Vocabulary Practice

A. 毎週(まいしゅう)すること Household chores and other activities

りょうりを します
(to) fix a meal

せんたくを します
(to) do laundry

そうじを します
(to) clean /dust a room

アルバイトを します
(to) have a part-time job

しごとを します
(to) work

しんぶんを よみます
(to) read a newspaper

かいものに いきます
(to) go shopping

メールを かきます
(to) write e-mail

先生に ききます
to ask the teacher

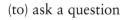

しつもんします

(to) ask a question

日本語(ご)で はなします

(to) talk in Japanese

でんわを
します／かけます
(to) make a phone call

Activity 1

Charades. Work in groups of three or four. Take turns performing an action from the list below while the rest of the group try to guess the expression.

ごはんを　たべます
りょうりを　します
せんたくを　します
そうじを　します
シャワーを　あびます
おふろに　はいります
しゅくだいを　します
コーヒーを のみます

アルバイトを　します
しんぶんを　よみます
かいものに　いきます
メールを　かきます
日本語(ご)で　はなします
テレビを　みます
ともだちに でんわを かけます
先生に しつもん します

Activity 2

Work in pairs. Ask each other what things you do every day, sometimes, not very often, and never. List each of your partner's activities in the appropriate box.

Example: A: ～さんは 毎日(まいにち) あさごはんを たべますか。
B: いいえ、たべません。
A: そうですか。じゃあ、ひるごはんは たべますか。

	パートナーの こたえ
毎日(まいにち) します。	
ときどきします。	
あまりしません。	
ぜんぜんしません。	

B. 休(やす)みの日に すること Things to do on a day off

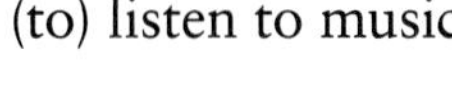

おんがくを ききます
(to) listen to music

コンサートに いきます
(to) go to a concert

ピクニックに いきます
(to) go on a picnic

うんどうします
(to) exercise

テニスを します
(to) play tennis

ジョギングを します
(to) go jogging

プールで およぎます
(to) swim in the pool

でかけます
(to) go out

ともだちに／と あいます
(to) meet a friend

ともだちを まちます
(to) wait for a friend

さんぽを します
(to) take a walk

あそびます
(to) play, (to) have fun

ゲームを します
(to) play a game

うちで ゆっくりします
(to) relax at home

てがみを かきます
(to) write a letter

ざっしを よみます

(to) read a magazine

パーティを します

(to) have a party

ともだちを
うちに よびます

(to) invite / call a friend over

C. きもちや ようすを あらわす ことば　Adjectives of emotion and condition

いそがしい	busy	つまらない	boring
うれしい	happy	やさしい	easy, kind
おもしろい	interesting	むずかしい	difficult
かなしい	sad	たのしい	fun
ざんねん（な）	sorry, regrettable	大変（たいへん）（な）	tough
ひま（な）	free, idle, with nothing to do		
だいじょうぶ(な)	all right, no problem		

Vocabulary Notes

- (お) げんきですか
げんきですか and its polite version おげんきですか can be translated as *How are you?*, but this expression is not used in the same way as in English. げんきですか／おげんきですか is used when you have not seen someone you know for an extended period of time. In function, its sense is closer to *How have you been?* For daily greetings, use おはよう（ございます), こんにちは, こんばんは.
- ざんねん vs. すみません
Both ざんねん and すみません may be translated as *sorry*, but their usage is very different. すみません is used for apologizing, but ざんねん merely expresses regret, disappointment, or sympathy (and may also function as an adjective). For example, if you are not able to finish your homework by the due date, you might say すみません to your teacher. The teacher might then reply ざんねんですね, to express his/her disappointment. すみません can also be used to approach someone (meaning *Excuse me. / Pardon me.*), or to express thanks. ざんねん cannot be substituted in these instances.

ダイアローグ
Dialogue

はじめに　Warm-up

しつもんに　こたえて下さい。Answer these questions in Japanese.

1. 週末(しゅうまつ)は　うちで　よく　何(なに)を　しますか。
2. 週末(しゅうまつ)は　よく　どこに　あそびに　いきますか。
3. 休(やす)みの日に　よく　でかけますか。どこへ　いきますか。
4. 休(やす)みの日に　よく　何(なに)を　しますか。

週末(しゅうまつ)は　どうでしたか。　*What did you do over the weekend?*

Ueda and Li meet in class on Monday.

上田：　リーさん、おはようございます。

リー：　あ、上田さん、おはようございます。週末(しゅうまつ)は
　　　　どうでしたか。

上田：　とても　たのしかったです。

リー：　それは　よかったですね。

上田：　ええ、みちこさんと　しぶやに　かいものに　いって、

リー：　ええ、

上田：　コンサートへ　いきました。

リー： そうですか。

上田： リーさんの 週末(しゅうまつ)は どうでしたか。

リー： いそがしくて あまり おもしろくなかったです。

先週(せんしゅう)は しゅくだいが たくさんあって、大変(たいへん)でした。

上田： そうですか。じゃあ、週末(しゅうまつ)は うちに いましたか。

リー： ええ、うちで ずっと べんきょうしました。

上田： それは 大変(たいへん)でしたね。

リー： ええ。

上田： じゃあ、来週(らいしゅう)の 週末(しゅうまつ)も いそがしいですか。

リー： いいえ、来週(らいしゅう)は あまり いそがしくありません。

上田： じゃあ、うちに あそびに きませんか。

リー： ありがとう。ほんとうに いいんですか。

上田： ええ。土曜日(どようび)は どうですか。

リー： ええ、土曜日(どようび)は 大丈夫(だいじょうぶ)です。

上田； じゃあ、土曜日(どようび)の あさ、でんわしてくれませんか。

リー： わかりました。じゃあ、でんわします。

Dialogue Phrase Notes

- The それ in それは よかったですね in line 5 refers to Ueda's statement that she had fun. It does not refer to any physical object in the scene. Similarly, the それ in それは 大変(たいへん)でしたね in line 15 refers to Ueda's having gone to a concert.
- Li interjects ええ while Ueda is talking in line 7. This ええ is the あいづち you learned about in Chapters 2 and 3. In this case, he is signaling to Ueda that he is following her story and wants her to continue. Similarly, Ueda says ええ in line 21 after Li's utterance. あいづち are generally used at phrase boundaries, for example, immediately after the て-form of verbs as shown in this dialogue, or after the conjunction が.
- ずっと means *for a long time*. In this context, it suggests *all day long*.
- ほんとうに いいんですか means *Are you sure?*
- あとで means *later*.
- In Japanese, あそびに きませんか is often used to invite a friend to get together or hang out, as in Ueda's invitation in line 23.

ダイアローグの後(あと)で Comprehension

A. Read each statement and circle はい if the statement is true or いいえ if it is false.

1. はい いいえ リーさんは 日曜日(にちようび)に べんきょうしました。
2. はい いいえ リーさんは 土曜日(どようび)に でかけました。
3. はい いいえ リーさんは おもしろい えいがを みました。
4. はい いいえ 上田さんは キムさんと コンサートに いきました。
5. はい いいえ 上田さんは 先週(せんしゅう)の 週末(しゅうまつ)に かいものを しました。

B. しつもんに こたえて下さい。 Answer these questions.

1. 上田さんは 先週(せんしゅう) 何(なに)を しましたか。
2. リーさんは 何(なに)を しましたか。
3. リーさんは 来週(らいしゅう)の 週末(しゅうまつ) いそがしいですか。
4. リーさんは 来週(らいしゅう) 何(なに)を しますか。

日本の文化(ぶんか)
Japanese Culture

Japanese Colleges and College Life

According to a 2005 government survey, nearly all Japanese students (97.6%) attend high school after completing junior high, and about a half of them (51.5%) will continue on to college or junior college. Most of those who do enroll in college attend school full-time, spending four to five days a week in class, and depend financially on their parents.

Japanese college class sizes tend to be large. As there are few graduate teaching assistants, professors themselves do most of the teaching. Undergraduates usually spend four years at college. Though most liberal arts students earn the necessary credit hours to graduate by the end of their junior year, they usually continue their course work through senior year. Job hunting starts junior year, and most students enter the workforce immediately upon graduation.

Traditionally, graduate schools in Japan have been regarded as institutions dedicated to producing academicians and researchers. Since Japanese law and medical schools accept students directly from high schools, in contrast with the

U.S. system, these are not considered graduate programs. Professional degrees were not available in Japan before 2002. Due to a series of educational reforms, however, over 120 institutions now offer MBAs as well as master's degrees and PhDs in a range of other fields. As a result, the number of graduate students in Japan is on the rise—currently, about 15% of college graduates. Over 80% of graduate students do not take a break from their studies after earning an undergraduate degree.

Another factor that has shaped college life in Japan today is the economic depression that began in the early 1990s and lasted through 2005. A decade-long job shortage caused many students to prioritize their studies much higher than their social lives at school. (**Zenkoku Daigaku Seikatsu Kyoodoo Kumiai** 2005). Still, most Japanese college students engage in a variety of extra-curricular activities, such as participating in college clubs, doing volunteer work, hanging out with friends, and traveling domestically and internationally. Over three-quarters of students work part-time during the school year as well as on spring break and summer vacation. The average student has a weekly budget of approximately 37,000 yen (about US$320 in 2006) that is put toward dining out, clothing purchases, online communications, and savings. (**Tokyo FM**, 2005).

文法（ぶんぽう）
Grammar

I. Using the particles と and に

A. Particle と

The particle と has two separate usages that are conceptually related.

1. と , *together with, with*

The first usage indicates association between two items and is translated as *with* or *together with*. For example:

私（わたし）は	チョイさんと	べんきょうしました。	*I studied with Ms. Choi.*
リーさんは	田中さんと	えいがを　みました。	*Mr. Li watched a movie with Mr. Tanaka.*
私（わたし）は	ペギーさんと	でんわで　はなします。	*I talk with Peggy on the phone.*
中山さんは	ともだちと	かいものに　いきます。	*Mr. Nakayama goes shopping with a friend.*

2. と , *and*

The second usage is to connect two or more nouns.

スミスさんと	私（わたし）は	学生です。	*Mr. Smith and I are students.*
そうじと	せんたくを	しました。	*I did cleaning and laundry.*
しんぶんと	ざっしを	よみました。	*I read a newspaper and a magazine.*
金曜日（きんようび）と	土曜日（どようび）に	ここへ　きます。	*I will come here on Friday and Saturday.*
ナイフと	フォークで	たべます。	*(I) eat with a knife and a fork.*

All of the above examples show that the particle と connects nouns only. It cannot be used to connect two or more sentences, or verb or adjective phrases.

Use the て-form of verbs (see p. a-230, Grammar III) or the conjunction そして to connect sentences and verb phrases.

そうじを　して、　せんたくも　しました。
I did the cleaning and the laundry.

そうじをしました。 そして、せんたくも　しました。
I cleaned the house. Then I did the laundry.

B. The particle に

So far, you have learned three functions of the particle に: に for time as in 土曜日(どようび)に (*on Saturday*) and いちじに (*at one o'clock*); に for goals/destinations, as in 学校に いきます (*go to school*) ; and に for the location of a person or object, as in うちに あります/います (*It/Someone is in my house.*) This chapter introduces two more usages of the particle に, but they are related to に used for goals.

1. に to (recipient, target, goal, destination)

に can indicate the recipient or the target person to which an action is directed.

	Noun	Particle	
私(わたし)は	ともだち	に	てがみを かきます。

I will write a letter to a friend.

ともだちに	でんわを かけます。	*I make a phone call to a friend.*
りょうしんに	メールを かきます。	*I write e-mail to my parents.*
先生に	ききます。	*I ask my teacher.*
先生に	しつもんします。	*I ask my teacher a question.*
先生に	はなします。	*I talk to/tell my teacher.*
ともだちに	あいます。	*I meet my friends.*

Notes

- に in this usage indicates the endpoint of an action, so it is conceptually related to the goal 〜に/へ いきます/きます/かえります. However, unlike the above usage, 〜に/へ いきます/きます/かえります cannot take a person as a goal.
- In some cases, the particle と association (with) is used instead of に with verbs like あいます and はなします. Although the English translation does not differentiate between に or と, the meaning is very different in Japanese. When に is used, the action is uni-directional, so 先生に はなします indicates that the speaker is telling something or speaking to the teacher, but not having a conversation. Conversely, と indicates bi-directional orientation, so 先生と はなします indicates that the speaker and the teacher collaboratively engage in conversation.

  先生に はなします　*I speak to/tell something to the teacher.*
  先生と はなします　*I converse with the teacher.*

  Similarly, ともだちに あいますis used when the speaker goes to the friend to talk or bumps into the friend on the street, but ともだちと あいます suggests that the speaker and the friend have made a prior arrangement before meeting each other.

---

2. Purpose に いきます／きます／かえります／でかけます

に can also indicate the purpose for going somewhere. It is used with the verbs いきます, きます, かえります and でかけます. The purpose may be a noun indicating an activity such as かいもの and コンサート.

アリソンさんは かいものに でかけました。 *Alison went shopping.*
リーさんは コンサートに いきます。 *Mr. Li is going to a concert.*

When purpose is represented by a verbal expression such as テニスを します or ごはんを たべます に should be attached to the verb stem (the part of verb that comes before ます).

	Verb stem	Particle	Verb of movement
ごはんを	たべ	に	でかけます。

I'm going out to eat.

Note いきます, きます, かえります and でかけますare commonly used with an expression of a desination such as としょかんに／へ いきます. When combined with the purpose, the sentence can have more than one に, such as としょかんに べんきょうしに いきます (*go to the library to study*) .

うちに <u>ねに</u> かえります。 *I am going home to take a nap.*
上田さんに <u>あいに</u> きました。 *I came to see Ms. Ueda.*
上田さんに <u>あいに</u> ここに きました。 *I came here to see Ms. Ueda.*

キム： あ、どこへ いきますか。
What are you doing tomorrow?
田中： たいいくかんに およぎに いきます。
I am going to the gym to swim.
キム： そうですか。
I see.

話(はな)してみましょう　Conversation Practice

Activity 1

The pictures below show what Mr. Suzuki did last week. Complete the following statements using the appropriate particles.

Example:

鈴木(すずき)さん／ともだち／でんわ／かけました。
鈴木(すずき)さんは　ともだちに　でんわを　かけました。

1. 鈴木(すずき)さん／ともだち／としょかん／べんきょうしました。
2. 鈴木(すずき)さん／ともだち／デパート／かいもの／いきました。
3. 鈴木(すずき)さん／かのじょ (*girlfriend*) ／でんわ／はなしました。
4. 鈴木(すずき)さんの　かのじょ／鈴木(すずき)さんの　うち／あそび／きました。
5. 鈴木(すずき)さんの　かのじょ／鈴木(すずき)さん／りょうり／しました。
6. 鈴木(すずき)さんの　かのじょ／鈴木(すずき)さん／ゲーム／しました。
7. 鈴木(すずき)さん／かのじょ／メール／かきました。

Activity 2

Based on each situation, create a sentence stating a purpose, using a verb stem + に　いきます／きます／かえります.

Example: 昨日（きのう）　スーパーへ　いきました。そして、アルバイトを　しました。
昨日（きのう）　スーパーへ　アルバイトを　しに　いきました。

1. たいいくかんへ　いきました。およぎました。
2. アパートに　かえります。そして、ゆっくり　します。
3. ここに　きました。そして、りょうりを　しました。
4. としょかんへ　いきました。そして、しんぶんを　よみました。
5. 先生の　けんきゅうしつ (*office*) に　いきます。そして、しつもんします。
6. このカフェに　よく　きます。そして、ともだちに　あいます。

Activity 3

Work in groups of three. One person chooses a place in the box but does not tell anyone. The other two ask questions about the purpose of going there and try to figure out which place it is. The person who has chosen the place will answer はい or いいえ. Take turns.

としょかん	たいいくかん	ラボ	きょうしつ	本屋（や）	こうえん
ぎんこう	ゆうびんきょく	カフェ	コンビニ	びょういん	こうばん
デパート	ともだちのうち	日本	中国（ちゅうごく）	かんこく	フランス
スペイン	オーストラリア	カナダ	メキシコ	アメリカ	イギリス

Example: B chooses としょかん

A: うんどうしに　いきますか。

B: いいえ。

C: 本を　よみに　いきますか

B: はい。

C: としょかんですか。

B: はい、そうです。

Activity 4

Based on the sentences you completed in Activity 1, narrate Mr. Suzuki's day. Try to use transition words like そして, when you can. To make the story sound more natural, try to fill in some information such as when Mr. Suzuki went out and came back, and when his girlfriend visited him and went home.

II. Commenting about the past, using polite past adjectives and the copula verb です

In Chapter 4, adjectives were introduced to describe the physical characteristics of an object. Another common use of adjectives is to comment on objects and events in the present and the past. This chapter introduces the past tense forms of adjectives and the copula verb です. Like the present forms, the formation of past tense forms differs depending on the adjective type.

A. い -adjectives

The past affirmative form of い-adjectives is formed by replacing い with かったです. The past negative form is formed by replacing い with くありませんでした or くなかったです. いい becomes よかったです in the affirmative form and よくありませんでした or よくなかったです in the negative form.

Dictionary form	Polite affirmative forms		Polite negative forms	
	Present	Past	Present	Past
あかい *(red)*	あかいです *(It is red.)*	あかかったです *(It was red.)*	あかくありません あかくないです *(It is not red.)*	あかくありませんでした あかくなかったです *(It was not red.)*
いい *(good)*	いいです *(It is good.)*	よかったです *(It was good.)*	よくありません よくないです *(It is not good.)*	よくありませんでした よくなかったです *(It was not good.)*

B. な -adjectives and the copula verb です

The ending of the な-adjectives and the copula verb are very similar. In both cases, you will change です to でした for the past affirmative form, じゃありません／じゃないです to じゃありませんでした／じゃなかったです for the past negative form.

Dictionary form	Polite affirmative forms		Polite negative forms	
	Present	Past	Present	Past
きれい *(pretty)*	きれいです *(It is pretty.)*	きれいでした *(It was pretty.)*	きれいじゃありません きれいじゃないです *(It is not pretty.)*	きれいじゃありませんでした きれいじゃなかったです *(It was not pretty.)*
ゲーム *(game)*	ゲームです *(It is a game.)*	ゲームでした *(It was a game.)*	ゲームじゃありません ゲームじゃないです *(It is not a game.)*	ゲームじゃありませんでした ゲームじゃなかったです *(It was not a game.)*

スミス：週末(しゅうまつ)は　どうでしたか。
How was your weekend?

山下：とても　たのしかったです。
It was really fun.

スミス：そうですか。よかったですね。
I see. I'm glad to hear that. (literally, *that was good.*)

上田：パーティは　どうでしたか。
How was the party?

リー：とても　にぎやかでした。
It was very lively.

上田：山田先生と　はなしましたか。
Did you talk with Professor Yamada?

リー：いいえ、先生は　いませんでした。
No, he wasn't there.

上田：そうですか。ざんねんでしたね。
I see. That's too bad.

チョイ：今日(きょう)、いそがしいですか。
Are you busy today?

本田：ええ、テストが　あります。
Yes, I have a test.

チョイ：そうですか。大変(たいへん)ですね。
I see. That's tough!

話(はな)してみましょう　Conversation Practice

Activity 1

Change the adjectives into both the past tense affirmative form and the past tense negative form. Pay attention to the two kinds of adjectives, い -adjectives and な -adjectives. Use とても with the affirmative form and あまり with the negative form.

Example: 大きい
とても　大きかったです。　あまり　大きくありませんでした。

1. おもしろい
2. きれい
3. うれしい
4. いい
5. たのしい
6. かなしい
7. ざんねん
8. 大変(たいへん)
9. ひま
10. げんき
11. にぎやか
12. むずかしい

Activity 2

Chat with a partner about events and occasions listed in the chart below. Discuss which ones were interesting, easy, difficult, etc., and complete the chart.

Examples: **1.** A: 日本語(ご)の テストは どうでしたか。

B: とても やさしかったです。

A: そうですか。よかったですね。

2. A: 日本語(ご)の テストは どうでしたか。

B: あまり よくなかったです。／
とても むずかしかったです。

A: そうですか。ざんねんでしたね。／大変(たいへん)でしたね。

	私	パートナー
日本語(ご)の テスト		
日本語(ご)の じゅぎょう		
週末(しゅうまつ)		
パーティ		

Activity 3

With your partner, take turns asking about life in high school (高校生活(こうこうせいかつ)) as well as about your high school classes and teachers. Fill in the chart as you ask and answer questions.

Example: A: 高校生活(こうこうせいかつ) は どうでしたか。

B: とても たのしかったです。

A: そうですか。よかったですね。

B: ～さんの 高校生活(こうこうせいかつ)は どうでしたか。

A: わたしの 高校生活(こうこうせいかつ)も とても よかったです。

	私(わたし)	パートナー
高校生活(こうこう せいかつ)		
じゅぎょう		
先生		

III. Connecting verb and adjective phrases and sentences using the て -form of verbs; making requests using the て -form

Chapter 1 introduced request forms such as きいて下さい and みて下さい, in which 下さい roughly means *please*. The forms きいて and みて are the て-forms of the verbs ききます and みます, respectively. Also, Chapter 5 introduced the phrase あるいて　いきます, in which あるいて is the て-form of あるきます (*to walk*) and indicates how the speaker goes from one place to another. You may have also noticed headings such as はなして　みましょう (*Let's try speaking*) and きいて　みましょう (*Let's try listening*) in the chapters of this textbook. The form みましょう means *let's try*, and the preceding て-forms indicate what to try out. These are only a few uses of the て-form. As you continue to study Japanese, you will learn a variety of structures that use this form. This section explains the formation of the て-form of verbs and three request forms using the て-form and 下さい／下さいませんか／くれませんか.

A. Verb て -forms

The て-form of る-verbs and irregular verbs is easy to form. All you have to do is to replace ます with て.

Verb class		Polite affirmative form	て -form
る -verbs	to eat	たべます	たべて
	to watch	みます	みて
	to make a phone call	かけます	かけて
Irregular verbs	to come	きます	きて
	to do	します	して
	to study	べんきょうします	べんきょうして

The て-form of う-verbs is more complicated. There are five basic patterns and they are determined by the sound before ます, as shown in the chart below. The て-form of the verb いきます is いって though it is an う-verb. This is considered an exception.

Verb class		Polite affirmative form	て -form	Formation Patterns
う -verbs	to talk	はなします	はなして	し→して
	to listen	ききます	きいて	き→いて
	to swim	およぎます	およいで	ぎ→いで
	to take (a bath), enter	はいります	はいって	り、い、ち→って
	to say	いいます	いって	
	to wait	まちます	まって	
	to read	よみます	よんで	み、び、に→んで
	to call	よびます	よんで	
	to die	しにます	しんで	
	to go	いきます	いって	Exception

B. 〜て下さい／〜て下さいませんか／〜てくれませんか

〜て下さい, 〜て下さいませんか and 〜てくれませんか are all used to make a request. Each expression generally indicates a polite request, but 〜て下さい is the most forceful form among the three forms because it is a command form. While a social superior such as your teacher or someone much older than you may use 〜て下さい to ask you to do something, it would be rude for you to say 〜て下さい to your social superior. Instead, use 〜て下さいませんか, a more polite request form commonly used for a social superior. 〜てくれませんか is less formal than 〜て下さいませんか, so it can be used with someone of equal social status or similar age.

To a social inferior:

CD を	きいて下さい。	*Please listen to the CD.*
こくばんを	みて下さい。	*Please look at the chalkboard.*
本を	よんで下さい。	*Please read the book.*

To a social superior:

先生、 かんじを かいて下さいませんか。
Could you write the kanji?

先生、もういちど いって下さいませんか。
Could you say it again?

先生、あしたまで まって下さいませんか。
Could you wait until tomorrow?

To a peer:

上田さん、あした　メールしてくれませんか。
Could you e-mail me tomorrow?

上田さん、としょかんへ　いってくれませんか。
Could you go to the library?

上田さん、この　てがみを　よんでくれませんか。
Could you read this letter?

話(はな)してみましょう　Conversation Practice

Activity 1

Your teacher gives you one of the following commands in Japanese. Act out the command.

Example: Your teacher says ここに　きて下さい.
You walk toward the teacher.

1. Come here.
2. Go to the back of the room.
3. Read the textbook.
4. Look at the chalkboard.
5. Write your name in Japanese.
6. Speak Japanese to a classmate next to you.
7. Turn in your work. (しゅくだいを　だします。)
8. Make a phone call.

Activity 2

Working with a partner, make the requests in Activity 1, using ～てくれませんか. Your partner will act out. You can create your own request if you like.

Example: You say ここに　きてくれませんか.
Your partner walks toward you.

Activity 3

Use the table below to make a request to the addressee. Pay attention to the relationship between you and your addressee and choose ～て下さい or ～て下さいませんか or ～てくれませんか.

Example: 先生 wants students to speak Japanese.

日本語(ご)で はなして下さい。

	You	Your addressee	Request
Example	先生	学生	Speak Japanese
1	学生	学生	Invite/call Tanaka-san
2	学生	先生	Write e-mail to you
3	学生	先生	Read this letter
4	先生	学生	Turn in the homework
5	学生	学生	Clean up the room
6	いしゃ (doctor)	かんじゃ (patient)	Walk every day
7	いしゃ (doctor)	かんじゃ (patient)	Relax at home
8	大学院生(いんせい)	大学の先生	Meet me next week
9	学校 1 の先生 (teacher at a school)	学校 2 の先生 (teacher at another school)	Write a letter to school

Activity 4

Work with a partner. Create dialogues in which you make requests in each of the following situations, using ～て下さい or ～てくれませんか.

Example: You are a teacher, and you are taking our students on a field trip tomorrow. So you want them to come to school at 7 a.m.

明日(あした)のあさ 7じに 学校へきて下さい。

1. You are sick and can't go to school. You want your roommate to call your teacher.
2. You want to use **kanji** to write your name. Ask your teacher to write your name in **kanji**.
3. You are a teacher. Your students performed very poorly on the test and you want them to study.
4. You have a visitor, who looks younger than you. But you are busy with work so you want him/her to wait for you here.
5. Your neighbor comes to your house to discuss a neighborhood dispute with you. She/he is at the door. Invite him/her in.

IV. Connecting phrases, using the て -forms of verbs and adjectives

A. The て-form of verbs indicating "and"

Another basic usage of the て-form is to connect phrases. As was mentioned in Grammar I, A-2 (p. a-223), the particle と cannot be used to connect two or more sentences or phrases. The て-form is used instead. Note that the て-form by itself does not express when the action takes place or has taken place. The timing of the action is determined by the phrase at the end of the sentence. For example, テレビを <u>みて</u>、ね<u>ます</u> indicates that the speaker goes or will go to bed after watching TV, but テレビを <u>みて</u>、ね<u>ました</u> indicates that he/she went to bed after watching TV.

しんぶんを <u>よんで、</u>学校に いきます	*I read the newspaper and go to school .*
おんがくを <u>きいて、</u>ねます。	*I listen to the music and go to bed.*
うちに <u>かえって、</u>ゆっくりしました。	*I went home and relaxed.*
ともだちを <u>よんで、</u>ゲームを しました。	*I called my friend and played a game.*
いぬの さんぽを <u>して、</u>でかけました。	*I walked my dog and went out.*
アルバイトが <u>あって、</u>いそがしかったです。	*I had to work part-time and was busy.*
田中さんが <u>いて、</u>にぎやかでした。	*Mr. Tanaka was there, and/so it was lively.*

Phrases connected by the て-form may indicate a chronological relationship or a cause-effect relationship, because the て-form loosely connects phrases without specifying how they should be related.

B. The て-form of adjectives indicating "and"

The て-form of adjectives and the copula verbs can connect phrases as well. The formation of the adjective て-form is relatively simple. い（です）is replaced by くて for い-adjectives, です is replaced by で for な-adjective and the copula verb. The て-form of いい is よくて.

い -adjectives	な -adjectives	Copula verb
たのし<u>いです</u> *(it is fun.)*	にぎやかです *(it is lively.)*	休(やす)みです *(It is a day off.)*
たのし<u>くて</u> *(it is fun, and)*	にぎやか<u>で</u> *(it is lively, and)*	休(やす)み<u>で</u> *(It is a day off, and)*

上田さんは やさし<u>くて、</u> きれいです。
Ms. Ueda is kind and pretty.

リーさんは　げんきで、　おもしろいです。
Mr. Li is cheerful and interesting.

かんじは　むずかしくて、　大変です。
Kanji is difficult and tough.

パーティは　にぎやかで、　たのしかったです。
The party was lively and fun.

ひまで、　うちに　います。
I have nothing to do and stay at home.

しごとで、　フランスへ　いきます。
I am going to France for work.

さびしくて、　ともだちに　でんわしました。
I was lonely, and/so I called my friend.

話してみましょう Conversation Practice

Activity 1

The following illustrations show what Ms. Yamamoto did last Sunday. Describe her activities using the て-form of verbs.

Example: あさ　8じに　おきて、うんどうを　しました。

8:00 A.M.

8:30 A.M.

About 9:00 A.M.

9:30 A.M.

About 10:00 A.M.

11:00 A.M.

About 11:30 A.M.

12:00 P.M.

12:15 P.M.

12:30 P.M.

ABOUT 4:00 P.M.

6:00 P.M.

7:00 P.M.

8:00 P.M.

ABOUT 11:00 P.M.

Activity 2

Comment on the following things using the て-form of adjectives.

Example: えいごのじゅぎょう
えいごのじゅぎょうは　やさしくて、おもしろいです。

1. 日本語(ご)
2. そうじ
3. せんたく
4. アルバイト
5. おんがく
6. うんどう
7. コンピュータ・ゲーム

Activity 3

With a partner, discuss a movie, a TV program (テレビばんぐみ) you've seen, a concert you've attended, or some music you have listened to recently. Comment on the experiences using the て-form. Then complete the chart.

Example: A: さいきん (*recently*) どんな　えいがを　みましたか。
B: ハリー・ポッターを　みました。
A: どうでしたか。
B: とても　おもしろくて、よかったですよ。

Category	Type/Title	How was it?
えいが		
コンサート		
テレビばんぐみ		
おんがく		

V. Extending an invitation using ませんか

The negative question form of a verb ～ませんか is often used to extend an invitation. It conveys the idea in English of *won't you* ～, or *why don't we* ～. ～ませんか is often used with the phrase いっしょに (*together*) when the speaker wants to invite someone for an activity.

いっしょに ジョギングを しませんか。
Why don't we go jogging together?

今度(こんど)の 休(やす)みに いっしょに ピクニックに いきませんか。
Why don't we go to a picnic on the next day off?

私(わたし)と いっしょに べんきょうしませんか。
Won't you study with me?

Notes

- Before extending an invitation, the speaker often checks the listener's availability or interest, or willingness. Because an overt rejection can often strain a relationship, Japanese people tend to avoid creating a situation in which a person may have to reject an offer or an invitation.

  ジョンソン： 今度(こんど)の 休(やす)みは いそがしいですか。
  Are you busy during the next holiday?

  木村(きむら)： いいえ、いそがしくありません。
  No, not really.

  ジョンソン： じゃあ、およぎに いきませんか。
  Then, why don't we go swimming?

  山田： テニスは よく しますか。
  Do you play tennis often?

  上田： ええ、しますよ。
  Yes, I do.

  山田： じゃあ、土曜日(どようび)に テニスを しませんか。
  Well, why don't we play tennis on Saturday?

- Japanese people often avoid saying no explicitly to an invitation in order not to hurt other people's feelings. When you cannot accept an invitation, it's customary to apologize for not being able to accept it, and then give a reason. If you don't want to give a specific reason, use the following phrases.

  すみません、ちょっと つごうが わるくて。
  Sorry, I'm a little busy. (literally, *Sorry, it's a little inconvenient.*)

すみません、ちょっと ようじが あって。
Sorry, I have some errands/business to attend to.

- Some common expressions for accepting an invitation are:

いいですね。	*That sounds great.*
ええ、ぜひ。	*Yes, I'd love to.* (literally, *Yes by all means.*)
ええ、いいですよ。	*Yes, that would be fine.*

話(はな)してみましょう　Conversation Practice

Activity 1

Work with a partner. Look at the following drawings and extend an invitation to each activity. Your partner will accept your invitation by saying ええ、いいですよ, いいですね or ええ、ぜひ.

Example: A: 〜さん、いっしょに かいものに いきませんか。
B: ええ、いいですよ。

Activity 2

Work with the class. In the chart below, write three activities that you want to do with someone on each day of this weekend. Invite at least one person for each activity. If someone invites you to do an activity, either accept using one of the phrases you've just learned, or decline the invitation politely if you're not interested.

Example: You have written えいがを　みる for 金曜日(きんようび).

A: 金曜日(きんようび)に　えいがを　みませんか。

B: ええ、いいですよ。

or　すみません、ちょっと　つごうが　わるくて。

ちょっと　ようじが　あって。

～曜日(ようび)	すること (Activities to invite for)	なまえ (Person who has agreed)
金曜日(きんようび)		
土曜日(どようび)		
日曜日(にちようび)		

Activity 3

Invite a partner to do the following activities together. Before extending your invitation, ask about his/her availability and/or interest.

Example: A: 今週(こんしゅう)の　金曜日(きんようび)は　いそがしいですか。

B: いいえ、いそがしくないですよ。

A: じゃあ、いっしょに　パーティに　いきませんか。

B: いいですね。

1. いっしょに　かいものに　いきます。
2. いっしょに　おんがくを　ききます。
3. いっしょに　しゅくだいを　します。
4. いっしょに　えいがを　みます。
5. いっしょに　こうえんの　そうじを　します。

Supplementary Note

In Japanese, verbal expressions can be abbreviated using です when the meaning can be guessed from context. This use of です appears often in response to a wh-question.

田中：だれを　よびましたか。
Who did you invite?
ペギー：上田さんと　アリソンさんです。
Ms. Ueda and Alison.

木村(きむら)：いつ　かえりますか。
When will you come back?
リー：来週(らいしゅう)の　火曜日(かようび)です。
Next Tuesday.

山中：だれと　はなしましたか。
Who did you talk to?
チョイ：スミスさんです。
Mr. Smith.

In English, you can simply use nouns such as people's names without a verb, but in Japanese it sounds abrupt and can be rude to omit the verb, especially in formal conversations. In cases like this, です can be used instead of more specific verbal expressions.

This is true in the classroom where the instructor asks many questions. You should try to respond to your teacher with the verb from the question or with です when it is appropriate to do so. (But be careful not to overuse です because excessive repetition may be interpreted as a lack of interest in class!)

聞く練習(きれんしゅう) Listening

上手(じょうず)な聞(き)き方(かた) Listening Strategy

Making sense of missing pronouns

Just as in writing, pronouns are often omitted in a conversation when they can be inferred from the context. Imagine that two people are talking with each other. If one person asks a question without an overt subject pronoun, the missing subject is likely to be *you*. If that person then makes a statement without a subject, the subject is most likely to be the speaker himself/herself. As you become more proficient with the language, you will understand who is mentioned without having to listen for subject pronouns.

A. だれの はなし？ **Whose story is it?**

Listen to the following short dialogues. In each of the conversations, the subject in the man's speech is either *I* or *you*, but it's missing. Identify the missing subjects.

1. I you **4.** I you
2. I you **5.** I you
3. I you

B. 私(わたし)の 生活(せいかつ)

Listen to the following conversations, then the statements about them. Circle はい if a statement is true, or いいえ if it is false.

1. a. はい いいえ **d.** はい いいえ **g.** はい いいえ
b. はい いいえ **e.** はい いいえ **h.** はい いいえ
c. はい いいえ **f.** はい いいえ

2. a. はい いいえ **d.** はい いいえ
b. はい いいえ **e.** はい いいえ
c. はい いいえ **f.** はい いいえ

聞き上手 話し上手
き じょうず はな じょうず
Communication

Communication Strategy

Using そうですか and そうですね

The expressions そうですか and そうですね are used often in conversation. These expressions are instrumental in making a conversation go smoothly. However, it is sometimes difficult to know which one to use. There are two そうですか: one with a falling intonation and one with a rising intonation. そうですか with a falling intonation means "I see" (*and I didn't know that*). It is used when you have just received new information. It is often preceded by ああ. そうですか with a rising intonation means "Is that so?" It is used to question what you have just heard, and is commonly preceded by えっ (*What!?*).

そうですね is usually spoken with a falling intonation. It means "That's right" so it would not be appropriate to say そうですね when you have just heard something new. そうですね is often preceded by ええ or はい.

練習 Practice
れんしゅう

1. Listen to the six short conversations. After each one, put a check mark in the box that corresponds to the correct meaning of そうですか／そうですね in the context of the conversation.

	1	2	3	4	5	6
I see.						
Is that so?						
That's right.						

2. Working with a partner, read the sentences below one at a time, and choose one of these three phrases as your reply. More than one answer may be correct, as long as you know why you have chosen it.

ああ、そうですか。 えっ、そうですか。 ええ、そうですね。

1. 山田先生は いい 先生です。
2. 山田先生は れきしの 先生です。
3. ブラウンさんは 日本人のともだちと でかけました。
4. このしゅくだいは むずかしかったですね。
5. 昨日は いそがしかったですね。
   きのう
6. 明日 日本に いきます。
   あした

漢字
かんじ
Kanji

Kanji derived from pictures and symbols (2)

月 (moon)

火 (fire)

水 (water)

木 (tree)

金 (gold)

土 (earth)

末 (end; tree with a focal point at the top)

今	今	now いま　コン	ノ 人 𠆢 今 今(いま)、何時(なんじ)ですか。　今週(こんしゅう)　今日(きょう)
私	私	I; private わたし・わたくし　シ	私(わたし)は日本人です。
月	月	moon, month つき　ゲツ・ガツ	月曜日(げつようび)
火	火	fire ひ　カ	火曜日(かようび)
水	水	water みず　スイ	水曜日(すいようび)
木	木	tree き　モク	一 十 才 木 木曜日(もくようび)　木(き)があります。
金	金	gold, money, metal かね　キン	金曜日(きんようび)

Kanji	Meaning	Readings	Examples
土	earth, soil, ground	つち ト・ド	土曜日(どようび)
曜	day of the week	ヨウ	月曜日(げつようび) 火曜日(かようび) 水曜日(すいようび) 木曜日(もくようび) 金曜日(きんようび) 土曜日(どようび)
何	what	なに・なん	何曜日(なんようび) 何(なん)ですか。 何時(なんじ)ですか。
週	week	シュウ	今週(こんしゅう)の週末(しゅうまつ) 先週(せんしゅう)
末	end	すえ マツ	週末(しゅうまつ)に何(なに)をしますか。
休	to rest	やす(む) キュウ	休(やす)みの日に何をしますか。

読(よ)めるようになった漢字(かんじ) (Kanji and compounds you can now read).

今 今日(きょう) 今日(こんにち)は 今晩(ばん) 今週 来週(らい) 先週 私 月曜日 火曜日 水曜日 木曜日 木 金曜日 土曜日 日曜日 何をしますか。 何ですか。何曜日 何時(じ) 週末 今度(こんど) 大変(たいへん)な 大丈夫(だいじょうぶ)です 毎週(まい) 休みの日

日本人の名前(なまえ)：金田(かねだ) 鈴木(すずき)

練習(れんしゅう) Practice

Read the following.

1. 日曜日 月曜日 火曜日 水曜日 木曜日 金曜日 土曜日
2. 大川：「中田さんは今週の週末に何をしますか。」
   本田：「土曜日に山にいきます。」
3. 先週の月曜日は休みでした。
4. 上田：「本田さんは何年生ですか」。
   本田：「私は日本大学の３年生です。」
5. 中川：「今日のごご、何をしますか。」
   山中：「アルバイトがあります。」

読む練習 (よ れんしゅう)
Reading

上手な読み方 (じょうず よ かた) Reading Strategy

Identifying missing nouns

In Japanese, it is not necessary to repeat nouns or pronouns in writing if they can be inferred from context. These omitted nouns are most likely to be either the subject or the topic, although they can be any other type of noun such as an object, place, or time. For example, in the sentences, 私は　学生です。三年生です。, the topic of the second sentence, 私は is missing because it is mentioned in the first sentence and can be inferred. This type of deletion makes a paragraph more cohesive. As you become more proficient with the language, this will become second nature to you.

読む前に (よ まえ) Pre-reading

A. Identify any missing nouns in the following sentences.

1. 先週の日曜日は　はちじに　おきました。そして、くじごろ　でかけました。
2. キムさんは　昨日(きのう)　しゅくだいを　しませんでした。でも、今日　しました。
3. アリスさんに　でんわを　かけました。てがみも　かきました。
4. パーティには　鈴木(すずき)さんを　よびました。でも、田中さんは　よびませんでした。

B. In Japanese, jot down five activities that you do often on weekends.

大川さんの週末

ことばの リスト (Vocabulary)

[Sentence +] から	Because [+ sentence]
汚(きたな)い	dirty
ですから	so
はやく	early

先週の土曜日に両親(りょうしん)が私に会(あ)いに来(き)ました。とてもうれしかったですが、忙(いそが)しくて大変(たいへん)でした。木曜日と金曜日にテストがあって時間(じかん)がなかったから、アパートはとても汚(きたな)かったです。ですから、土曜日の朝早(あさはや)く起(お)きて、掃除(そうじ)と洗濯(せんたく)をしました。それから、スーパーに買(か)い物(もの)に行(い)きました。

12時(じ)ごろに両親(りょうしん)が私のアパートに来(き)ました。少(すこ)し話(はなし)をして、アパートの近(ちか)くのショッピング・センターに行(い)って、昼(ひる)ご飯(はん)を食(た)べました。その後(あと)、買(か)い物(もの)をして、キャンパスに行(い)きました。図書館(としょかん)で上田さんに会(あ)いましたから、いっしょに図書館(としょかん)のカフェに行(い)って、コーヒーを飲(の)んで話(はなし)をしました。両親(りょうしん)は5時(じ)ごろ帰(かえ)りました。

読(よ)んだ後(あと)で Comprehension

A. しつもんに こたえて下さい。Answer these questions in Japanese.

1. 大川さんの 週末は どうでしたか。
2. 大川さんは 金曜日に 何を しましたか。
3. 大川さんは 土曜日の あさ 何を しましたか。
4. 大川さんは だれと 昼(ひる)ご飯(はん)を 食(た)べましたか。
5. どこで 食(た)べましたか。
6. 土曜日の ごご、何を しましたか。

B. Identify any missing nouns for each sentence of the reading.

C. Write a letter to a friend in Japan describing your weekend activities.

総合練習
そうごうれんしゅう
Integration

山田さんとさとうさんの一日 A Day in the Lives of Ms. Yamada and Mr. Sato

The illustration below shows a typical day for two Japanese college students, Ms. Yamada and Mr. Sato. Ms. Yamada lives with her parents. Mr. Sato lives in an apartment because he is from another area of Japan. In groups of four or five, complete the following tasks.

1. Describe what each student does in a day.
2. Compare and contrast Ms. Yamada's and Mr. Sato's routines.
3. Discuss simlarities and differences between their daily routines and your own.

ロールプレイ Role Play

You are conducting a telephone survey of people's daily routines. With a partner, come up with five questions that you would like to ask. Then, pretend to make a phone call. Ask to speak with someone (your partner) politely. Once he/she comes to the phone, say すみません。アンケートちょうさなんですが、いいですか。(*Excuse me. I am doing a survey. May I . . . ?*) Ask the five questions and take notes. Once the call is complete, reverse roles with your partner. Compare notes with several people in the class to see if your routines share anything in common.

APPENDIX A

PITCH ACCENTS

Whereas Enlish uses stress (or loudness) for accent, Japanese uses two relative pitches: high and low. Standard Japanese has the following rules.

1. The first mora (or syllable) and the second mora must have different pitches. Thus, a word always begins with either a low-high or a high-low combination.

2. Once the pitch goes low, it will never go up within a word.

3. For an N-mora word, there are N + 1 accent patterns. This becomes obvious when a particle follows a noun.

Common patterns

One-mora word

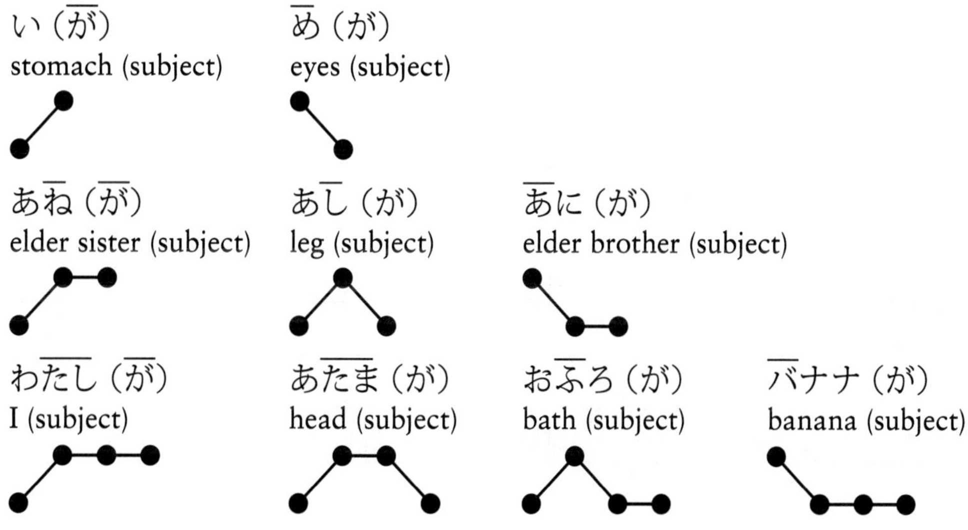

APPENDIX B

VERB CONJUGATIONS

			Irregular Verb	Irregular Verb	る - verb	う - verb
Dictionary Form			くる (to come)	する (to do)	たべる (to eat)	いく (to go)
Plain	Present	Affirmative	くる	する	たべる	いく
		Negative	こない	しない	たべない	いかない
	Past	Affirmative	きた	した	たべた	いった
		Negative	こなかった	しなかった	たべなかった	いかなかった
Polite	Present	Affirmative	きます	します	たべます	いきます
		Negative	きません	しません	たべません	いきません
	Past	Affirmative	みました	しました	たべました	いきました
		Negative	きません でした	しません でした	たべません でした	いきません でした
Volitional	Plain		こよう	しよう	たべよう	いこう
	Polite		きましょう	しましょう	たべましょう	いきましょう
Potential	Plain		こられる	できる	たべられる	いける
	Polite		こられます	できます	たべられます	いけます
Conditional			くれば	すれば	たべれば	いけば
て - form			きて	して	たべて	いって

う - verb	う - verb	う - verb	う - verb	う - verb
およぐ (to swim)	かえる (to go home)	かく (to write)	のむ (to drink)	はなす (to talk)
およぐ	かえる	かく	のむ	はなす
およがない	かえらない	かかない	のまない	はなさない
およいだ	かえった	かいた	のんだ	はなした
およがなかった	かえらなかった	かかなかった	のまなかった	はなさなかった
およぎます	かえります	かきます	のみます	はなします
およぎませn	かえりません	かきません	のみません	はなしません
およぎました	かえりました	かきました	のみました	はなしました
およぎません でした	かえりません でした	かきません でした	のみません でした	はなしません でした
およごう	かえろう	かこう	のもう	はなそう
およぎましょう	かえりましょう	かきましょう	のみましょう	はなしましょう
およげる	かえれる	かける	のめる	はなせる
およげます	かえれます	かけます	のめます	はなせます
およげば	かえれば	かけば	のめば	はなせば
およいで	かえって	かいて	のんだ	はなして

APPENDIX C

ADJECTIVE AND COPULA CONJUGATIONS

			い - adjective おおきい (big)	い - adjective しずか（な） (quiet)	Copula だ / です (be)
Plain	Present	Affirmative	おおきい	しずかだ	N だ
		Negative	おおきくない	しずかじゃない	N じゃない
	Past	Affirmative	おおきかった	しずかだった	N だった
		Negative	おおきくなかった	しずかじゃなかった	N じゃなかった
Polite	Present	Affirmative	おおきいです	しずかです	N です
		Negative	おおききないです / おおきくありません	しずかじゃないです / しずかじゃありません	N じゃないです / N じゃありません
	Past	Affirmative	おおきかったです	しずかでした	N でした
		Negative	おおきくなかったです / おおきくありませんでした	しずかじゃなかったです / しずかじゃありませんでした	N じゃなかったです / N じゃありませんでした
Prenominal	おおきい（だいがく）			しずかな（ひと）	N の
Conditional	おおきければ			しずかなら・しずかだったら	N なら /N だったら
て - form	おおきくて			しずかで	N で

APPENDIX D
COUNTERS AND TIME EXPRESSIONS

Common Counters				
	General Counter ～つ	People ～にん	Bound Objects (book, magazine, etc.) ～さつ	Cylindrical Objects (pen, umbrella, etc.) ～ほん
1	ひとつ	ひとり	いっさつ	いっぽん
2	ふたつ	ふたり	にさつ	にほん
3	みっつ	さんにん	さんさつ	さんぼん
4	よっつ	よにん	よんさつ	よんほん
5	いつつ	ごにん	ごさつ	ごほん
6	むっつ	ろくにん	ろくさつ	ろっぽん
7	ななつ	しちにん	ななさつ	ななほん
8	やっつ	はちにん	はっさつ	はっぽん
9	ここのつ	くにん	きゅうさつ	きゅうほん
10	とお	じゅうにん	じゅっさつ じっさつ	じゅっぽん じっぽん
11	じゅういち	じゅういちにん	じゅういっさつ	じゅういっぽん
12	じゅうに	じゅうににん	じゅうにさつ	じゅうにほん

Specific Time				
	Month ～がつ	Day ～にち	Time (o'clock) ～じ	Time (minute) ～ふん
1	いちがつ	ついたち	いちじ	いっぷん
2	にがつ	ふつか	にじ	にふん
3	さんがつ	みっか	さんじ	さんぷん
4	しがつ	よっか	よじ	よんぷん
5	ごがつ	いつか	ごじ	ごふん
6	ろくがつ	むいか	ろくじ	ろっぷん
7	しちがつ	なのか	しちじ	ななふん
8	はちがつ	ようか	はちじ	はっぷん
9	くがつ	ここのか	くじ	きゅうぷん
10	じゅうがつ	とおか	じゅうじ	じゅうぷん、じっぷん
11	じゅういちがつ	じゅういちにち	じゅういちじ	じゅういっぷん
12	じゅうにがつ	じゅうににち	じゅうにじ	じゅうにふん
14		じゅうよっか (14)		
20		はつか (20)		
24		にじゅうよっか (24)		

Extent					
	Year ～ねん	Month ～かげつ	Week ～しゅうかん	Day ～にち	Hour ～じかん
1	いちねん	いっかげつ	いっしゅうかん	いちにち（かん）	いちじかん
2	にねん	にかげつ	にしゅうかん	ふつか（かん）	にじかん
3	さんねん	さんかげつ	さんしゅうかん	みっか（かん）	さんじかん
4	よねん	よんかげつ	よんしゅうかん	よっか（かん）	よじかん
5	ごねん	ごかげつ	ごしゅうかん	いつか（かん）	ごじかん
6	ろくねん	ろっかげつ	ろくしゅうかん	むいか（かん）	ろくじかん
7	しちねん ななねん	ななかげつ	ななしゅうかん	なのか（かん）	しちじかん
8	はちねん	はちかげつ はっかげつ	はっしゅうかん	ようか（かん）	はちじかん
9	きゅうねん くねん	きゅうがげつ	きゅうしゅうかん	ここのか（かん）	くじかん
10	じゅうねん	じゅうかげつ じっかげつ	じゅっしゅうかん じっしゅうかん	とおか（かん）	じゅうじかん
11	じゅういちねん	じゅういっかげつ	じゅういっしゅうかん	じゅういちにち（かん）	じゅういちじかん
12	じゅうにねん	じゅうにかげつ	じゅうにしゅうかん	じゅうににち（かん）	じゅうにじかん
14				じゅうよっか（かん）(14)	
20				はつか（かん）(20)	
24				にじゅうよっか（かん）(24)	

APPENDIX E

DEMONSTRATIVE WORDS（こ そ あ ど）

	こ series	そ series	あ series	ど series
	Close to both speaker and listener	Closer to listener than to speaker; moderately away from both	Away from both speaker and listener	Interrogative
Adjective	この～ (this ～)	その～ (that ～)	あの～ (that ～)	どの～ (which ～)
Pronoun	これ (this thing)	それ (that thing)	あれ (that thing)	どれ (which thing)
Location	ここ (this place)	そこ (that place)	あそこ (that place)	どこ (where)
Direction	こちら (this way)*	そちら (that way)	あちら (that way)	どちら (which way)
Manner	こう (this way)	そう (that way)	ああ (that way)	どう (how)

* こちら can be used for "this person" (polite)

APPENDIX F

KANJI LIST

	Kanji		Kun-reading	On-reading	Examples
1	大	4	おお(きい)	ダイ	大学、大きい、大学院(いん)、大学院(いん)生
2	学	4	まな(ぶ)	ガク、ガッ	学生、学校、学生、～学
3	校	4		コウ	学校、高(こう)校
4	先	4	さき	セン	先生、先週(せんしゅう)
5	生	4	なま、う(まれる)	セイ	学生、先生、一年(いちねん)生、留(りょう)学生、生活(かつ)
6	山	5	やま	サン、ザン	山川(やまかわ)さん、富士山(ふじさん)、山(やま)の上(うえ)
7	川	5	かわ、がわ	セン	小川(おがわ)さん、川中(かわなか)さん、ミシシッピー川(がわ)
8	田	5	た、だ	デン	上田(うえだ)さん、田中(たなか)さん
9	人	5	ひと	ジン、ニン	日本人(にほんじん)
10	上	5	うえ、かみ	ジョウ	テーブルの上(うえ)
11	中	5	なか	チュウ	へやの中(なか)、中国(ちゅうごく)
12	下	5	した	カ、ゲ	まどの下(した)
13	小	5	ちい（さし、）	ショウ	小(ちい)さいへや
14	日	5	ひ、び	ニチ、ニ、ジツ、カ	日本(にほん)、昨日(きのう)、今日(きょう)、明日(あした)
15	本	5	もと	ホン、ボン、ポン	山田(やまだ)さんの本(ほん)、日本

	Kanji		Kun-reading	On-reading	Examples
16	今	6	いま	コン	今、何時ですか。、今週、今日 いま なんじ こんしゅう きょう
17	私	6	わたし、わたくし	シ	私は日本人です。 わたし
18	月	6	つき	ゲツ、ガツ	月、月曜日 げつようび
19	火	6	ひ	カ	火曜日 かようび
20	水	6	みず	スイ	水曜日 すいようび
21	木	6	き	モク	木曜日 もくようび
22	金	6	かね	キン	金曜日 きんようび
23	土	6	つち	ト、ド	土曜日 どようび
24	曜	6		ヨウ	日曜日 にちようび
25	何	6	なに、なん		何曜日、何ですか。、何時ですか。 なんようび なん なんじ
26	週	6		シュウ	今週の週末、先週 こんしゅう しゅうまつ せんしゅう
27	末	6	すえ	マツ	週末 しゅうまつ
28	休	6	やす（む）	キュウ	休みの日 やす ひ

JAPANESE-ENGLISH GLOSSARY

This glossary contains all Japanese words that appear in the vocbulary list of each chapter. They are listed according to **gojuuon-jun** (Japanese alphabetical order). Each entry follows this format: word written in kana, word written in kanji, part of speech, English meaning, and chapter number where the word first appears. If the chapter number is followed by the letter P, the word is designated as supplementary vocabulary. Other abbreviations are identical to the labels used in each chapter's vocabulary list.

adv.	adverb	*conj.*	conjunction	*q. word*	question word
い*-adj.*	い-adjective	*inter.*	interjection	*pref.*	prefix
な*-adj.*	な-adjective	*count.*	counter	*suf.*	suffix
う*-v.*	う-verb	*n.*	noun	*part.*	particle
る*-v.*	る-verb	*exp.*	expression	*cop. v.*	copula verb
irr. v.	irregular verb	*demo.*	demonstrative	*number*	number

あ

あいます（会います） う*-v.* (to) meet, 6
あおい（青い） い*-adj.* blue, 4
あかい（赤い） い*-adj.* red, 4
あがってください（上がって下さい） *exp.* Please come in., 5
あかるい（明るい） い*-adj.* bright, 5
あさ（朝） *n.* morning, 3
あさごはん（朝御飯） *n.* breakfast, 3
あさって（明後日） *n.* the day after tomorrow, 3
アジアけんきゅう（アジア研究） *n.* Asian studies, 2
あした（明日） *n.* tomorrow, 3
あそこ *demo.* over there; that place (far away from both speaker and listener), 4
あそびます（遊びます） う*-v.* (to) play, 6
あたらしい（新しい） い*-adj.* new, 4
あの *demo.* that Noun over there, 5
あのう *inter.* uh, well, 2
アパート *n.* apartment , 4
あびます（浴びます） る*-v.* (to) take (a shower) シャワーを あびます take a shower. The dictionary form is あびる., 3
あまり *adv.* very (always used with a negative form), 4
アメリカ *n.* America, U.S., 2
ありがとうございます。 *exp.* Thank you., 1
あります う*-v.* (to) be held, (to) have The dictionary form is ある., 3
あるいて（歩いて） *exp.* on foot , 5
あるきます（歩きます） う*-v.* (to) walk The dictionary form is あるく., 6
アルバイト *n.* part time job , 6
あれ *demo.* that object over there; that, 4
あれは にほんごで なんと いいますか。 *exp.* How do you say that (over there) in Japanese?, 1

い

いい　い-*adj.* good, 4
いいえ　*inter.* no, don't mention it, you're welcome, 2
いいえ、そうじゃありません *exp.* No, that's not so., 2
いいえ、わかりません。*exp.* No, I don't understand it., 1
いいます（言います）　う-*v.* (to) say, 6
いきます（行きます）　う-*v.* (to) go　The dictionary form is いく., 3
イギリス　*n.* England, 2
いす（椅子）　*n.* chair, 5
いそがしい（忙しい）　い-*adj.* busy, 6
いち（一）　*number* one, 3
いちじ（一時）　*time exp.* one o'clock, 2
いちねんせい（一年生）　*n.* freshman, first-year student　(The suffix せい may be dropped), 2
いつ　*q. word* when, 3
いっしょに（一緒に）　*adv.* together, 6
いって　ください。　*exp.* Please say it. / Repeat after me., 1
いつも　*adv.* always, 3
いぬ（犬）　*n.* dog, 5
いま（今）　*adv.* now, 2
います　る-*v.* to be; to exist (used for an animate beings). Dictionary form is いる., 4
いらっしゃい *exp.* Welcome! Come in., 5

う

うえ（上）　*loc. n.* on; above; over, 5
うしろ（後ろ）　*loc. n.* bchind; back of, 5
うち（家）　*n.* home, 3
うれしい（嬉しい）　い-*adj.* happy, 6
うんどう（運動）*n.* (physical) exercises, 6

え

え（絵）　*n.* picture, 5
えいが（映画）　*n.* movie, 3
えいご（英語）　*n.* English, 2
えき（駅）　*n.* station, 4
えんぴつ（鉛筆）　*n.* pencil, 4

お

お～　*pref.* polite prefix おなまえ　polite form of なまえ (name), 2
オーストラリア　n. Australia, 2
おおきい（大きい）　い-*adj.* big, 4
おおきい　こえで　いってください。*exp.* Please speak loudly. (Teacher's request), 1
おおきい　こえで　おねがいします。*exp.* Please speak loudly. (Student's request), 1
おきます（起きます）　る-*v.* (to) get up, (to) wake up　The dictionary form is おきる., 3
おしいれ（押し入れ）　*n.* Japanese-style closet; storage space, 5
おじゃまします（お邪魔します）　*exp.* Thank you. (literally, *I will intrude on you*) (said before going inside someone's house or apartment), 5

おととい（一昨日） *n.* the day before yesterday, 3
おはようございます。 *exp.* Good morning. / Hello., 1
おはよう。 *exp.* Good morning. / Hello. (casual), 1
おふろ（お風呂） *n.* bath, 3
おもしろい（面白い） い-*adj.* interesting, 6
およぎます（泳ぎます） う-*v.* (to) swim, 6
おんがく（音楽） *n.* music, 6

か

か *part.* question marker, 2
かいて ください。 *exp.* Please write., 1
かいもの（買い物） *n.* shopping, 6
かえります（帰ります） う-*v.* (to) return, (to) go home The dictionary form is かえる., 3
かかります う-*v.* to take (time), it costs, 5
かきます（書きます） う-*v.* (to) write, 6
がくしょく（学食） *n.* school cafeteria (a shortened form of 学生しょくどう), 5
がくせい（学生） *n.* student, 2
がくせいかいかん（学生会館） *n.* student union, 5
かけます る-*v.* (to) make (a phone call) でんわを かけます, 6
がっこう（学校） *n.* school, 3
かなしい（悲しい） い-*adj.* sad, 6
カナダ *n.* Canada, 2
かばん（鞄） *n.* luggage, bag, 4
カフェ *n.* coffee shop, café (more recent word), 4
かようび（火曜日） *n.* Tuesday, 3
から *part.* from, 5
〜から きました。 *exp.* came from 〜 [casual], 2
かわ（川） *n.* river, 5
かんこく（韓国） *n.* South Korea, 2

き

き（木） *n.* tree, 5
きいて ください。 *exp.* Please listen., 1
きいろい（黄色い） い-*adj.* yellow, 4
ききます（聞きます / 聴きます） う-*v.* (to) ask; (to) listen to, 6
きっさてん（喫茶店） *n.* coffee shop (more traditional word), 4
きのう（昨日） *n.* yesterday , 3
きます（来ます） *irr. v.* (to) come, 3
きゅう、く（九） *number* nine, 3
きょう（今日） *n.* today, 3
きょうかしょ（教科書） *n.* textbook, 4
きょうしつ（教室） *n.* classroom, 5
きれい（な） な-*adj.* clean; pretty; neat, 4
ぎんこう（銀行） *n.* bank, 4
きんようび（金曜日） *n.* Friday, 3

く

くじ (九時) *time exp.* nine o'clock, 2
くらい (暗い) い*-adj.* dark, 5
〜ぐらい、〜くらい *suf.* about duration, quantity, 5
クラス *n.* class, 3
くるま (車) *n.* car, 5
くろい (黒い) い*-adj.* black, 4

け

けいえいがく (経営学) *n.* management/business administration, 2
ゲーム *n.* game, 6
けしゴム (消しゴム) *n.* eraser, 4
げつようび (月曜日) *n.* Monday, 3
げんき (な)(元気 (な)) な*-adj.* healthy, cheerful, lively (person), 6

こ

〜ご (〜語) *suf.* language にほんご Japanese language, 2
ご (五) *number* five, 3
こうえん (公園) *n.* park, 4
こうがく (工学) *n.* engineering, 2
こうこう (高校) *n.* high school, 2
こうばん (交番) *n.* police box, 4
コーヒー *n.* coffee, 3
こくばん (黒板) *n.* blackboard, chalkboard, 5
ここ *demo.* here; this place, 4
ごご (午後) *n.* p.m., afternoon, 2
ごじ (五時) *time exp.* five o'clock, 2
ごぜん (午前) *n.* a.m., forenoon, morning, 2
こちら *n.* this person, this way, 2
こちらこそ。*exp.* It is I who should be saying that. Thank YOU., 2
この *demo.* this Noun, 5
このへん (この辺) *n.* this area, 4
ごはん (御飯) *n.* meal, cooked rice, 3
ごめんください (御免下さい) *exp.* Excuse me; Anyone home?, 5
これ *demo.* this object, this, 4
これは　にほんごで　なんと　いいますか。*exp.* How do you say this in Japanese?, 1
〜ごろ *suf.* about 〜 (used only with a time expression), 3
こん〜 (今〜) *pref.* this こんしゅう、こんばん, 3
コンサート *n.* concert, 6
こんしゅう (今週) *n.* this week, 3
こんど (今度) *n.* next time, 6
こんにちは。 *exp.* Good afternoon. / Hello., 1
こんばん (今晩) *n.* tonight, 3
こんばんは。 *exp.* Good evening. / Hello., 1
コンビニ *n.* convenience store, 4
コンピュータ *n.* computer, 5

さ

ざっし（雑誌） *n.* magazine, 6
さびしい（寂しい） い-*adj.* lonely, 6
さようなら。／さよなら。 *exp.* Good-bye., 1
〜さん *suf.* Mr./Mrs./Miss/Ms. 〜, 1
さん（三） *number* three, 3
さんじ（三時） *time exp.* three o'clock, 2
ざんねん（な）（残念（な）） な-*adj.* sorry, regrettable, 6
さんねんせい（三年生） *n.* junior, third-year student (The suffix せい may be dropped.), 2
さんぽ（散歩） *n.* (to take) a walk さんぽ（を） します to take a walk, 6

し

〜じ（〜時） *suf.* 〜 o'clock, 2
〜じかん *suf.* 〜 hours, 5
しごと（仕事） *n.* job, 6
じしょ（辞書） *n.* dictionary, 4
しずか（な）（静か（な）） な-*adj.* quiet, 5
した（下） *loc. n.* under; beneath, 5
しちじ（七時） *time exp.* seven o'clock, 2
しつもん（質問） *n.* question しつもん（を）します (to) ask a question, 6
しつれいします。 *exp.* Good-bye. / Excuse me., 1
じてんしゃ（自転車） *n.* bicycle, 5
します *irr. v.* (to) do The dictionary form is する, 3
じゃあ、また。 *exp.* See you later. (literally, *Well then, again.*), 1
しゃしん（写真） *n.* photograph, 5
シャワー *n.* shower, 3
じゅう（十） *number* ten, 3
じゅういちじ（十一時） *time exp.* eleven o'clock, 2
じゅうじ（十時） *time exp.* ten o'clock, 2
じゅうにじ（十二時） *time exp.* twelve o'clock, 2
しゅうまつ（週末） *n.* weekend, 3
じゅぎょう（授業） *n.* class, course, 3
しゅくだい（宿題） *n.* homework, 3
しゅっしん（出身） *n.* one's native country, hometown, birthplace, alma mater, 2
ジョギング *n.* jogging, 6
しろい（白い） い-*adj.* white, 4
〜じん（〜人） *suf.* 〜 nationality アメリカじん, 2
しんぶん（新聞） *n.* newspaper, 6

す

すいようび（水曜日） *n.* Wednesday, 3
スーパー *n.* supermarket, 4
スペイン *n.* Spain, 2
（あのう、）すみません。 *exp.* (Eh,) Excuse me., 1
すみません。 *exp.* I am sorry. / Excuse me., 1

せ

〜せい（〜生） *suf.* 〜 student だいがくせい　college student いちねんせい　freshman, 2
せいかつ（生活） *n.* life, living, 3
ぜひ（是非） *adv.* I'd love to, by all means, 6
せまい（狭い） い-*adj.* cramped; narrow, 5
ゼロ（ゼロ） *number* zero, 3
せんこう（専攻） *n.* major, 2
せんしゅう（先週） *n.* last week, 3
せんせい *n.* Teacher, 1
〜せんせい *suf.* Professor 〜, 1
ぜんぜん（全然） *adv.* not at all (used with negative form of verb), 3
せんたく（洗濯） *n.* laundry, 6

そ

そうじ（掃除） *n.* cleaning, 6
そうじゃないです *exp.* No, that's not so., 2
そうですか *exp.* Is that so? I see., 2
そこ *demo.* there; that place (close to the listener or slightly removed from both speaker and listener), 4
そと（外） *loc. n.* outside, 5
その *demo.* that Noun, 5
ソファ *n.* sofa, 5
それ *demo.* that object; that (close to the listener or slightly removed from both speaker and listener), 4
それは　にほんごで　なんと　いいますか。 *exp.* How do you say that in Japanese?, 1

た

たいいくかん（体育館） *n.* gym, 5
だいがく（大学） *n.* college, university, 2
だいがくいんせい（大学院生） *n.* graduate student, 2
だいがくせい（大学生） *n.* college student, 2
だいじょうぶ（な）(大丈夫（な）) な-*adj.* all right, no problem, 6
たいてい *adv.* usually, 3
たいへん（な）(大変（な）) な-*adj.* tough, 6
たいわん（台湾） *n.* Taiwan, 2
たかい（高い） い-*adj.* tall, high, 4
たてもの（建物） *n.* building, structure, 4
たのしい（楽しい） い-*adj.* fun, 6
たべます（食べます） る-*v.* (to) eat　The dictionary form is たべる., 3
だれ *q. word* who, 4
たんす（箪笥） *n.* chest; drawers, 5

ち

ちいさい（小さい） い-*adj.* small, 4
ちかく（近く） *loc. n.* near; vicinity, 5
ちゃいろい（茶色い） い-*adj.* brown, 4
ちゅうごく（中国） *n.* China, 2

ちょっと　つごうが　わるくて（ちょっと都合が悪くて）*exp.* I'm a little busy. (literally, *Sorry, it's a little inconvenient.*), 6
ちょっと　ようじが　あって（ちょっと用事があって）*exp.* Sorry, I have some errands/ business to attend to., 6

つ

つぎ（次） *n.* next, 3
つくえ（机） *n.* desk, 5
〜って　なんですか。*exp.* What does 〜 mean?, 1
〜って　いいます。 *exp.* Colloquial version of 〜と　いいます。, 2
つまらない　い-*adj.* boring, 6

て

で　*part.* at, in, on, etc. (location of action or event)　としょかんで　べんきょうします。, 3
で　*part.* by means of, by, with, 5
テーブル　*n.* table, 5
でかけます（出かけます） る-*v.* (to) go out, 6
てがみ（手紙） *n.* letter, 6
です　*cop. v.* (to) be, 2
テスト　*n.* test, 4
テニス　*n.* tennis テニスを　します to play tennis, 6
デパート　*n.* department store, 4
テレビ　*n.* TV, 3
でんわ（電話） *n.* telephone, 5
でんわばんごう（電話番号） *n.* telephone number, 3

と

と　*part.* with, together with (association), 6
と　*part.* and (exhaustive listing), 6
〜と　いいます。／〜って　いいます。 *exp.* You call it 〜. / You say 〜, 1
ドア　*n.* door, 5
トイレ　*n.* toilet; restroom, 5
どういたしまして。 *exp.* You are welcome., 1
どうも　*adv.* very, 4
どうも　ありがとう　*adv.* Thank you very much, 4
どうも　すみません　*adv.* I'm very sorry, 4
ときどき（時々） *adv.* sometimes, 3
とけい（時計） *n.* clock; watch, 5
どこ　*q. word* where, 2
ところ（所） *n.* place, 5
としょかん（図書館） *n.* library, 3
どちら　*q. word* where (more polite than どこ), which way, 2
とても　*adv.* very (always used with an affirmative form), 4
となり（隣） *loc. n.* next to, 5
どの　*demo.* which Noun, 5
どのぐらい、どのくらい　*exp.* how long, how much, how many, 5

ともだち（友達） *n.* friend, 6
どようび (土曜日) *n.* Saturday, 3
どれ *q. word* which one, 4
どんな *q. word* what kind of, 4

な
なか (中) *loc. n.* in; inside, 5
なな、しち (七) *number* seven, 3
なに／なん (何) *q. word* what, 2
なまえ (名前) *n.* name, 2

に
に (二) *number* two, 3
に *part.* at, on, in (point in time) 10じに ねます。, 3
に *part.* to (goal, activity + に) クラスに いきます。, 3
に *part.* in order to; for (purpose), 6
に *part.* to (goal, receiver), 6
にぎやか (な)(賑やか (な)) な*-adj.* lively (place or event), 6
にじ (二時) *time exp.* two o'clock, 2
にちようび (日曜日) *n.* Sunday, 3
にねんせい (二年生) *n.* sophomore, second-year student (The suffix せい may be dropped.), 2
にほん (日本) *n.* Japan, 2

ね
ねこ (猫) *n.* cat, 5
ねます (寝ます) る*-v.* (to) go to bed The dictionary form is ねる., 3
〜ねん (〜年) *suf.* year いちねん first year, 2

の
の *part.* noun modifier marker (of), ('s), 2
ノート *n.* notebook, 4
のみます (飲みます) う*-v.* (to) drink The dictionary form is のむ., 3

は
は *part.* topic marker, 2
〜は にほんごで なんと いいますか。 *exp.* How do you say 〜 in Japanese?, 1
パーティ *n.* party, 6
はい（ええ）、そうです。 *exp.* Yes, that's so., 2
はい、わかりました。 *exp.* Yes, I understand it., 1
はい／ええ *inter.* yes, 2
はいります (入ります) う*-v.* (to) take (a bath), (to) enter The dictionary form is はいる.
おふろに はいります take a bath., 3
はじめまして。〜です。どうぞ よろしく。 *exp.* How do you do? I am 〜 . Pleased to meet you., 1
バス *n.* bus, 5
はち (八) *number* eight, 3
はちじ (八時) *time exp.* eight o'clock, 2

はなします (話します) う-*v.* (to) talk, 6
はやい (速い) い-*adj.* fast; quick, 5
はん (半) *time exp.* half past いちじはん 1:30, 2
はん (〜半) *suf.* half past, 2
ばん (晩) *n.* night, evening, 3
ばんごはん (晩御飯) *n.* supper, dinner, 3

ひ
ピクニック *n.* picnic, 6
ビジネス *n.* business, 2
ひだり (左) *loc. n.* to the left; left side, 5
ビデオ *n.* video, 5
ひと (人) *n.* person, 5
ひま (な)(暇 (な)) な-*adj.* free, idle, unscheduled, 6
びょういん (病院) *n.* hospital, 4
ひる (昼) *n.* afternoon, 3
ビル *n.* building, 4
ひるごはん (昼御飯) *n.* lunch, 3
ひろい (広い) い-*adj.* spacious; wide, 5

ふ
ふとん (布団) *n.* futon, 5
フランス *n.* France, 2
プール *n.* pool, 6
ふるい (古い) い-*adj.* old, 4
〜ふん (〜分) *count.* 〜 minute, (for) 〜 minute, 3
ぶんがく (文学) *n.* literature, 2

へ
へ *part.* to (direction) がっこうへ いきます。, 3
ベッド *n.* bed, 5
へや (部屋) *n.* room, 5
ペン *n.* pen, 4
べんきょう (勉強) *n.* study, 3
べんきょうします (勉強します) *irr. v.* (to) study The dictionary form is べんきょうする , 3

ほ
ボールペン *n.* ball point pen, 4
ぼく (僕) *pron.* I (normally used by males), 2
ほん (本) *n.* book, 3
ほんだな (本棚) *n.* bookshelf, 5
ほんや (本屋) *n.* bookstore, 4

ま
まい〜 (毎〜) *pref.* every まいしゅう まいあさ まいばん まいにち, 3
まいあさ (毎朝) *n.* every morning, 3

まいしゅう（毎週） *n.* every week, 3
まいにち（毎日） *n.* every day, 3
まいばん（毎晩） *n.* every night, 3
まえ（前） *loc. n.* in front of; in the front, 5
まち（町） *n.* town, 4
まちます（待ちます） う-*v.* (to) wait, 6
まで *part.* until, to, 5
まど（窓） *n.* window, 5

み

みぎ（右） *loc. n.* to the right, 5
みて ください。 *exp.* Please look at it., 1
みます（見ます） る-*v.* (to) see, (to) watch The dictionary form is みる., 3

む

むずかしい（難しい） い-*adj.* difficult, 6

め

メール *n.* email, 6
メキシコ *n.* Mexico, 2

も

も *part.* similarity marker (also, too), 2
もう いちど いってください。 *exp.* Please say it again. (Teacher's request), 1
もう いちど おねがいします。 *exp.* Please say it again. (Student's request), 1
もう すこし ゆっくり おねがいします。 *exp.* Please say it slowly., 1
もくようび（木曜日） *n.* Thursday, 3
もの（物） *n.* thing (tangible), 5

や

～や（～屋） *suf.* store (e.g. ほんや bookstore), 4
やさしい（易しい、優しい） い-*adj.* easy, kind, 6
やすみ（休み） *n.* rest; absence, a day off, 6
やすみのひ（休みの日） *n.* a day off; holiday, 6
やま（山） *n.* mountain, 5

ゆ

ゆうびんきょく（郵便局） *n.* post office, 4
ゆうめい（な）(有名（な）) な-*adj.* famous, 4
ゆっくり *adv.* slowly, ゆっくりします, to relax; to, 6

よ

～ようび（～曜日） *suf.* days of the week, 3
よく *adv.* often, well, 3
よこ（横） *loc. n.* next to; at the side of, 5
よじ（四時） *time exp.* four o'clock, 2
よねんせい（四年生） *n.* senior, fourth-year student (The suffix せい may be dropped.), 2

よびます (呼びます)　う-*v.* (to) call (someone); (to) invite, 6
よみます (読みます)　う-*v.* (to) read　The dictionary form is よむ., 3
よん、し (四)　*number* four, 3
よんで ください。 *exp.* Please read., 1

ら

らいねん (来年)　*adv.* next year, 2
ラボ (ラボ)　*n.* laboratory, 5

り

りっぱ (な)(立派 (な))　な-*adj.* fine; splendid, 4
りゅうがくせい (留学生)　*n.* foreign student, 2
りょう　*n.* dormitory, 4
りょうしん (両親)　*n.* parents, 6
りょうり (料理)　*n.* meal; cuisine りょうりをします to fix a meal, 6

れ

れい (零)　number zero, 3
れきし (歴史)　*n.* history, 2
レストラン　*n.* restaurant, 4

ろ

ろく (六)　*number* six, 3
ろくじ (六時)　*time exp.* six o'clock, 2

わ

わかりましたか。 *exp.* Do you understand it?, 1
わたし (私)　*pron.* I (used by both males and females), 2

を

を　*part.* direct object marker　ほんを　よみます。, 3

ENGLISH-JAPANESE GLOSSARY

A

a day off; holiday　やすみのひ (休みの日)　*n.*, 6
a.m., forenoon, morning　ごぜん (午前)　*n.*, 2
about ～ (used only with a time expression)　～ごろ *suf.*, 3
about duration, quantity　～ぐらい *suf.*, 5
afternoon　ひる (昼)　*n.*, 3
all right, no problem　だいじょうぶ (な)(大丈夫 (な))　な-*adj.*, 6
always　いつも *adv.*, 3
America, U.S.　アメリカ *n.*, 2
and (exhaustive listing)　と *part.*, 6
apartment　アパート *n.*, 4
Asian studies　アジアけんきゅう (アジア研究)　*n.*, 2
(to) ask; (to) listen to　ききます (聞きます / 聴きます)　う-*v.*, 6
at, in, on, etc. (location of action or event)　としょかんで　べんきょうします。　で *part.*, 3
at, on, in (point in time)　10じに　ねます。　に *part.*, 3
Australia　オーストラリア *n.*, 2

B

ball point pen　ボールペン *n.*, 4
bank　ぎんこう (銀行)　*n.*, 4
bath　おふろ (お風呂)　*n.*, 3
(to) be　です *cop. v.*, 2
(to) be held, (to) have　The dictionary form is ある．ありますう-*v.*, 3
bed　ベッド *n.*, 5
behind; back of　うしろ (後ろ)　*loc. n.*, 5
bicycle　じてんしゃ (自転車)　*n.*, 5
big　おおきい (大きい)　い-*adj.*, 4
black　くろい (黒い)　い-*adj.*, 4
blackboard, chalkboard　こくばん (黒板)　*n.*, 5
blue　あおい (青い)　い-*adj.*, 4
book　ほん (本)　*n.*, 3
bookshelf　ほんだな (本棚)　*n.*, 5
bookstore　ほんや (本屋)　*n.*, 4
boring　つまらない い-*adj.*, 6
breakfast　あさごはん (朝御飯)　*n.*, 3
bright　あかるい (明るい)　い-*adj.*, 5
brown　ちゃいろい (茶色い)　い-*adj.*, 4
building　ビル *n.*, 4
building, structure　たてもの (建物)　*n.*, 4
bus　バス *n.*, 5
business　ビジネス *n.*, 2
busy　いそがしい (忙しい)　い-*adj.*, 6

by means of, by, with　で *part.*, 5

C

(to) call (someone); (to) invite　よびます（呼びます）　う-*v.*, 6
came from ～ [casual]　～から　きました。 *exp.*, 2
Canada　カナダ *n.*, 2
car　くるま（車） *n.*, 5
cat　ねこ（猫） *n.*, 5
chair　いす（椅子） *n.*, 5
chest; drawers　たんす（箪笥） *n.*, 5
China　ちゅうごく（中国） *n.*, 2
class　クラス　*n.*, 3
class, course　じゅぎょう（授業） *n.*, 3
classroom　きょうしつ（教室） *n.*, 5
clean; pretty; neat　きれい（な）　な-*adj.*, 4
cleaning　そうじ（掃除） *n.*, 6
clock; watch　とけい（時計） *n.*, 5
coffee　コーヒー *n.*, 3
coffee shop (more traditional word)　きっさてん（喫茶店） *n.*, 4
coffee shop, café (more recent word)　カフェ *n.*, 4
college student　だいがくせい（大学生） *n.*, 2
college, university　だいがく（大学） *n.*, 2
(to) come　きます（来ます） *irr. v.*, 3
computer　コンピュータ *n.*, 5
concert　コンサート *n.*, 6
convenience store　コンビニ *n.*, 4
cramped; narrow　せまい（狭い）　い-*adj.*, 5

D

dark　くらい（暗い）　い-*adj.*, 5
the day after tomorrow　あさって（明後日） *n.*, 3
the day before yesterday　おととい（一昨日） *n.*, 3
days of the week　～ようび（～曜日） *suf.*, 3
department store　デパート *n.*, 4
desk　つくえ（机） *n.*, 5
dictionary　じしょ（辞書） *n.*, 4
difficult　むずかしい（難しい）　い-*adj.*, 6
direct object marker　ほんを　よみます。　を *part.*, 3
(to) do　The dictionary form is する　します *irr. v.*, 3
Do you understand it?　わかりましたか。 *exp.*, 1
dog　いぬ（犬） *n.*, 5
door　ドア *n.*, 5
dormitory　りょう *n.*, 4
(to) drink　The dictionary form is のむ．のみます（飲みます）　う-*v.*, 3

E

easy, kind やさしい（易しい，優しい） い-*adj.*, 6
(to) eat The dictionary form is たべる．たべます（食べます） る-*v.*, 3
eight はち（八） *number*, 3
eight o'clock はちじ（八時） *time exp.*, 2
eleven o'clock じゅういちじ（十一時） *time exp.*, 2
e-mail メール *n.*, 6
engineering こうがく（工学） *n.*, 2
England イギリス *n.*, 2
English えいご（英語） *n.*, 2
eraser けしゴム（消しゴム） *n.*, 4
every day まいにち（毎日） *n.*, 3
every morning まいあさ（毎朝） *n.*, 3
every night まいばん（毎晩） *n.*, 3
every week まいしゅう（毎週） *n.*, 3
every まいしゅう まいあさ まいばん まいにち まい〜（毎〜） *pref.*, 3
(Eh,) Excuse me. （あのう、）すみません。 *exp.*, 1
Excuse me; Anyone home? ごめんください（御免下さい） *exp.*, 5
exercise (physical) うんどう（運動） *n.*, 6

F

famous ゆうめい（な）(有名（な）) な-*adj.*, 4
fast; quick はやい（速い） い-*adj.*, 5
fine; splendid りっぱ（な）(立派（な）) な-*adj.*, 4
five ご（五） *number*, 3
five o'clock ごじ（五時） *time exp.*, 2
foreign student りゅうがくせい（留学生） *n.*, 2
four よん、し（四） *number*, 3
four o'clock よじ（四時） *time exp.*, 2
France フランス *n.*, 2
free, idle, unscheduled ひま（な）(暇（な）) な-*adj.*, 6
freshman, first-year student (The suffix せい may be dropped.) いちねんせい（一年生） *n.*, 2
Friday きんようび（金曜日） *n.*, 3
from から *part.*, 5
fun たのしい（楽しい） い-*adj.*, 6
futon ふとん（布団） *n.*, 5

G

game ゲーム *n.*, 6
(to) get up, (to) wake up The dictionary form is おきる．おきます（起きます） る-*v.*, 3
(to) go The dictionary form is いく．いきます（行きます） う-*v.*, 3
(to) go out でかけます（出かけます） る-*v.*, 6
(to) go to bed The dictionary form is ねる．ねます（寝ます） る-*v.*, 3
good いい い-*adj.*, 4
Good afternoon. / Hello. こんにちは。 *exp.*, 1
Good evening. / Hello. こんばんは *exp.*, 1

Good morning. / Hello. おはようございます。 *exp.*, 1
Good morning. / Hello. (casual) おはよう。 *exp.*, 1
Good-bye. さようなら。／さよなら。 *exp.*, 1
Good-bye. / Excuse me. しつれいします。 *exp.*, 1
graduate student だいがくいんせい（大学院生） *n.*, 2
gym たいいくかん（体育館） *n.*, 5

H

half past はん（～半） *suf.*, 2
half past いちじはん 1:30 はん（半） *time exp.*, 2
happy うれしい（嬉しい） い-*adj.*, 6
healthy, cheerful, lively (person) げんき（な）(元気（な）) な-*adj.*, 6
here; this place ここ *demo.*, 4
high school こうこう（高校） *n.*, 2
history れきし（歴史） *n.*, 2
home うち（家） *n.*, 3
homework しゅくだい（宿題） *n.*, 3
hospital びょういん（病院） *n.*, 4
～ hours ～じかん *suf.*, 5
How do you do? I am ～. Pleased to meet you. はじめまして。～です。どうぞよろしく。 *exp.*, 1
How do you say ～ in Japanese? ～は　にほんごで　なんと　いいますか。 *exp.*, 1
How do you say that (over there) in Japanese? あれは　にほんごで　なんと　いいますか。 *exp.*, 1
How do you say that in Japanese? それは　にほんごで　なんと　いいますか。 *exp.*, 1
How do you say this in Japanese? これは　にほんごで　なんと　いいますか。 *exp.*, 1
how long, how much, how many どのぐらい／どのくらい *exp.*, 5

I

I (normally used by males) ぼく（僕） *pron.*, 2
I (used by both males and females) わたし（私） *pron.*, 2
I am sorry. / Excuse me. すみません。 *exp.*, 1
I'd love to, by all means ぜひ（是非） *adv.*, 4
I'm a little busy. (literally, *Sorry, it's a little inconvenient.*) ちょっと　つごうが　わるくて（ちょっと都合が悪くて）*exp.*, 6
I'm very sorry どうも　すみません *adv.*, 4
in front of; in the front まえ（前） *loc. n.*, 5
in order to; for (purpose) に *part.*, 6
in; inside なか（中） *loc. n.*, 5
interesting おもしろい（面白い） い-*adj.*, 6
Is that so? I see. そうですか *exp.*, 2
It is I who should be saying that. Thank YOU. こちらこそ。 *exp.*, 2

J

Japan にほん（日本） *n.*, 2
Japanese-style closet; storage space おしいれ（押し入れ） *n.*, 5
job しごと（仕事） *n.*, 6
jogging ジョギング *n.*, 6

junior, third-year student (The suffix せい may be dropped.) さんねんせい（三年生） *n.*, 2

L

laboratory ラボ(ラボ) *n.*, 5
language にほんご Japanese language ～ご(～語) *suf.*, 2
last week せんしゅう(先週) *n.*, 3
laundry せんたく(洗濯) *n.*, 6
letter てがみ(手紙) *n.*, 6
library としょかん(図書館) *n.*, 3
life, living せいかつ(生活) *n.*, 3
literature ぶんがく(文学) *n.*, 2
lively (place or event) にぎやか(な)(賑やか(な)) な-*adj.*, 6
lonely さびしい(寂しい) い-*adj.*, 6
luggage, bag かばん(鞄) *n.*, 4
lunch ひるごはん(昼御飯) *n.*, 3

M

magazine ざっし(雑誌) *n.*, 6
major せんこう(専攻) *n.*, 2
(to) make (a phone call) でんわを かけます かけます る-*v.*, 6
management/business administration けいえいがく(経営学) *n.*, 2
meal, cooked rice ごはん(御飯) *n.*, 3
meal; cuisine りょうりをします to fix a meal りょうり(料理) *n.*, 6
(to) meet あいます(会います) う-*v.*, 6
Mexico メキシコ *n.*, 2
～ minute, (for) ～ minute ～ふん(～分) *count.*, 3
Monday げつようび(月曜日) *n.*, 3
morning あさ(朝) *n.*, 3
mountain やま(山) *n.*, 5
movie えいが(映画) *n.*, 3
Mr./Mrs./Miss/Ms. ～ ～さん *suf.*, 1
music おんがく(音楽) *n.*, 6

N

name なまえ(名前) *n.*, 2
～ nationality アメリカじん ～じん(～人) *suf.*, 2
(one's) native country しゅっしん(出身) *n.*, 2
near; vicinity ちかく(近く) *loc. n.*, 5
new あたらしい(新しい) い-*adj.*, 4
newspaper しんぶん(新聞) *n.*, 6
next つぎ(次) *n.*, 3
next time こんど(今度) *n.*, 6
next to となり(隣) *loc. n.*, 5
next to; at the side of よこ(横) *loc. n.*, 5
next year らいねん(来年) *adv.*, 2
night, evening ばん(晩) *n.*, 3

nine きゅう、く（九） *number*, 3
nine o'clock くじ（九時） *time exp.*, 2
no, don't mention it, you're welcome いいえ *inter.*, 2
No, I don't understand it. いいえ、わかりません。 *exp.*, 1
No, that's not so. いいえ、そうじゃありません *exp.*, 2
No, that's not so. （そうじゃないです） *exp.*, 2
not at all (used with negative form of verb) ぜんぜん（全然） *adv.*, 3
notebook ノート *n.*, 4
noun modifier marker (of), ('s) の *part.*, 2
now いま（今） *adv.*, 2

O

～ o'clock ～じ（～時） *suf.*, 2
often; well よく *adv.*, 3
old ふるい（古い） い-*adj.*, 4
on foot あるいて（歩いて） *exp.*, 5
on; above; over うえ（上） *loc. n.*, 5
one いち（一） *number*, 3
one o'clock いちじ（一時） *time exp.*, 2
outside そと（外） *loc. n.*, 5
over there; that place (far away from both speaker and listener) あそこ *demo.*, 4

P

p.m., afternoon, ごご（午後） *n.*, 2
parents りょうしん（両親） *n.*, 6
park こうえん（公園） *n.*, 4
part time job アルバイト *n.*, 6
party パーティ *n.*, 6
pen ペン *n.*, 4
pencil えんぴつ（鉛筆） *n.*, 4
person ひと（人） *n.*, 5
photograph しゃしん（写真） *n.*, 5
picnic ピクニック *n.*, 6
picture え（絵） *n.*, 5
place ところ（所） *n.*, 5
(to) play あそびます（遊びます） う-*v.*, 6
Please come in. あがってください（上がって下さい） *exp.*, 5
Please listen. きいて ください。 *exp.*, 1
Please look at it. みて ください。 *exp.*, 1
Please read. よんで ください。 *exp.*, 1
Please say it again. (Student's request) もう いちど おねがいします。 *exp.*, 1
Please say it again. (Teacher's request) もう いちど いってください。 *exp.*, 1
Please say it slowly. もう すこし ゆっくり おねがいします。 *exp.*, 1
Please say it. / Repeat after me. いって ください。 *exp.*, 1
Please speak loudly. (Student's request) おおきい こえで おねがいします。 *exp.*, 1
Please speak loudly. (Teacher's request) おおきい こえで いってください。 *exp.*, 1

Please write. かいて ください。 *exp.*, 1
police box こうばん (交番) *n.*, 4
polite prefix おふろ お (御～) *pref.*, 3
polite prefix おなまえ polite form of なまえ (name) お～ *pref.*, 2
pool プール *n.*, 6
post office ゆうびんきょく (郵便局) *n.*, 4
Professor ～ ～せんせい *suf.*, 1

Q

question しつもん (を) します (to) ask a question しつもん (質問) *n.*, 6
question marker か *part.*, 2
quiet しずか (な)(静か (な)) な*-adj.*, 5

R

(to) read The dictionary form is よむ. よみます (読みます) う*-v.*, 3
red あかい (赤い) い*-adj.*, 4
rest; absence, a day off やすみ (休み) *n.*, 6
restaurant レストラン *n.*, 4
(to) return, (to) go home The dictionary form is かえる. かえります (帰ります) う*-v.*, 3
river かわ (川) *n.*, 5
room へや (部屋) *n.*, 5

S

sad かなしい (悲しい) い*-adj.*, 6
Saturday どようび (土曜日) *n.*, 3
(to) say いいます (言います) う*-v.*, 6
school がっこう (学校) *n.*, 3
school cafeteria がくしょく (学食) (a shortened form of 学生しょくどう) *n.*, 5
See you later. (literally, *Well then, again.*) じゃあ、また。*exp.*, 1
(to) see, (to) watch The dictionary form is みる. みます (見ます) る*-v.*, 3
senior, fourth-year student (The suffix せい may be dropped.) よねんせい (四年生) *n.*, 2
seven なな、しち (七) *number*, 3
seven o'clock しちじ (七時) *time exp.*, 2
shopping かいもの (買い物) *n.*, 6
shower シャワー *n.*, 3
similarity marker (also, too) も *part.*, 2
six ろく (六) *number*, 3
six o'clock ろくじ (六時) *time exp.*, 2
slowly, ゆっくりします, to relax; to ゆっくり *adv.*, 6
small ちいさい (小さい) い*-adj.*, 4
sofa ソファ *n.*, 5
sometimes ときどき (時々) *adv.*, 3
sophomore, second-year student (The suffix せい may be dropped.) にねんせい (二年生) *n.*, 2
Sorry, I have some errands/business to attend to. ちょっと ようじが あって (ちょっと用事があって) *exp.*, 6
sorry, regrettable ざんねん (な)(残念 (な)) な*-adj.*, 6

South Korea かんこく (韓国) *n.*, 2
spacious; wide ひろい (広い) い-*adj.*, 5
Spain スペイン *n.*, 2
station えき (駅) *n.*, 4
store (e.g. ほんや bookstore) 〜や (〜屋) *suf.*, 4
student がくせい (学生) *n.*, 2
Student union がくせいかいかん (学生会館) *n.*, 5
〜 student だいがくせい college student いちねんせい freshman 〜せい (〜生) *suf.*, 2
study べんきょう (勉強) *n.*, 3
(to) study The dictionary form is べんきょうする べんきょうします (勉強します) *irr. v.*, 3
Sunday にちようび (日曜日) *n.*, 3
supermarket スーパー *n.*, 4
supper, dinner ばんごはん (晩御飯) *n.*, 3
(to) swim およぎます (泳ぎます) う-*v.*, 6

T

table テーブル *n.*, 5
Taiwan たいわん (台湾) *n.*, 2
(to) take (a bath), (to) enter The dictionary form is はいる . おふろに はいります take a bath. はいります (入ります) う-*v.*, 3
(to) take (a shower) シャワーを あびます take a shower. The dictionary form is あびる. あびます (浴びます) る-*v.*, 3
to take (time), it costs かかります う -*v.*, 5
(to) talk はなします (話します) う-*v.*, 6
tall, high たかい (高い) い-*adj.*, 4
Teacher せんせい *n.*, 1
telephone でんわ (電話) *n.*, 5
telephone number でんわばんごう (電話番号) *n.*, 3
ten じゅう (十) *number*, 3
ten o'clock じゅうじ (十時) *time exp.*, 2
tennis テニスを します to play tennis テニス *n.*, 6
test テスト *n.*, 4
textbook きょうかしょ (教科書) *n.*, 4
Thank you. ありがとうございます。*exp.*, 1
Thank you. (literally, *I will intrude on you*) (said before going inside someone's house or apartment) おじゃまします (お邪魔します) *exp.*, 5
Thank you very much どうも ありがとう *adv.*, 4
that Noun その *demo.*, 5
that Noun over there あの *demo.*, 5
that object over there; that あれ *demo.*, 4
that object; that (close to the listener or slightly removed from both speaker and listener) それ *demo.*, 4
there; that place (close to the listener or slightly removed from both speaker and listener) そこ *demo.*, 4
thing (tangible) もの (物) *n.*, 5
this area このへん (この辺) *n.*, 4
this Noun この *demo.*, 5
this object, this これ *demo.*, 4

this person, this way こちら *n.*, 2
this week こんしゅう（今週） *n.*, 3
this こんしゅう、こんばん こん〜（今〜） *pref.*, 3
three さん（三） *number*, 3
three o'clock さんじ（三時） *time exp.*, 2
Thursday もくようび（木曜日） *n.*, 3
to (goal, activity + に) クラスに いきます。 に *part.*, 3
to (direction) がっこうへ いきます。 へ *part.*, 3
to (goal, receiver) に *part.*, 6
to be; to exist (used for an animate beings). Dictionary form is いる．います る-*v.*, 4
to the left; left side ひだり（左） *loc. n.*, 5
to the right みぎ（右） *loc. n.*, 5
today きょう（今日） *n.*, 3
together いっしょに（一緒に） *adv.*, 6
toilet; restroom トイレ *n.*, 5
tomorrow あした（明日） *n.*, 3
tonight こんばん（今晩） *n.*, 3
topic marker は *part.*, 2
tough たいへん（な)(大変（な)) な-*adj.*, 6
town まち（町） *n.*, 4
tree き（木） *n.*, 5
Tuesday かようび（火曜日） *n.*, 3
TV テレビ *n.*, 3
twelve o'clock じゅうにじ（十二時） *time exp.*, 2
two に（二） *number*, 3
two o'clock にじ（二時） *time exp.*, 2

U

uh, well あのう *inter.*, 2
under; beneath した（下） *loc. n.*, 5
until, to まで *part.*, 5
usually たいてい *adv.*, 3

V

very どうも *adv.*, 4
very (always used with a negative form) あまり *adv.*, 4
very (always used with an affirmative form) とても *adv.*, 4
video ビデオ *n.*, 5

W

(to) wait まちます（待ちます） う-*v.*, 6
(to) walk あるきます（歩きます） う-*v.*, 6
(to take) a walk さんぽ（を） します to take a walk さんぽ（散歩） *n.*, 6
Wednesday すいようび（水曜日） *n.*, 3
weekend しゅうまつ（週末） *n.*, 3
Welcome! Come in. いらっしゃい *exp.*, 5

what なに／なん（何） *q. word*, 2
What does ～ mean? ～って　なんですか。 *exp.*, 1
what kind of どんな *q. word*, 4
when いつ *q. word*, 3
where どこ *q. word*, 2
where (more polite than どこ), which way どちら *q. word*, 2
which Noun どの *demo.*, 5
which one どれ *q. word*, 4
white しろい（白い） い-*adj.*, 4
who だれ *q. word*, 4
window まど（窓） *n.*, 5
with, together with (association) と *part.*, 6
(to) write かきます（書きます） う-*v.*, 6

Y

year いちねん first year ～ねん（～年） *suf.*, 2
yellow きいろい（黄色い） い-*adj.*, 4
yes はい／ええ *inter.*, 2
Yes, I understand it. はい、わかりました。 *exp.*, 1
Yes, that's so. はい（ええ）、そうです。 *exp.*, 2
yesterday きのう（昨日） *n.*, 3
You are welcome. どういたしまして。 *exp.*, 1
You call it ～/You say ～ ～と　いいます。／～って　いいます。 *exp.*, 1

Z

zero ゼロ、れい（ゼロ、零） *number*, 3

INDEX